THE AUTHORS

David Blunkett was born in 1947. He is a graduate of Sheffield University and holds a further education teaching certificate, as well as the National Certificate in business studies. He served as a trade-union activist while working for the East Midlands Gas Board, and later became a tutor on industrial relations.

He has held a number of positions in local government, including the first chair of the Local Government Information Unit and deputy chair of the Association of Metropolitan Authorities. In 1970 he was elected to Sheffield City Council, becoming its leader in 1980. He is a member of the Labour Party National Executive Committee and chairs its Local Government Committee. He was elected Member of Parliament for Sheffield Brightside in June 1987.

David Blunkett is married and has three sons.

Keith Jackson, born in 1937, is Senior Tutor at Northern College in South Yorkshire. Since graduating from Oxford University, his career has been in adult education, with the Workers' Educational Association, Liverpool University and Northern College.

He has been involved in local government since the 1960s, in the Potteries, on Merseyside and in Sheffield. In Liverpool he played an active part in the voluntary and community movement of the late 1960s and early 1970s. In Sheffield his activities include being a founder member of the Employment Forum which led to the formation of the council's Employment Department. He represents his union, ASTMS, at ward, constituency district, and district executive level of the Labour Party.

Keith Jackson is married with a daughter and two sons.

DEMOCRACY IN CRISIS

The Town Halls Respond

David Blunkett
and Keith Jackson

THE HOGARTH PRESS
LONDON

This book is dedicated to the city and the people of Sheffield

Published in 1987 by
The Hogarth Press
Chatto & Windus Ltd
30 Bedford Square, London WC1B 3RP

British Library Cataloguing in Publication Data

Blunkett, David
Democracy in crisis: the town halls
respond.
1. Local government – Great Britain
2. Great Britain – Politics and government
– 1979
I. Title   II. Jackson, Keith, *1947*–
352.041   JS3173

ISBN 0 7012 0777 9

Printed in Finland by
Werner Söderström Oy

Contents

Acknowledgements

Our thanks are due to a number of organisations: Sheffield City Library Service, the staff of the Sheffield City Council Department of Employment and Economic Development (particularly Richard Money), the City of Sheffield Treasury Department, Judy Mallaber and the staff in the Local Government Information Unit, the Centre for Local Economic Strategy, and the Association of Metropolitan Authorities.

We have also been helped by many colleagues, trade unions and community groups, but we must mention for their direct contributions (any errors are, of course, ours and not theirs): Bob Fryer and colleagues at the Northern College (both academic and secretarial), Mo Mowlam, John Grayson, Richard Caborn, M.P., Michael Barrett-Brown and Mike Ward.

The circumstances of writing this book required more than the usual secretarial help and we want to thank particularly Joyce Keen of Sandygate Secretarial Services, and also Jean Marples, Karen Gascoign and Christine Hirst. And Julia Velacott contributed invaluable editorial work.

Finally, we are grateful to Valda Waterfield for her wisdom, common sense, practical help and a reminder to me (David) that real life goes on outside the town hall. And to Ruth, Helen, David (Jackson) and the rest of our families who never gave up on us.

DAVID BLUNKETT

KEITH JACKSON

Preface

Democracy in Crisis was at the printers when Margaret Thatcher called the General Election of 1987. The publishers suggested that we write a Preface in order to take this into account. In our view the conduct of the election and its outcome vindicated the argument we present and increase the importance of its being taken seriously. A further Conservative victory with just over 40 per cent of the national vote took formal parliamentary representation another step away from democracy. A major part of the subsequent Queen's Speech was based on the strange notion of 'bringing power to the people' by weakening the role of local government (Nicholas Ridley, Secretary of State for the Environment, *Guardian*, 19 June 1987). In practice, this meant that when the majority of the people in the cities had expressed their preferences through democratic local elections and in national parliamentary elections against the Government, the Conservatives would use the power of a national state to dismantle local democratic institutions themselves. It also implied bribing the electorate into collusion – by injecting state resources into the cities through centrally imposed institutions, having previously taken such resources away from the elected bodies which represented local people.

The Conservatives presented this election as a major event in the clash of forces in society. It was a crucial test of their ability to reap the fruits of their 'radical' strategy, introduced in 1979. In the run-up to the election, Mrs Thatcher reminded the nation that she was not merely concerned with gaining another term of office to act on behalf of the British people, but wanted to continue along a crusading path: 'We are well on the way', she told the *Sunday Express*, 'to making Britain a country safe from socialism.' (17 May 1987). What Margaret Thatcher meant by socialism increasingly became anything which blocked the Conservatives' progress.

The conduct of the 1987 election and the contents of the

Queen's Speech on 25 June, therefore, should help to reduce the surprise which readers might feel on finding that the first and last chapters of a book on local government and local politics are devoted largely to broad national and international political issues. Why on earth, they might have asked, do we include references to the Mont Pelerin Society of right-wing activists, founded in Switzerland decades ago? In the approach to Mrs Thatcher's third term, the reasons were more obvious as the general threat to democracy became increasingly apparent and the associated attack on local politics was declared more openly than in 1979 and 1983.

Margaret Thatcher claimed in her foreword to the 1987 Conservative manifesto that 'Together we are building One Nation of free, prosperous and responsible families and people. A Conservative dream is, at last, becoming a reality.' We begin, by contrast, with the argument that Britain is more divided than ever before, that large sections of the population, young and old, are dispirited and struggling for an opportunity to use their energies and talents responsibly, both at work and in the community, and that for many this Conservative period has been a bad dream, if not a nightmare. 'Once again, our economy is strong,' said the Conservatives, but, as we show in Chapter 1, it has become unbalanced and less subject to control by the people of Britain than ever before. The Conservative manifesto sought to justify its claim in a supporting document, *Our First Eight Years*, but we believe that an examination of its presentation of the facts shows it to be grossly misleading. The reader can judge whether we have used our evidence with more attention to reality – concerning employment, industry, crime and the police, the quality of life, freedom and democracy.

Local politics was subject to the same process of misinformation and distortion by Conservatives and their immediate supporters as were other aspects of public policy. The manifesto claimed, 'Our rate-capping legislation – so bitterly opposed by the Labour, SDP and Liberal parties in Parliament – has protected ratepayers from huge rate increases. This year alone, 20 councils will be rate-capped – 19 of them Labour and one controlled by Liberals and the SDP – saving ratepayers several hundred million pounds.' There was no indication here that many of the Government's own supporters had been opposed to the Rates Act, and that the rate increases condemned by the Government were due to grant loss and penalty imposed by Westminster. Any pretence that the Act was an even-handed measure concerned with the control of public spending was abandoned in a rhetorical onslaught on those committed to public spending.

We emphasise on the first page that this book is not a party political tract. Thus, while the campaign highlighted the significance for the Conservatives of undermining local government, it also demonstrated the opposition's caution in responding to Conservative deception when they failed to emphasise the achievements of local politics. The Labour manifesto gave some comfort to hard-pressed Councils in promising to overturn the worst Conservative legislation and recognising the value of local economic initiatives. It did not, however, offer an alternative view of the vital role of local democracy in the future, or show that it recognised the extent of the growing threat. Despite all the evidence that people trust their Council as much as, or more than their House of Commons, there was a nervous reaction from Labour to press caricatures of 'loony left' Councils. The Alliance went further. They adopted the media's hectoring tone in their manifesto's first page, referring to 'extremists of the left' on Local Councils which the Labour Party would have to 'keep the lid on', while failing to acknowledge that the Alliance itself controlled one Council which had been rate-capped for so-called extremism. There should have been a measured demonstration from the opposition of the realities of local policies on housing, employment, transport, education, equality and leisure in those rate-capped and other hard-pressed Councils across the country.

Opposition leaders did not stress during the campaign that the Government's own Audit Commission had praised some rate-capped Councils as models of prudence. No emphasis was given to the absurdity of the Conservative Manifesto's charge that the Widdicombe Report 'painted a disturbing picture of the break down of democratic processes in a number of Councils', when the Report actually praises many of them for expanding the scope of democratic debate. The Alliance claim that 'some Labour controlled Boroughs failed to co-operate with the police in combatting crime'. No one brought to the fore a letter from a police chief to Bernie Grant, leader of Haringey Council and parliamentary candidate for Tottenham, a major figure in press demonology, wishing him well for the election and thanking him for his help in maintaining good policing and establishing better relations between the police and young people (*Guardian*, 4 May 1987).

By their caution, opposition political leaders were contributing to a climate provoked by those sections of the popular press which subjected Local Councils to what is known as 'rubbishing' – mixing innuendo with untruth to give the impression of absurdity, as when the *Daily Star* and the *Sun* alleged that one Council had forbidden 'Baa Baa Black Sheep' to be sung by children in schools because it was offensive to the black community (*Guardian*, 4 May 1987). The real problem was that the climate was such that people could believe it to be true. Individuals who have been called 'the loony left' did sometimes act with less sensitivity to people's concerns than they might have done, sometimes to the point of silliness, but they were less dangerous to the future well-being of our democracy than the extremists who were now clearly in control of the Government's programmes. What we have seen are classic methods of destabilising democracy. The way was being opened for new inroads into liberty by discrediting local government before dismantling it further.

After the assault on local government finance, housing, municipal enterprise, transport and other services over the last eight years, it became the turn of education. Before the election was announced the Government abandoned the negotiating machinery for teachers' pay and conditions, declared its intention of taking polytechnics and colleges of higher education out of the local democratic framework and put forward the idea of setting up centrally-funded city technology colleges for a selected few. The Conservative manifesto then proposed allowing state schools to 'opt out' of local democratic accountability, to be funded directly by Whitehall and run by governors and headteachers. Confusion in Conservative ranks over whether these schools should be fee paying or not indicated that, in seeking to set up a market model for education, ideological determination was overriding serious consideration about how it would work in practice.

Following an election conducted in this way, it was easy for the Conservatives to smoothly repeat the pattern of the previous eight years. This had involved reiterating misleading information about Councils so that people would think it must be true and using financial regulations and the letter of the law against local government, whilst itself transgressing constitutional law and good financial practice. Thus, Nicholas Ridley now claimed: 'I really don't think the Government can go on being blamed for dereliction in certain parts of the older urban areas when you have Councils which can be infuriating beyond belief in their planning decisions, when their rates are sky high, and when they operate such an anti-business attitude' (*Guardian*, 19 June 1987). By these means, the Conservatives would justify the steady demolition of democratically accountable local public services. A housing bill would seek to dismantle council housing, taking no account of the excellent homes built by Councils when sufficient resources had been available to them. Another bill would force Councils to hand over six of their functions to private business so that they could make profits on the rates with no accountability when services were inadequate. It would also ban Councils' so-called 'political propaganda', much of which had been recognised as a means of extending informed democracy. A further bill would abolish domestic rates in favour of a Poll Tax, increasing the tax burden on those least able to pay. Finally, the Secretary for the Environment proposed more urban development corporations, the new undemocratic quangos which would take over cities like Leicester or Nottingham – 'Places of that sort and smaller areas of bigger cities' (*Guardian*, as above) – to handle planning, housing, education and rates.

During the weekend on which the likely contents of the Queen's Speech were released, it was reported that several Councils faced a new threat of surcharge actions after the collapse of creative accountancy deals, and that there were continuing possibilities of surcharge against those delaying setting a rate in 1985. Councils had taken these steps only to maintain public services on behalf of their people, hoping that the Government would recognise its case, and were then labelled 'irresponsible'. But who would challenge the Government's irresponsibility in its use of public monies? It is difficult to see how the Audit Commission or the court, using the same criteria as they had for Councils, could have justified Government activities in selling off assets built up over the years, since the Government was not taking into account tax payers' interests nor properly carrying out what the Law Lords called 'fiduciary duties' when they decided against a local authority's transport policies in 1985.

People may wonder how we can talk about the crisis in, or the destabilising of, democracy in Britain, the mother of Parliaments. We believe the evidence has accumulated for some years. For example, in February, 1985, '20/20 Vision' on Channel 4 screened an interview with an MI5 worker who pointed out that the infiltration of voluntary organisations like CND was being stepped up in the 1980s, and employees recruited for work of this kind increased in number, apparently after political pressure. *Guardian* reporters, following up evidence of the same kind, noted that in trade unions and similar bodies 'infiltrators are used to supply information, but also to influence events' (*Guardian*, 19 April 1984).

Finally, in the run-up to the 1987 election, right-wing Conservatives were beginning to be more confident in justifying apparent subversion. Ten years ago would there not have been a more forceful denunciation by our elected representatives if an admittedly right wing, but none the less reputable, newspaper, like the *Sunday Telegraph*, had printed such a clearly subversive editorial as that on 3 May 1987? Under the headline, 'But Did Those MI5 Plotters "Have A Case"', the editor wrote, 'The ugly suspicion must arise that quite a number of sane and honorable people have found reason for concluding that desperate measures were justified to get rid of the Wilson Government . . . Of course, they have no constitutional rights to indulge in destabilisation. What they did, if they did do it, was outrageous.' Nevertheless, an enquiry 'might establish not only MI5's madness, but also the method in it . . . given a reasonably healthy body politic . . . MI5 should not dream of plotting'. Mr Worsthorne concludes that the electorate may not be trusted democratically to choose healthy politics unless they choose Conservative, and, since he was confident they would do so in 1987, MI5 could rest at ease. The *Sunday Telegraph* is not a Government mouthpiece, but in the 1970s right-wing outriders, including Peregrine Worsthorne, produced outrageous statements, on unemployment and the trade unions, for example, which prepared people for what would soon be 'respectable' government policy in the 1980s. Or, to put it another way, what would have been the political reaction in the run-up period to an election if an equivalent paper of the Left, with similar circulation to that of the *Sunday Telegraph*, had produced an editorial virtually justifying secret service destabilisation of an elected government? In this book, we had to recognise the link between what was happening to local democracy and the undermining of a broader range of liberties in this way.

It is for these reasons that we have spelled out the international scale of the challenge to democracy in a book on local government. We believe that it is the only way satisfactorily to answer the question posed by many people over recent years, as to why

Mrs Thatcher's Government has spent so much time on local government finance and local government powers, even to the point of stepping outside the constitution. The answer lies in a vision of the world, not of particular cities. The Conservative manifesto claimed that 'Britain is, once again, giving a lead in world affairs . . . no democracy has a better record than Britain in standing up to the terrorists, who threaten the most basic values of civilised life' (Conservative manifesto, pp. 71, 74). In practice, Mrs Thatcher has not been a voice for Britain, but for the policies of President Reagan and international finance. Along with the United States President, she has supported terrorists like the Contras in Nicaragua, not stood up to them, even though they have been fighting a democratically supported government whose election was validated by the United Nations, the Common Market and even a Conservative representative. She has urged caution in support of the people of South Africa seeking self-determination because it spells danger for international business. And the 'radicalism' of the Conservatives has required not courage or patriotism but its opposite, economic surrender. Behind all the waving of the flags, Britain's economy, its democracy and its freedom have all been put second to international economic interests. Whatever the benefits for some in material terms, and the spoils are likely to be divided unequally, British people will be less in control of their own destiny following the Thatcher years. Local politics has tried to offer an alternative way forward and that is why the argument in this book has to go beyond local government, as normally understood.

Whilst election results profoundly affect the climate and atmosphere in which debate is possible and alternatives are feasible, the issues remain the same. For people who pursue a cause like democracy, temporary setbacks give rise to the need to rethink strategy and approach, but they do not spell terminal illness for the principles for which they stand. All those interested in the long-term future of this country, and the world, would do well to lift their eyes from the immediate results of the British general election to focus on the long-term pattern of events which can be discerned, and on how the tide and climate of opinion can be influenced in favour of a civilised democracy.

Introduction

There is a crisis at the heart of British democracy. Freedom and the right to dissent have been curtailed. This arises from the fact that it is in the interests of international capital to turn as many human activities as possible into a commodity which can be bought and sold. Freedom, for the Conservative Party in the 1980s, has meant the freedom to buy and sell – the 'magic of the market place', as it has been called – small comfort for those who have little with which to buy and little to sell. People like the bustle and bargaining of their local markets, but the international market, dominated by transnational companies and financial institutions, offers the opposite of such direct personal contact and choice. The international market is becoming the arena which determines every aspect of the nation's political decision making.

Focusing attention on market 'freedom' also creates an illusion which hides the meaning of true personal liberty and choice, and diverts attention from the fact that they have been whittled away in the 1980s. The market offers people the freedom to choose a car of this colour or that colour, it also increases the opportunity for more people to buy cars. These are important considerations but they do not offer the opportunity to all the people to determine the life they want to live and how they want to live it. These are the decisions which should be given priority, even if the advertising moguls, with their enormous resources, try to persuade us differently. Democracy is the means by which people can make these decisions.

This book is not a party political tract. The issues transcend the immediate contest between parties. In the end it should be the people who decide what kind of politics they want and what kind of direction they want the country to take. The Conservative Party has been directly responsible for the erosion of freedom. The SDP/Liberal Alliance would put the market before democracy in the final analysis. Nor do we hold any brief for those Labour parliamentarians, councillors or party members who have not built defences against the international political tide, which has moved against democracy, social justice and economic good sense. Local democratic politics has been increasingly exposed to the force of this tide.

In order to foster an extension of the international market into every aspect of the nation's life, the Conservatives concentrated political power at the centre of the parliamentary system, not merely opposing but seeking to destroy any challenge to its purpose which might arise from the exercise of democratic freedoms, fought for over the centuries. Their attack on the trade unions was declared in advance and was remorselessly pursued. As early as 27 May 1978, the *Economist* gave details of the final report of the Conservative Party's policy group on the nationalised industries, drafted by the radical rightwinger, Nicholas Ridley MP. The Ridley Plan clearly outlined a five-part strategy for dealing with any trade union opposition to Tory policies, anticipating and preparing for the coal industry to be the most likely battleground. What followed in the 1980s indicated that the plans were well prepared.

Confrontation with local government was less well prepared and heralded by the Conservative Party, following more from the logic of its policies than from a carefully thought-out strategy.[1] It was not so easy, even for the radical Right, to challenge local government and local democracy, which have strong support in important sections of the Conservative Party. The first and most public reason for challenging local democracy concerned public spending policy. In effect, a switch was achieved between the balance of central and local taxation. In the first five years of the Thatcher government, the equivalent of 4p off income tax was removed from grants and subsidies to local government. By 1986, taking the equivalent to what had been provided in grants in 1979 – updated for inflation – there had been a staggering £17 billion reduction in the government contribution to local services. The intention was clear: public services would be cut. Local and not central government would be blamed for the inevitable increase in local rates (even in areas which agreed to implement massive cutbacks), and public provision would become discredited in the eyes of the electorate.

The methods used became increasingly sophisticated: cutting the total amount available to local government; changing the system of distribution to individual authorities; penalising 'over-spending' authorities. Having tried coercion and psychological warfare, the government resorted to direct central control. Through the operation of the 1984 Rates Act, they were to fix levels of expenditure and the amount which local authorities could raise in rates. This deprived local communities of powers which they had had since 1601. Finally the GLC and the metropolitan counties were abolished in 1986.

The second reason that local government came under attack was more fundamental and ideological. Many councils and political leaders opposed the government's broad strategy. They had started to develop alternatives and to win popular support, even in the face of large rate increases made necessary by the reduction in government grant. The proposals to abolish the GLC and the six metropolitan counties owed more to political motives than to a desire to streamline and reconstruct local government.

At each stage, local government fought back. But given the ultimate power invested in central government, it can always have the final say – so the GLC and the metropolitan counties were abolished despite resistance, and the Rates Act became law. However, the opposition outside Parliament built itself into British politics in a way which could have profound consequences. There was more widespread support for the institutions of local government than the government had anticipated and stronger feelings for the welfare state than it might have hoped. People must decide what they want to do about this.

Much has been written about the way in which particular institutions in local government have been dismantled, particularly the Greater London Council.[2] The clash between Liverpool City Council and the government has also been examined in detail.[3] The aim of this book is to look at the overall ideological conflict between central and local government and at the implications of this for British politics and society, particularly as suggested by the policies adopted by a number of Labour councils. Our intention is therefore not simply to offer a study of local government, but to reflect on the shift that local government has made in the 1980s from the political attitudes prevailing since 1945, into a rudimentary opposition movement against the ruling party in Westminster. If we draw heavily on Sheffield's past and present for illustration, it is because we started by interpreting our own experience.

Chapters 1 to 6 seek to demonstrate how the measures adopted by the Conservative government to contain local politics were more than an attempt to reduce public expenditure. Defence of local democracy in the 1980s has not simply been about the relationship between central and local government, nor about old-style centralism versus decentralised participative democracy; it amounts to a clash between political democracy and 'economic democracy'. Though Margaret Thatcher's government embarked on a programme to diminish the role and power of local government, it was not simply in order to replace it with the central state. It was motivated by a much deeper and more fundamental commitment to the interests of private and corporately owned wealth. These already dominate society through their economic power. The Conservatives intended to curtail the counteracting force which is provided by democratic political institutions.

How best to respond to profound economic and social change has always been a central issue in politics. What is remarkable in recent years is the speed and scale of such change, and the forceful stance which the government has taken in responding to and shaping events – on the one hand offering a definite vision of a future in which freedom is equated with how much you have to spend in the marketplace, and on the other playing on fears and uncertainty to achieve its ends.

Rapid change often creates a feeling of uncertainty and a loss of direction. People not only fear financial insecurity for themselves and those around them, but they also feel threatened by changing standards of behaviour, of culture and of individual as well as collective status and role. One set of changes often triggers or exaggerates others. In such circumstances, benchmarks for what is acceptable in social relationships fade, moral codes tend to be undermined, and uncertainty about the future leads to immediate self-interest overriding cooperative ways of living. In a highly urbanised society where so many factors produce individualism and fragmentation, a recognition of interdependence is crucial for retaining a civilised future.

It is the purpose of democratic politics to give legitimate authority to economic and social institutions and relationships within the nation, which enable people to enjoy the most satisfying lives possible, taking into account the country's economic performance and its foreign political interests. In Chapter 1 we suggest that there has been consistent failure by parliamentarians to carry out this democratic purpose over recent decades. It would be inappropriate to attempt a 'state of the nation' survey, but it is important to indicate the scale of the political problem, one in which 'law and order', serious inequality within the country and growing inequality in the world cannot be treated as separate issues if a clear and more certain future is to be built by the British people.

Any suggestion that local government has the power to wield decisive political and economic influence over the country is obviously wrong. Indeed, the era of giant transnationals places serious constraints on even parliament's capacity to act effectively. Local government and local political action cannot on their own solve unemployment or provide for a major redistribution of resources, let alone create new relations between Britain and the rest of the world. However, politics is not simply concerned with taking decisions. It is also the means for setting an agenda for what should be done and how it can be achieved.

Local politics

We must make it clear what we mean by 'local politics', a phrase which is at the heart of our argument. For our present purpose we do not mean solely to imply activities in a particular locality which are conventionally called 'political', either in everyday or academic terms. Nor is the phrase merely intended to distinguish local from 'national politics', although Chapters 2 and 3 illustrate that there is some value in considering the contrast between the two. In fact these two chapters are an extended definition of the term 'local politics' as we use it. They sum up an important tradition in British politics which takes seriously the need *to build democracy*; since democracy is more than the mere right to cast a vote at elections. Active politics of this kind has commonly only been available to privileged elites and powerful interests. Local politics is about its extension so that people can run their own affairs, adopting an increasingly broad perspective as confidence in democracy grows. Clearly there are conservative and reactionary elements in local government and in local political affairs, but our contention is that the more active democracy is extended, the more the weaknesses and limitations of these elements will be exposed. We argue that it is more the political activities of international business and some sections of the media, rather than local politics, which manipulate events so as to encourage reactions based on fear, prejudice and uncertainty.

Chapters 2 and 3 therefore look at the nature and quality of local politics in Britain, and its ability to influence events over the long term by helping to shape such an agenda, through a combination of independent political organisational and administrative powers. We draw our evidence from history, not because we believe the past gives authority to what people do now and in the future, but because there are strong grounds for holding on to some of the basic principles of democratic practice which have been established. The fundamental social changes created by the Industrial Revolution were accompanied by pressure for political power from below which began to present a democratic counterweight to the owners and controllers of industry and commerce, and to provide collective answers to the problems which change brought. Along with the growth of trade unions, cooperative and community organisations and political parties, local government was significant in extending democratic involvement and providing services which used collective resources to fight disease, poor housing and industrial squalor. Today, central government is actively engaged in reversing the cooperative advances which followed the Industrial Revolution, at a time when technological advance gives rise to an economic and social upheaval of enormous proportions. Rather than democratic structures being used to help plan and manage the impact of such change, the representative and participative machinery for democratic action has actually been undermined.

It will be clear that our concept of local politics is wider than the formal system of local government, and that we do not disregard the significance of broader democratic movements in pointing the way towards a more civilised society, such as those for peace and for the preservation and better use of the environment. We include trade unions, who are too often portrayed as mere defenders of the status quo, and who have indeed been forced on the defensive by recent government policies and the economic recession. Chapters 4 to 6 show why the radical Conservatives of the 1980s recognised the particular danger presented by new initiatives in local politics in the broadest sense. In short, local politics was providing a means by which democratic practices could create policies in the interests of the vast majority of people in local communities, not only by highlighting the inadequacies of private enterprise but also by demonstrating that the politics of the marketplace are in no way natural or inevitable.

In Chapter 7 we describe the political manoeuvring between

local government and Westminster as the Conservatives sought to impose their will by technical means within the system of local government finance. Problems were created for both central and local government when the political issues were presented in these technical terms, but it was an inevitable consequence of the fact that local government is, to a considerable degree, constitutionally an agent of central government. Initially, at least, Margaret Thatcher's government did not want its own supporters to think that they were seriously prepared to dismantle traditional constitutional relations or remove local powers. In local politics it took time before the full implications of the cumulative measures became apparent, even to those who eventually decided to organise the unprecedented local government campaign which is described in Chapter 8.

Today there is more hope in looking for the possibility of a reasonable future for Britain in enterprising town halls and county halls than in Westminster. That is the theme of this book. It is not about local government in the conventional, constitutional sense – it is about locally based politics in which it is possible for politicians to listen as well as talk. Indeed it argues that too sharp a distinction between 'electors' on the one hand and politicians on the other is unhelpful, because democracy requires everyone to take on political rights and responsibilities. The argument presented here is for debate with people who are not prepared to hand democracy over to Westminster or businessmen and accountants; who believe it is possible for government to be both active and responsive, democratic as well as purposeful, and who know that the new economic era demands such politics.

It may be considered that a book giving so much attention to a city like Sheffield, and similar urban areas, is only relevant to the industrial north and midlands. We shall argue that this is not so, (and there are many local authorities in the South-East[4] who have been involved in the local politics we describe). Its significance overrides the simple north–south divide, or the inner city preoccupation, which have misleadingly been presented as the nub of the British problem over the past two decades.

The defence of local government concerns the two most important questions of the future, other than the issue of survival in a nuclear age. It involves the true nature of public and private resources – questioning the short-sighted idea that public spending uses up wealth while private spending creates wealth. It also concerns the nature of democracy – how collective action can retain and develop its rightful place alongside electoral representation. Conservative governments from 1979 abused their constitutional powers over local government for their own political ends. Deliberately or not, they undermined an important element in the British democratic system whose very strength has been indicated by the tenacity of its resistance.

1

The Challenge to Democracy

The world economic recession has put great pressure on democracy in many countries. Confrontation between Margaret Thatcher's Conservative government and many local councils in Britain during the 1980s has to be understood in this context. Since the 1979 manifesto, the Conservatives have persistently warned Britain about the serious political and economic problem which the recession posed to this country: 'This election is about the future of Britain – a great country which seems to have lost its way.'[1] Yet the direction in which the Conservatives chose to lead the country accelerated the pace at which Britain has been underdeveloped by the same economic forces and policies that underdevelop the Third World, and has led to an erosion of democracy and liberty. The ideological confrontation that is now so clear between central and local government came about when local politics in some parts of the country began to develop a different political agenda for their own communities and to challenge the government's policies in practice. To understand why local politics developed in this way we have to look at the scale of the problem that British society faces, the failure of successive governments to address it, and some of the evidence which is beginning to accumulate of what the future will be like in Britain if Conservative policies were allowed to continue.

The end of empire

What position should Britain hold in the world, economically and politically, without an empire to buttress its economy? For over 200 years a British sense of wellbeing and material prosperity has depended on the possession of an empire – giving our small island a special status in the world. Other nations, like Japan, have lost an empire but have moved on to create a new political and economic role in the world. We would not wish to emulate

Japan's policies and methods, but it is important to recognise that hanging on to Britain's imperial legacy inhibits the development of a new international perspective and that this has serious consequences for the quality of life in this country.

Reducing the gap between rich and poor in the world must be at the centre of domestic as well as international politics. In the early 1970s a quarter of the world's population controlled 90 per cent of its scientific capacity, 70 per cent of its meat and 80 per cent of its protein. Even when some of the less developed countries have been able to improve their economic position, the gap has widened in relation to the more developed countries. The countries where this is not the case have mainly been those where industrial development has been stimulated for strategic or political reasons, such as South Korea or Singapore.

The following table, which uses World Bank GNP per capita data, shows the average annual growth rates which would be required in the period 1984 to 2000 in each of the listed countries for their GNP per capita in 2000 to equal a half or even a third of that enjoyed by the United States in 1984.

		(% per annum)			
	GNP per capita 1984 US$	Full Per capita income of US	Half Per capita income of US	Third Per capita income of US	Actual growth rate 1965–84
Singapore	7,260	2·9	0·2	−1·3	7·8
Venezuela	3,410	6·0	3·2	1·6	0·9
Mexico	2,040	8·1	5·2	3·6	2·9
Malaysia	1,980	8·2	5·4	3·7	4·5
Brazil	1,720	8·8	5·9	4·3	4·6
Thailand	860	11·7	8·8	7·1	4·2
Nigeria	730	12·4	9·5	7·8	2·8
Egypt	720	12·5	9·5	7·8	4·3
Philippines	660	12·9	9·9	8·2	2·6
Zambia	470	14·4	11·4	9·6	−1·3
Sri Lanka	360	15·5	12·5	10·8	2·9
Kenya	310	16·2	13·1	11·4	2·1
India	260	17·0	13·9	12·2	1·6
Tanzania	210	18·0	14·9	13·1	0·6

Growth rate of per capita income required to reach US level by the year 2000

Source: World Bank, *World Development Report*, 1986.

When the Independent Commission on International Development Issues, chaired by Willy Brandt, produced its report *North–South: a Programme for Survival*, in 1980, their conclusion was clear:

Current trends point to a sombre future for the world economy and international relations. A painful outlook for the poorer countries with no end to poverty and hunger; continuing world stagnation combined with inflation; international monetary disorder; mounting debts and deficits; protectionism; major tensions between countries competing for energy, food and raw materials; growing world population and more unemployment in north and south; increasing threats to the environment and the international commons through deforestation and desertification, overfishing and overgrazing, the pollution of air and water. And overshadowing everything the menacing arms race.[2]

Brandt calls for policies which recognise the 'mutuality of interests' between north and south, and points to the results which 'can only be achieved if you put together moral conviction with something which has to do with your children'. In our view, this generation is already suffering from the consequences of the failure to combine morality and realism. British economic policy helps to create poverty and social division both overseas and at home.

In *How Europe Underdeveloped Africa*, Walter Rodney's argument applies not only to Africa:

So long as foreigners own land, mines, factories, banks, insurance companies, means of transportation, newspapers, power stations, etc., then for so long will the wealth of Africa flow outwards into the hands of those elements. In other words, in the absence of direct political control, foreign investment ensures that the natural resources and the labour of Africa produce economic value which is lost to the continent.[3]

Britain and the USA held between them three-quarters of world stock in direct company investment in the late 1960s. These two imperial powers, of the nineteenth and twentieth centuries respectively, were then drawing nearly half their income from past investment in underdeveloped countries. Most of that income does not go back to increase the wealth of the Third World but boosts trade in the richer countries. Trade in the poorer countries grows slowly by comparison. Third World countries are forced to borrow, at increased interest rates. As one economist, André Gunter Frank, noted in 1986, 'the current world debt represents a tenfold multiplication from what it was when the world economic crisis began in 1973'. Interest payments on a growing debt at rising rates lead to countries having to borrow to service previous debts. 'The Third World debt today is a new form of taxation without representation . . . The poor had no representation in the political decisions to borrow or use the money and they derived scarcely any benefit from it. Yet now . . . they are being asked to foot the bill.' Even Henry Kissinger, former US Secretary of State, 'was moved to observe with alarm how developed countries, foreign banks, and the International Monetary Fund and World banks dictate terms'.[4]

If this situation is to change in favour of the Third World, major adjustments must be made in Britain. The Brandt Report has been criticised by Altaf Ganhar, among others, because it did not recognise sufficiently the domestic situation in the richer nations:

The entire argument in the report is based on the premise of inter-dependence and mutuality of north–south interests. But the premise remains unsubstantiated . . . Surely the politicians and industrialists in the north are aware that growing exports to the developing countries create new jobs in their economies? But these jobs do not always go to the persons who lose employment when marginal industries have to close down in the face of cheaper and better products imported from the Third World. The north has to adopt adjustment policies to phase out workers from the uneconomic sectors and absorb them into more sophisticated and rewarding sectors of the economy. But such adjustments can only be planned on a long-term basis and the needs of the south require immediate satisfaction. It is this incompatibility of time-scales which has brought about the present north south stalemate.[5]

Ganhar's pessimism seems justified, and Britain is becoming increasingly less capable of generating support for the necessary readjustments. Many sections of the British population have begun to experience the process of underdevelopment. The links between the economic deprivation and political oppression dominating so much of Africa, Asia and Latin America, and what happens now in many parts of Britain, are beginning to emerge. Conditions may be far less acute here than in the Third World, but they are still unacceptable in the midst of great wealth and lead to defensive and parochial reactions to industrial change. Achieving change by democratic means is an urgent priority.

The international pattern of increasing riches and increasing poverty, of development and underdevelopment, has become clearly apparent in Britain. The empire made the City of London the financial centre of the world and its institutions have been determined to retain their influence. British economic policy has been dominated by their requirements – maintaining the free flow of capital or determining currency values and interest rates so that profits can be made by depositing, buying and selling money rather than investing in production of goods and services. Speaking on Granada's 'World in Action' programme on 6 December 1986, a leading industrialist portrayed a casino and betting-shop economy in which finance used to be the handmaid of industry but now industry has become the football of finance. Major manufacturing undertakings such as the General Electric Company prefer to keep their capital liquid for speculation rather than invest in research and production. 'The biggest talking point in the City for several years has, of course, been the fate of GEC's £1.6 billion cash mountain . . . Mr Nicholas Edwards, Secretary of State for Wales, has accused it of turning itself into a financial institution on the back of government contracts, instead of risking its own resources to develop and market new products aggressively', wrote Guy de Jonquieres in the *Financial Times*, 13 April 1985, but GEC has been precisely in line with government policy. Transnational companies and conglomerates sell off industrial plant and lay off workers to amass capital for speculative profit making.

In addition to encouraging its extension, the Conservative governments of the 1980s have actively engaged in the casino economy. In 1986, the government spent £300 million of taxpayers' money on advertising and managing, through the City of London, the sale of British Gas, with no benefits to industry either through investment or pricing policies. The Managing Director of Forgemasters in Sheffield (in other contexts a critic of public ownership) said on the same 'World in Action' programme that his firm's £6 million a year bill for gas would not be eased in any way by the sale, and a private monopoly would be less accountable to industrial and domestic users than a public one had been. As in the case of British Telecom, the sale of public assets results mainly in the accumulation of profits through share transactions.

There has clearly been sufficient wealth available to reshape Britain's economy. After the Conservative government removed exchange controls in 1979, private investment abroad rose dramatically. Overseas portfolio investment by UK companies rose from £12 billion in 1979 to almost £90 billion by December 1985. The UK's stock of overseas assets is estimated to have been 25 per cent of gross domestic product (GDP) at the end of 1985, compared with 6 per cent of GDP in 1979. The financial institutions of the City of London have maintained and even expanded their international role, bequeathed from imperial days, but they do not contribute effectively to the needs of the domestic economy. Strongly encouraging the City of London, with all the pomp and circumstance which surrounds its political role, has been distinctly unpatriotic. Most recently the de-regulation of the London Stock Exchange in 1986 (the so-called Big Bang), was a further attempt to maintain its world-wide significance against the pressure of international, mainly United States, securities firms. In the new de-regulated arrangement, continuing U.S. pressure along with that of the even more heavyweight Japanese financial interests, could be expected to wrest even more control of their economy from the British people if no counteracting political force was exerted. Financial decisions would take no account whatsoever of the needs of British communities. The government measured Britain's economic health by the state of its financial institutions, but what is good for finance capital is not necessarily good for Britain.

When capital is used in this way it cannot be used at home. In 1980 total investment in British industry represented a smaller percentage of national income per head of population than in any other OECD country except Portugal, and this followed a long period of similar underinvestment and renewal, as shown in the following table.

British communities have the lifeblood drained from them. The gap widens between old industrial areas starved of investment

	1963	1968	1973	1978	1983
United States	17·9	18·1	19·1	19·5	16·9
Japan	31·5	33·2	36·4	30·8	28·5
Germany	25·6	22·4	23·9	20·8	20·8
France	22·1	23·3	23·8	21·4	19·6
United Kingdom	16·8	19·4	20·1	18·6	16·5
Italy	24·0	20·3	20·8	18·7	18·0
Canada	20·5	21·5	22·4	22·2	19·4
Total OECD	20·6	21·1	23·2	22·1	19·7

Gross investment in British industry as a percentage of GDP

Source: Organisation for Economic Cooperation and Development (OECD), *Economic Outlook*, and House of Lords Select Committee on Overseas Trade, 1985.

and new growth areas. The traveller who moves from Hampshire to the Dearne Valley in South Yorkshire, or from East Anglia to Merseyside, can see ready physical evidence of the crisis. The Family Expenditure survey figures for 1986 illustrate a distinct geographical pattern of inequality. They reveal that total average spending each week in 1984–5 was £181.53 in the southeast, £142.17 in Yorkshire and Humberside and as low as £131.16 in the north. The gap has widened since 1979, the most rapid increase being between the years 1979 and 1981. For example, in 1979, household expenditure in the southeast was £17.51 per week higher than in Yorkshire and Humberside. Since that date expenditure has increased by 76 per cent in the southeast compared with 69 per cent in Yorkshire and Humberside, and we must bear in mind that figures of average spending do not show the position of those who are worst off. (See Appendix 1.)

Although there are clear geographical differences, it is not really a north–south divide, or even a west–east polarisation as others suggest, that should concern us. It is a widening gap between those who benefit from present investment patterns in industry, commerce and housing, and those who don't. The latter are workers and their families, young and old, who live in the areas which were once Britain's industrial base. People in Scotland, Wales, Northern Ireland and the north of England suffer most obviously, but there are also many in the west and southeast, where the surrounding wealth often makes the contrast starker. Levels of unemployment provide the most obvious evidence of the consequences. The graph below shows the numbers of unemployed nationally and the percentage level of unemployment. (The difference between the 'old' and 'new' calculations shows how the government has misrepresented the level of unemployment by changing the way it collects its figures on nineteen occasions.)

By the end of 1983 there were more people unemployed for one year or more than the entire unemployed population in 1975 (roughly 1 million), and by 1985 the number out of work for two years or more had almost reached the same figure at 0·8 million.

Long-term unemployment is concentrated in those areas which had previously contributed massively to Britain's wealth through manufacturing: the West Midlands, the north, Wales and Scotland. The employment census published in January 1987 showed that 94 per cent of jobs lost between 1979 and 1986 were north of a line between the Bristol Channel and The Wash. More

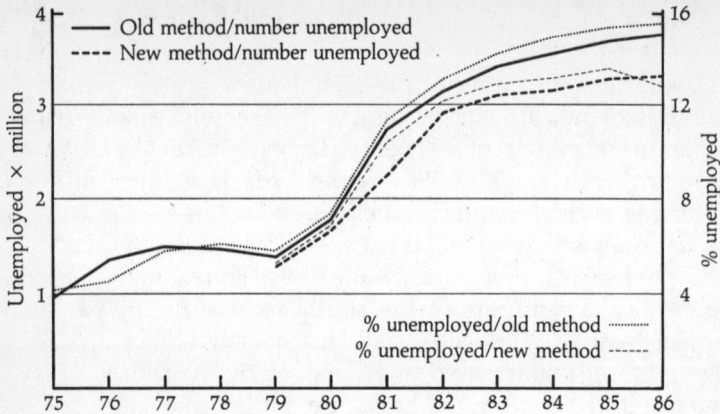

Source: Department of Employment Gazettes 1975–6.

than two-thirds of the service-sector jobs created since 1979 were in the more fortunate southeast. The northern regions lost almost 1·5 million manufacturing jobs in the same period but gained only 272,000 service jobs compared with 547,000 manufacturing jobs lost and 588,000 service-sector jobs gained in the south (about one-third of all manufacturing jobs lost in the Midlands, the north, Scotland and Wales went after 1979). Nationally there was a fall in investment from 1980 to 1987 of 18 per cent. The dramatic decline in manufacturing and construction jobs in this period (28 per cent) compares with an increase in Japan (4·9 per cent) and much smaller declines in the United States (2 per cent), West Germany (8·5 per cent) and Italy (9·4 per cent). In Sheffield, for example, once a premier special steels centre, 47,632 jobs were lost between the mid 1970s and the early 1980s in the manufacturing sector compared with 19,905 gained in the service sector, with a particularly rapid rise in unemployment from 1979, when Sheffield exceeded the national rate at which people were put out of work.[6]

Real material deprivation has become endemic in the worst areas. Andrew Arendt, writing in the *Financial Times* of 22 May 1986, summarised the 1985 publication of the government's *Regional Trends*:

Its statistics give a picture of dramatically different economic and social conditions. Below a line drawn between South Wales and the Wash, the southern picture is of a growing population, new housing stock and relative economic prosperity. Above the line a grim collection of statistics

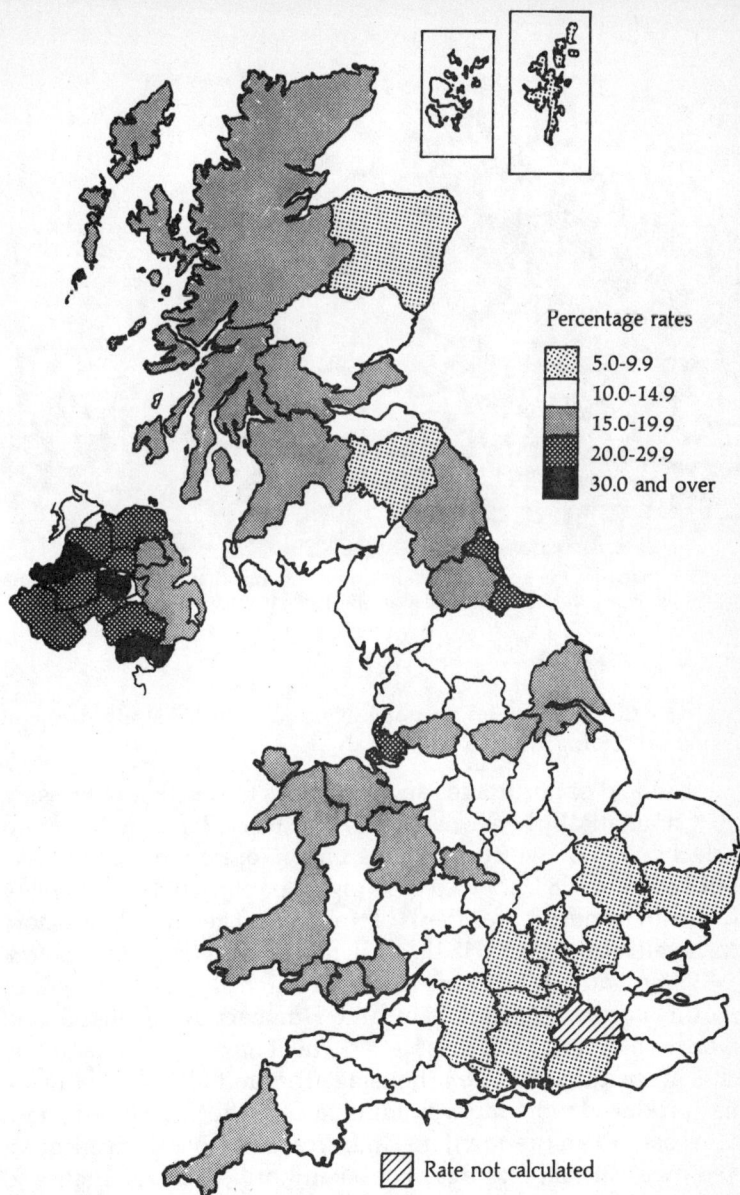

Percentage rates

5.0-9.9
10.0-14.9
15.0-19.9
20.0-29.9
30.0 and over

Rate not calculated

Unemployment in Britain, October 1985. Source: Department of Employment, *Regional Trends*, 1986.

1   The attack on the special steels industry: economic policies succeed in the
    1980s where the Luftwaffe failed in the 1940s (Carlisle Street, Sheffield).

portrays the north as an economically and socially deprived region
facing continuing industrial decline.

Educational opportunities and standards of health and housing
vary dramatically between regions. The Black Report in 1981, and
a DHSS report which the government preferred not to have
published in 1985, showed growing disparities in the availability
of health resources: 'residents of Hampstead get three times more
cash value from the NHS than the residents of Oldham.'[7] Before
1979, local authorities were producing high slum clearance rates
in the northwest, Yorkshire and Humberside, Scotland and
Northern Ireland. It is these areas which have been worst hit by
cuts in spending on public housing. The shift to private housing
has produced more rapid building rates in the prosperous south
and east, not in the worst housing areas. This has been encouraged by financial pressures on local authorities to raise rents and
reduce subsidies, through council house sales and through the
raising of the upper limits on mortgages qualifying for tax relief.
For those who cannot afford to buy, the situation deteriorates. In
August 1985 the Building Societies Association admitted that an

increase in home ownership was to a great extent due to the lack of decent rented accommodation. By July 1986 building societies were providing £3·8 billion for mortgages in one month, twice the annual total which the government allowed local authorities to borrow for housing investment. (See Appendix 2.)

Within the regions themselves, the widening gap between the comfortably off and the poor is unmistakable. For those in secure, well-paid employment, living standards rose in the first half of the 1980s through increases in real income and reductions in the higher rates of taxation, but for the unemployed and low paid, standards deteriorated.

The new Right (and more recently the SDP) have been politically astute in trying to unite suburb and countryside around the ideology of a property-owning democracy against the inner cities. In the latter, people who cannot afford the suburban residential life, or who do not want it, are increasingly thrown back on their own resources as public spending is cut. The dangers can be seen in both the shabby physical fabric of the inner city and the social tensions which have until recently been associated with urban life in the USA, and whose absence in Britain many Americans have so often noted with pleasure.

There is abundant evidence of the grimness of inner-city life in numerous reports. In one review the author summed up the stark reality behind the statistics:

It consists of a constant struggle to make ends meet. It is rich only in fear: fear of the next unpayable fuel bill; fear of another humiliating encounter with the officials in the DHSS offices; fear especially for the isolated elderly of robbery or physical violence; fear among the young and the black that once again they will be stopped and questioned by the police if they gather on the streets. There is little that offers hope. The prospects of better housing or some substantial improvement in the decaying environment of the inner city, appear remote and over it all hangs the imminence of yet more closures of the factories.[8]

In similar vein, the authors of *Faith in the City* – the report on urban deprivation commissioned by the Archbishop of Canterbury – wrote of their research:

We have been confronted with the human consequences of unemployment, which in some urban areas may be over 50 per cent of the labour force, and which occasionally reaches a level as high as 80 per cent – consequences which may be compounded by the effects of racial discrimination. We have seen physical decay, whether of older Victorian terraced housing or of inferior system-built blocks of flats, which has in places created an environment so degrading that some people have set fire to their own homes rather than be condemned to live in them indefinitely. Social disintegration has reached a point in some areas that shop windows are boarded up, cars cannot be left on the street, residents are afraid either to get out themselves, or to ask others in, and there is a pervading sense of powerlessness and despair.[9]

Occasionally the explosive political tensions of the inner cities force Westminster to take notice, through riot and civil disorder. But the inner-city obsession then obscures what is really happening. For the inner cities represent only the most uncomfortable and newsworthy evidence that whole sections of the economy are being written off as capital and technology move on, using the wealth created by communities now discarded. Mining, steel and engineering areas die in the same way as the inner cities.

Lost opportunities

It is a mistake to blame the Thatcher government alone for the present situation. The 1960s and 1970s saw successive failures by politicians from all parties to offer a perspective which could lead to popular support for a new direction as the various symptoms of Britain's problems presented themselves with increasing urgency.

The first but perhaps most dubious opportunity was presented by the European Economic Community. By the time of the 1975 referendum the potential value to Britain of membership of the EEC had already been eroded by the failure of successive previous governments to negotiate entry on terms that were fully advantageous to Britain. France agreed with Germany and the original founders to set up the Common Market as a treaty organisation and bargained accordingly; Britain then joined it as a club with rules to be observed. The common agricultural policy was France's price for agreement to the initial treaty. It ensured that the French farming community, a socially and politically important but technologically backward sector of its economy, could be restructured without too much strain and disorder. The cost was shared by Europe and as the years have progressed that cost has become immense and legendary. Cattle are slaughtered needlessly, new potatoes dyed blue and vegetables ploughed into the ground. (It is worth noting also that intensive agricultural policies in the Common Market and other industrialised countries have worsened the economic situation of primary producers in the Third World.)

When Britain joined the EEC, its older industrial areas were paying the price for their early development, and urgently needed reinvestment and restructuring. However, though 45 per cent of the community's agriculture is now designated as 'less-favoured agricultural areas which need special measures of assistance', there is no parallel industrial policy to meet Britain's need for industrial redevelopment. The Social Fund and the European Regional Development Fund are merely gestures in the right direction – totally inadequate because the political will is not there. Indeed the British government in the 1980s, due to its dislike of public spending in general and its political antagonisms towards the regions which would have benefited, did not fully deploy the resources which were available.

Britain's conditions of entry should have been stated plainly: payment for agriculture in France should have been matched by payment to restructure Britain's traditional industrial areas, the inner cities, whose problems are the product of Britain being the oldest industrial nation. Successful negotiations would have brought real benefits and an opportunity for wider social reconstruction; failure would at least have demonstrated more clearly the nature of the EEC and its inability to take into account Britain's needs.

A more major opportunity was missed in the mid-1960s when, for a time, it seemed that the Labour Party, led by Harold Wilson, an apparently radical prime minister without a public-school background, was willing to present a vision of a future which depended neither on Britain being a major world power, nor on its becoming an offshore tourist attraction. When Harold Wilson, in his 1964 election campaign, referred to the white heat of the new technological revolution, he was also reflecting the mood of the time, not just the views of the Left. The National Economic Development Committee argued under a Conservative government in 1963:

More rapid industrial and technological change will be required to achieve a faster rate of economic growth . . . Nevertheless, if the necessary development is to be carried out smoothly and to the best advantage, measures will have to be taken to facilitate mobility of labour and avoid the hardship of redundancy.[10]

In the same year, at the Labour Party Conference, Harold Wilson stated:

We are redefining and we are restating our socialism in terms of scientific revolution. But that revolution cannot become a reality unless we are prepared to make far-reaching changes in economic and social attitudes which permeate the whole of our society.

In calling for changes in industry, however, the government took little account of the need to develop democratic institutions alongside economic ones. Industry was certainly rationalised and the effects softened by redundancy payments, but there was no increase in strategically planned investment. There was a drastic reshaping of our cities, with urban motorways breaking up communities, large profits for the building industry, and a high-rise and property boom, but despite an improvement in housing conditions for some, the social costs for many people brought dissatisfaction and protest.

Social policies designed to facilitate change failed to recognise the scale of the problem. Public expenditure rose following criticisms of private affluence and public squalor.[11] Yet, despite many reports proposing reforms, the eventual resources were inadequate and poorly directed. There was the Milner Holland Report on Housing in Greater London (1965), reports on children in trouble ('Children, Family and the Young Offender', 1965, and 'Children in Trouble', 1968), the Plowden Report on inadequate primary schools (1966), the Maude (1967), Mallaby (1967) and Redcliffe Maude (1969) reports on local government, the Seebohm Report (1968) on local authority personal social services, and the Skeffington Report (1969) on people and planning. Most of them placed great stress on the need for more professionalism in handling social problems, along with increased social spending. Too much of the expansion went into managing the problems of those who experienced change, not enough into redistribution of resources to benefit people directly. The Seebohm Report was described as a 'social workers' charter', not a manifesto on behalf of the poor and dispossessed.

Welfare spending alone is no solution to Britain's problems. People have to experience the benefits. Democracy needs to extend beyond the ballot box so that people can recognise the spending as theirs – not state hand-outs, not jobs for social workers, but a collective use of resources in the collective interest. Handing social problems over to teachers and social workers produces a paternalistic rather than a liberating approach to welfare – 'looking after' people, 'handling' people, 'managing' people in difficult times of change. Both through its collusion with financial and business interests, and its over-reliance on handing down welfare, Labour eventually lost its chance of asserting the true place of public spending and collective provision in a civilised society.

Anthony Crosland's book, *The Future of Socialism*,[12] which had become the bible of a generation of Labour politicians, argued that the economic boom of the 1950s and the institutions of the welfare state heralded a new, classless, 'post-industrial' society. This view was no basis on which to deal with the problems which emerged in the late 1960s and 1970s when the conflicts of interest between classes, which Crosland had consigned to history, became increasingly obvious.

We do not refer here to class as it is often discussed in the press and public debate, in terms of cloth caps and distinctions between the manners and life style of middle class and manual workers. Most people today do not want to maintain these differences in their own lives. We mean the conflicting interests which people can easily recognise. There are, on the one hand, those whose lives are based on the ownership of great wealth and the power which goes with it, including people close to power in high management and the professions. On the other hand are the vast majority of people who do not benefit from the ownership of capital or wield such influence in society. It is this second group, which makes up most of the nation, for whom the welfare state is crucial. This is what we mean by the distinction between classes, and it is not modified in any way by the greater distribution of small peripheral shareholdings.

The expansion of public spending as a proportion of gross national product which had resulted from the growth of the welfare state heightened competition for scarce resources at the same time as Britain's poor economic performance was limiting the size of the cake. A low rate of growth affected the size of the cake available for distribution both in profits and in wages and social benefits. The long boom had increased both trade union membership and the power of trade unions on the shop floor – unions could now bring pressure to bear to improve conditions and resist change when it opposed their interests.

Strong political leadership was required from a Labour government to turn this strength away from wage bargaining alone, or resistance to industrial change, and towards a commitment to industrial restructuring and the social improvements it could lead to. This could only be achieved by government challenging the power of those who owned and controlled industry and finance. Instead, it was the voice of the financial interests which swayed Labour in defining the key problems: instead of low investment and inadequate planning becoming the focus of attention, high wages and high public spending were blamed as the economic situation worsened. Concentration on the balance of payments and exchange rate in the two years after the 1966 election debilitated the Labour government and diverted it from this task.

The third missed opportunity came in the 1970s with the possibilities of constructive use of oil revenues. In a radio broadcast after the October 1974 election Harold Wilson tried once more to unite the country behind him, despite his fragile majority of three:

Elections inevitably divide the nation, harsh things are said by political parties about each other, but all parties are agreed that this country faces the biggest crisis since the war.

Unfortunately, while all parties agreed that a crisis existed, the Labour Party failed to offer an alternative to the monetarist solutions which now dominated economic policy. Two years later, in 1976, Britain capitulated to the orders of the International Monetary Fund to cut back its public spending: the scene for the next decade was being set.

The long-term consequence was a Conservative victory in 1979 at a crucial time, when the new wealth from North Sea oil was beginning to flow. Some of us will remember school essay titles in the 1950s and 1960s which asked, 'What would Britain do if we had Arab oil?' But we cannot remember any answer which argued that we should pay millions of people subsistence wages for doing nothing. These discoveries of fossil fuel, which in the coal era had formed the bedrock of an empire, provided an opportunity of escaping from the consequences of barely-understood decline. Investment from oil could have been used to tackle the linked problems of industrial change and social upheaval. Facilitating changes 'from the age of the smokestack to the era of the microchip'[13] means something quite different from the notion of simply destroying manufacturing industry, which was what became in effect the regional policy of the Conservative government.

The size of this lost opportunity can easily be seen by comparing Britain with Norway, another European country with an offshore oil fortune. In the four years to 1983, Norway's industrial output increased by 15 per cent and unemployment remained at only 3 per cent during a world recession which the British government blamed for its 13 per cent unemployment. Most impressive of all was the Norwegians' ability to reverse the small growth in unemployment in their country in the early 1980s.

	1976	1980	1983	1985
Norway	2·7	1·5	3·8	2·9
United Kingdom	5·4	5·8	11·3	13·2

Unemployment (%) in the first quarter each year
Source: OECD, *Labour Force Statistics*, 1985, No. 2, and
OECD, *Main Economic Indicators*, April 1986.

Despite a modest recovery in 1985, the rate of growth of UK manufacturing output also lagged a long way behind that of Norway:

	1983	1984	1985	Jan. 1986
	Industrial production 1980 = 100			
Norway	107	113	117	121
United Kingdom	101·9	103·2	108·1	109·4

Comparative growth of production
Source: OECD, *Labour Force Statistics* 1985, No. 2, and
OECD, *Main Economic Indicators*, April 1986.

Oil has been used to improve the quality of life in Norway. In 1977 they had 1·8 doctors per 1,000 population (UK 1·5 per 1,000). By 1981 Norway's figure was up to 2·0 and the UK's down to 1·3. Infant mortality in a similar period dropped from 8·8 to 7·5 per 1,000, while the United Kingdom stayed the same at 11·8. Revenue from British oil has been soaked up by the cost of increased social security, allowing the government to expand public spending in its most wasteful form, neglecting any restructuring of the manufacturing base and merely providing an anaesthetic for enforced social readjustment.

The Thatcher era

Margaret Thatcher's government came onstage as a dramatic political consequence of the failure of the past. She presented a vision which combined sentimentality with calculated opportunism, popular rhetoric with profoundly undemocratic practices; it offered the hollowness of a future based on imperial nostalgia abroad and Victorian values at home. When the British people failed to see through this combination of rhetoric and ruthlessness, the great opportunity of North Sea oil was hopelessly lost.

The new leadership of the Conservative Party had recognised the scale of the British problem since the 1970s, and the 1979 and 1983 Conservative manifestos were based on a clear political perspective on how to proceed. 'Stranded on the middle ground' was Sir Keith Joseph's analysis in a pamphlet written in 1973: according to his precepts, we were neither properly socialist nor properly capitalist. The Conservatives must therefore get rid of the socialist element, which meant reducing public spending, letting international companies run as much of the country's industries and services as possible, overcoming any obstacle in the workforce, particularly in organised trade unions, ignoring any opposition and breaking the mould of the mixed economy for ever. Instead of building on pride in a way of life and protecting communities, the British Conservatives attacked their own people, blaming those who had created wealth for the country's economic ills.

There are many examples of the link between the government's prejudice against those industrial areas which give them few votes and their short-sighted economic policies towards them. The decimation of the coal industry has been the most dramatic example, but it is also easy to see the rundown of special steels and related engineering products as a result of this approach, not merely stemming from a decline in international demand. Government policies which led to the demolition of special steels and related engineering production have been little short of the sabotage of the British manufacturing industry and those communities that depend on it. There has been an unplanned reduction in capacity, a failure to distinguish between crude steel output and special or alloy steel, an unquestioning acceptance of the EEC quota system, which has protected special steels in other countries, and a dogmatic observance of EEC rules for phasing out government subsidies to the steel industry by 1985, unlike France, which announced that its major subsidy to nationalised producers would continue to 1987. Taking alloy and stainless-steel production together, the UK ranked fourth out of ten in 1975, but by 1984 it was ninth, well behind the EEC and European Free Trade Association competitors like France, Germany, Italy and Sweden.[14]

In line with their lack of concern for production, the Conservatives have made no attempt to stimulate the home market by public investment in railways, for example, or by developing an imaginative response to the problems of the British motor industry. The decline of the motor industry was already well under way when Mrs Thatcher won the general election in 1979 – between 1972 and 1979 car production fell from 1·9 to 1 million cars a year. Between 1979 and 1984 British Leyland reduced its break-even output from 1 million to 430,000 cars a year, while two multinational producers, General Motors (Vauxhall) and Peugeot (Chrysler), reduced their operations in the UK. The Japanese company Nissan opened an assembly plant in Sunderland with enormous government subsidy. Against this background the Conservative government opened negotiations to 'privatise' the rump of British Leyland. The Conservatives' preference for a sale to General Motors over a management buy-out, and the subsequent sale of British Leyland's truck division to DAF, not only displayed their ideological opposition to nationalised industries, but also their lack of imagination in responding to the needs of industry. For example, new developments in electronics and robotics could have led to falling economies of scale and improved product quality which would have made it easier for small and medium-sized producers to survive if they had been able to collaborate on developing new technologies.[15] It is in directions like this that oil revenues should have been turned.

Jim Prior summed up the attitude of his former Cabinet colleagues in 1986: 'Their attitude to manufacturing industry bordered on the contemptuous. They shared the view of all monetarists that we would be better suited as a nation to be a service economy and should no longer worry about production.'[16] The rundown of scientific and technical industry in Britain has left British industry at the mercy of other nations. Prejudice against and fear of that section of the nation employed in the traditional industrial areas has caused the government to sign away the finest legacy of those areas, namely the skills and community organisation built up over the last 150 years. In 1983, Britain became a net importer of manufactured goods for the first time since the beginning of the Industrial Revolution.

Margaret Thatcher and her more trusted colleagues have evolved a series of policy proposals which are changing the pattern of life and the political face of Britain for the foreseeable future. They have a clear, almost visionary picture of the future: the second coming of Adam Smith, prophet of free-market capitalism. They have been reshaping British society to conform to that picture.

The framework presents a Britain where large areas of northern England and Scotland, as well as the major cities, are of little

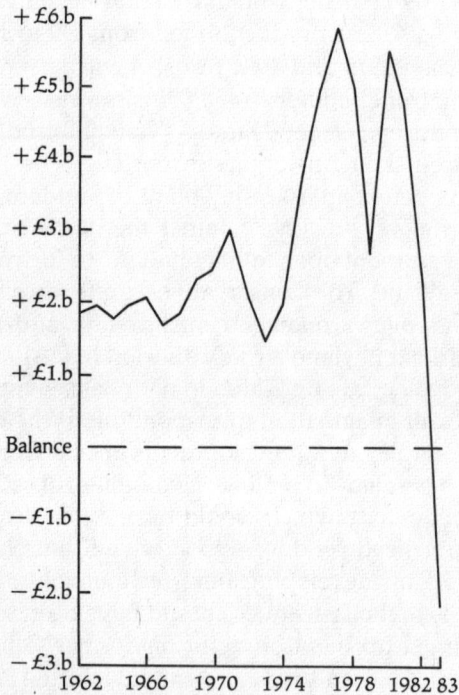

UK balance of trade in manufactures, 1962–83. Source: Written evidence submitted to the Select Committee on Overseas Trade, House of Commons Library, 1985.

By 1987 there was a trade deficit in manufactured goods of £8 billion, the consequences of which were reduced by oil revenue of £14 billion.

political significance to the Tory Party and can be ignored. In dealing with these areas, the lessons of the Depression have been learnt well, namely that demoralisation and fear lead to acquiescence if no alternative to the morality and politics of the market economy is presented. The Thatcher strategy is to destroy that alternative indirectly and directly – by creating unemployment, by removing the protection of trade unions and wages councils, by preventing councils from defending their communities, by preaching the need for low wages. Reductions in state benefits have been accompanied not by a drive to make work more financially attractive but by a campaign for people to 'price themselves back into work'. Employers have been encouraged to use the unemployment situation and the weakening of the trade unions as an opportunity to push down wages in the lower earnings bracket and to increase part-time and temporary contract employment. Privatisation of the public services has been almost wholly at the expense of lower-paid workers who have had their pay and conditions dramatically worsened. The poverty trap has tightened and the fringe or subeconomy has grown sharply.

Instead of being lifted out of benefits, more and more people have found themselves attempting to maximise their income through the labyrinth of local and national entitlements. As temporary, part-time and 'lump' employment has grown, so moonlighting has become more commonplace. The government and some sections of the press denounce 'scrounging' but ignore the drift into semi-corruption and corporate and individual theft from the common purse which goes with it. Traditional defensive responses to these issues from Labour or Liberal politicians, and well-meaning actions of past governments in tackling the symptoms but not the causes of poverty, enable the accusations and distortions of the Right to appear plausible. They appeal to those above the poverty line who see the moonlighting and resent the ever-increasing public outlay on benefits, caused in fact not chiefly by scroungers, but by high unemployment, demographic change and cuts in public services. At the same time little attention is given to the enormous tax relief available to the well off, including high mortgage relief, company cars and a whole range of tax-free company benefits which have to be paid for by the nation as a whole, either by making up loss of tax revenue or by costs to the consumer.

An economy with high levels of unemployment is only part of

the aim. Economic activity could be expected to increase, with a much smaller manufacturing sector, if the world recession picked up. Britain's low wages by international standards, and the inevitable limited increase in unit productivity which came from fewer workers on the job rather than better technology, would produce some 'growth' from an extremely low base. But the Conservatives' aim would not then be to create secure, decently paid jobs with reasonable conditions for everyone. Their true intentions were easy to read from claims of success in late 1986 and early 1987. More jobs, they said, had resulted from their management of the economy than was the case in any other EEC country, but of the million jobs announced by the Chancellor in his 1987 television budget statement on 24 March 700,000 were part-time or temporary, a fact he omitted to mention. Furthermore, the figure included a government guess at the number of self-employed workers, who were not part of previous statistical calculations. The overall number of full-time registered jobs actually fell, unlike most of our industrial competitors. The following week on Radio Four's 'Today' programme Lord Young quoted Beveridge's view in the 1940s that young people straight from school should not receive unemployment benefit, in order to justify forcing them onto MSC 'training' programmes in 1987. This was a way of reducing unemployment statistics, habituating youngsters to temporary low paid work but not providing quality training for skilled, permanent jobs. Alongside the unemployed, the new 'slimmed down' economy was to be built on large numbers of badly-paid workers in insecure jobs.

The Conservatives' approach to generating jobs has been both penny-pinching and wasteful. Writing for stockbrokers Simon and Coates, economists Davies and Metcalf calculated that to reduce the unemployment count by one person, the cost would be £47,000 in income tax cuts, £58,000 in VAT cuts, £26,200 and £15,000 respectively for investment in education and housing, or £2,200 and £1,400 respectively for non-jobs in the Community Programme and Youth Training Scheme.[17] This is 'bad housekeeping' in the national economy on a large scale. The evidence indicates that the Conservatives are happy to see an underdeveloped economy with severe imbalances and welcome the kind of society which has been forced on other nations in Africa, Asia and Latin America, where decisions in the international market had subverted peoples' political choices about what was in their national interest, as we have described earlier in this chapter.

Unemployment and poor employment weaken the trade union movement both in its bargaining power and in its political role. But the present Conservatives have a deeper purpose in attacking trade unions. They seek, we shall argue, to undermine the collective experience that comes from membership of and participation in trade union activity at all levels and from local politics.

Unemployment and poverty do not simply demoralise people – they separate and divide those in work from those out of work and the unemployed from each other as they strive to fend for themselves. The individual becomes vulnerable to subtle changes of perception. Forced to forget their pride as contributors to society at work and offered no dignified alternative, people become the victims of their own fantasy and self-questioning. 'Is unemployment a necessary evil which can't be helped? Am I partly to blame? Is the paint peeling from the walls in the children's school because my wages have been too high?' they ask themselves. 'It's a pity,' they begin to say, 'but now I'm retired the rest of the country can't possibly afford to pay for my comfort.' Or, 'I was beginning to feel a new woman, going out to work and getting to an evening class, but maybe my place really is back at home when he's out of work and Mum's getting old.'

Among Britain's black population British society is often written off. 'There is no hope in Babylon, black people just have to get back to Africa, it's their own place, black and white can't mix,'[18] while their white compatriots argue that 'these "coloured" people came here of their own free will, now there's no work they have to go back.' Statements like these are all too common and are evidence of a disordered and disillusioned society.

What kind of future?

North and South, then, were the more visible geographical dimensions of the growing divide between rich and poor, where whole communities could be seen to suffer. Millions of families and individuals were suffering increasing poverty in the more prosperous regions. Distributing tiny portions of shares to a few million people, from privatised public enterprise, to which all tax payers had contributed (making some of them, like gas, electricity and telecommunications, the most efficient sectors of British industry), was a device to hide the truth about inequality.

In 1986 the 50 per cent of the population at the lower end of the income scale owned 7 per cent of the nation's wealth whilst the top 5 per cent held 33 per cent. The post war trend towards greater equality was halted and probably reversed in the 1980s despite improved standards of living for most people in secure work.

Measured by any of the three official criteria – marketable wealth on its own, marketable wealth including state and occupational pension rights, or marketable wealth including only occupational pension rights – the share of the top 1 per cent and 5 per cent had stabilised or risen since 1980. This was largely due to the boom in the stock market concessions on Capital Gains and Capital Transfer tax, and larger pay increases at the top. (Inland Revenue Statistics, 1986, in the *Guardian*, 23 March 1986.) Ownership and the power to take decisions going with it remained firmly in the hands of the few, despite the overall improvement in living standards since the war. This is what class division in Britain means, not whether people recognise themselves as working class or middle class in sociological surveys or opinion polls. International business is using the opportunity of new technology to create a society in which a large core of people have secure, well paid jobs to whom the Conservatives can appeal to with tax handouts and 'share distribution' to secure the 40 per cent or thereabout of the votes which are needed to stay in power. There is then no need to take account of the rest, in electoral terms, as long as riot and disorder can be bought off by special cosmetic inner city projects and similar devices, or clamped down on by an increasingly military style police force.

Civil disorder became characteristic of the new society being offered in the 1980s. Two tragedies that occurred in June 1985, during sporting events far removed from formal politics, were symbols of social disorder. The terrible deaths in the Heysel football stadium in Brussels, when Liverpool fans started a fight with rival spectators, causing a wall to collapse on Italian supporters, led to international condemnation of the British. In the other football tragedy of that violent month, many people were burned to death in a blazing football stand at Bradford. The Bradford City chairman said in his statement that the club had considered installing fire-fighting equipment, and putting attendants on duty at the exits after kick-off, in case of an emergency. Unfortunately, fire-fighting equipment would become weapons for vandals and the attendants would be in danger of attack, standing on their own away from the crowd. Lives were at stake simply because decent conduct could not be relied on. These two dramatic instances, along with the unusable state of telephone boxes, vandalism and graffiti on other public facilities and buildings, and litter disfiguring the environment, were symbols of disorder in everyday life. We became not only the economic failure of Europe; we were its public disgrace.

Criminal statistics are notoriously difficult to interpret depending as much on the level of reporting as on the number of incidents, but the rate of reported crime had risen nationally by 50 per cent in the seven years to 1986. From 1979–86 criminal damage in England and Wales rose by 55 per cent and mugging by 20 per cent. Expenditure on the police rose by 40 per cent in real terms, but efficiency – as measured by detection rates – dropped from 42 per cent to 32 per cent. Since 1978 violent crimes had increased 44 per cent, burglaries 66 per cent, theft 39 per cent, and criminal damage 91 per cent. It is the poor who are most at risk from crime. They are also the most dependent on vandalised public facilities. In parts of inner-city Liverpool one household in four is burgled every year – in the suburbs of Liverpool it is one in 32. In the London Borough of Tower Hamlets there were 737 racially motivated assaults in under two and a half years (May 1982 to October 1984). Nor is crime the preserve of a 'criminal community'. A survey in Islington estimated that there are about 400 cases per annum of police assault on the public within the borough.[19]

Civil disorder is the symptom rather than the cause of our insecure and divided society. Sometimes this is expressed as a direct protest. The 1980s have seen frequent outbursts of rioting, petrol bombing and looting in more than 20 English towns and cities. Hundreds have been injured and the cost of damage has run into millions of pounds. The names of Toxteth, Brixton, St Pauls Bristol and others were familiar examples in 1981 and reflected in Handsworth and Broadwater Farm four years later.

A *Times* article of 10 July 1981 noted, four years before Heysel, that 'English football fans are bashing every Swiss head in sight' and saw 'the horrible events of the past week' as

only the latest symptoms of a deeper malaise – the fact that the government itself and the subsidiary organs of state . . . are suffering from a loss of authority. Those whom they are trying to control, whether black or white, no longer seem to share a positive vision of what this country is and what it might be to be British.

A sense of shared identity has never been as great in Britain as David Watt, the *Times* writer, assumed. Jingoism has too often been a substitute for patriotism, which should look forwards not backwards. A shared identity requires pride in a way of life which accords dignity to everyone, recognising freedoms and rights which have been won over the centuries and responding to the idea of building a civilised order in the present. And indeed there will be no stability and order in British society unless the social values and morality which regulate our lives provide the basis for a shared identity, a shared future for all the people, not merely a fortunate few. To achieve this shared identity, people's aspirations must be consistent with Britain's present economy and its place in the world today, not dependent on the would-be revival of past glories in a different world order.

Policies and attitudes towards Britain's black population are an acid test of success or failure in this. We have argued that the achievements, however flawed, of the postwar welfare state offered the British people an opportunity for reconstructing national life with a sense of pride and achievement. Similarly, the 'end of the Empire' might have been a civilised exercise in cooperation between black and white, who had been torn apart by imperialism. Unlike the migrant workers in other European countries, black migrant workers were originally offered a permanent home in Britain, as full Commonwealth citizens, part of British society, not a subordinate section with lesser legal rights and status. But as economic circumstances have changed and immigrant labour has no longer been needed, successive governments have regarded black people as a problem, an embarrassing relic of Empire.

The 1986 Nationality Act gave legal support to separate status for black and white. Racist and fascist organisations have explicitly linked the causes of Britain's present discontents with the 'loss of the Empire'. In a speech to the National Front Annual General Meeting in 1977, the NF chairman, John Tyndall, claimed that 'the leaders of the old parties had thrown away an empire and brought this country to the pawnbrokers'.[20] Despite a fall in electoral support for the National Front and other fascist parties in Britain from the quarter of a million votes they won in the local elections of 1977, other indicators (such as the substantial number of racist assaults) suggest that strongly racist attitudes are held by sizeable sections of the community. The presence of the far Right within the Tory Party offered a more 'respectable' home for their votes and public support for their attitudes.

Crude nationalism replaced any attempt to tackle inequalities and reduce tensions and divisions in the country. Attention focused on the enemy wherever it could be found, or even invented. The Falklands War was seized on as an opportunity to release pent-up frustrations among a people unsure of their place in the world and who were being offered no other way of taking pride in a common endeavour. The cost of the Fortress Falklands policy was £780 million in 1982–3, £629 million in 1983–4 and £632 million in 1984–5 with expenditure of a further £1.5 billion by 1988–9. Not for the first time public spending became available for war where it was considered wasteful for social and economic reconstruction. The enemy without had its inevitable flip side, 'the enemy within'.[21] Any stand taken in resistance to Conservative policies was opposed in the name of 'democracy' and 'freedom'. The right to free speech and political organisation outside Parliament is an important liberty, which must be preserved. The Conservatives, however, argued that any challenge to what Parliament does as the 'sovereign body' was self-evidently undemocratic; on the other hand, any action approved by a parliamentary majority in the interests of law and order was said to protect our 'freedom'.

The streets of our city are in turmoil . . . communists are seeking to destroy our country, the Soviet Union is threatening us with her might and the nation is in danger. Yes, danger from within and without. We need law and order, without it our nation cannot survive.

The words are those of Adolf Hitler in 1932, but a similar tone appeared with increasing stridency in statements from our leading politicians and officials in the 1980s. In July 1981, Margaret Thatcher, in a party political broadcast after the recent riots, said:

. . . a free society will only survive if we, its citizens, obey the law and teach our children to do so.

That is why violence must be stopped, the law must be upheld, people must be protected.

Then we can put these terrible events behind us, repair the damage and begin to rebuild confidence. That is the urgent priority.

It all sounds so reasonable, and who would disagree, but these sentiments were used as a cynical cover for more dangerous opinions to be expressed. On 14 July 1981, the *Daily Mail* echoed

Margaret Thatcher's mood in quoting Jim Jardine, the leader of the Police Federation:

It is time to stop 'pussyfooting' with rioters . . . I don't give a damn for the bleeding hearts, the so-called liberals and Marxist agitators who can do nothing but complain about brutality . . . I am sick to the stomach because in the last few days the police have not been able to stop the homes and livelihoods of ordinary, decent citizens from being destroyed.

History has shown how dangerous such escalations of prejudice can be to democracy. The natural and understandable fear of people wanting to live a peaceful and secure life was being exploited to gain support for measures to suppress what were clearly symptoms of a disordered society. The *Daily Mirror* reported, on 9 June 1981, a drastic 'save our cities' anti-riot plan being prepared by the Cabinet:

Its main and most startling feature would be to appoint American-style 'city bosses' to take control of Britain's crisis zones, with special powers to cut through red tape and bureaucracy and get things done quickly.

During the same month Patricia Hewitt wrote in *Rights* (May/June 1981), the journal of the National Council for Civil Liberties, 'In the last two months, hundreds of peaceful processions have been banned. Freedom of assembly is now at the mercy of the Home Secretary. . .' Three years later Lord Avebury, a Liberal, stated:

The government has rolled back the frontiers of freedom. Our prede-cessors would have recognised the government's reliance on 'law and order' and 'national security' as the justification for the new encroach-ments on the liberties of the subject. This is evident in the current Parliamentary Agenda which is replete with policing measures, the ban on trade union membership at GCHQ and in the use of the Official Secrets Act.[22]

By 1985 the media had been sucked into reflecting government propaganda rather than facts, so much so that the BBC reversed film which had been taken when mounted police attacked miners at Orgreave during the miners' strike, in order to make the victims appear guilty of the first offence. Gareth Pierce, writing in the *Guardian* on 12 August 1985, drew a stark parallel between the capacity for revulsion at state violence in the past, when violence was more commonplace, and the attitude of the media in the present day. At Peterloo, 150 years ago in similar circumstances and for similar motives, the army sent its cavalry into a peaceful crowd – the press, then, proved capable of outrage. Not surprisingly it was revealed in 1985 that the BBC had been engaged in secret vetting of the political opinions and affiliations of its journalists and producers, in conjunction with MI5.

The Conservative government tried to hide the facts about a divided society and economy on many occasions. In 1981 the Social Services Secretary Mr Patrick Jenkin attempted to suppress Sir Douglas Black's report on inequalities in health, publication being held up for two years. Only 273 copies of this public document were printed and only in cyclostyled form (less than one for every two members of parliament).[23] Its author was refused permission to hold a press conference. On 24 March 1987 Sir Brian Bailey, government appointee as chair of the new Health Education Authority which would replace the Health Education Council a week later, took the same step of banning a press conference by the HEC to launch its report, 'The Health Divide', because it was 'political dynamite' in an election year.[24]

The report stated that 'whether social position is measured by occupational class, or by assets such as house and car ownership, or by employment status a similar picture emerges. Those at the bottom of the social scale have much higher death rates than those at the top. This applies at every stage of life'. The less fortunate occupational classes had higher rates of chronic illness, their children had lower birth weights, shorter stature and were more generally likely to sicken. 'The unemployed and their families have considerably worse physical and mental health than those in work'. There was clear evidence that conditions had worsened markedly in the 1980s. Dr David Player, the outgoing director-general of the HEC, commented 'This is a review of research into inequalities of health, a scientific not a political document. The only possible political comment, with a small "p" is two sentences in the foreword by me where I say "such inequity is inexcusable in a democratic society which prides itself on being humane".'

Suppression of facts in this way has to be seen alongside the banning of trade unions at GCHQ, the prosecution of Clive Ponting for telling the truth about the Falklands Belgrano affair, the legal attempt in an Australian court to stop Peter Wright from publishing his memoirs, which included disturbing revelations that MI5 had worked to destabilise the Wilson Labour government, the vetting of workers in the BBC, and the increase in phone-tapping and the keeping of personal dossiers on people who might be considered critical of the government, which was repeatedly reported in Parliament and the press. Margaret Thatcher's book of speeches was published as a *Defence of Freedom*. This title could not have been more misleading.

In his story of the Belgrano Affair, *The Right to Know*, Clive Ponting identified the nub of the matter. How would it be decided during his trial, he said, what were the 'interests of the state' under the discredited Section 2 of the Official Secrets Act. 'Could this be left to the jury to decide at the end of the trial once they had heard all the evidence, or would the prosecution try to use the argument that "the interests of the State" had to be defined by the government of the day? If the latter definition was correct then "the interests of the State" would be the same as "the political interests of the Government". This would be a radical new departure in English law that would have profound implications and could, many people had argued, be the first step on the road to greater authoritarianism.'[25] Clive Ponting was acquitted but his case should not be seen in isolation from the general tendency. Conservative authoritarianism was the British version of President Nixon's Watergate, and President Reagan's Irangate. Britain's less open government makes it possible to suppress the truth without the obvious embarrassment of public lies and distortions.

Margaret Thatcher and her advisers shared their vision of the future, and their strategy, with international counterparts. Alvin and Heidi Toffler wrote in the *Sunday Times* about a meeting of President Reagan and his aides at the White House attended by social scientists and 'futurologists', in which the capacity of information technology to break up production and to move it away from centres where collective ideas had been developed since the Industrial Revolution, could finally destroy any notions of 'welfarism' still evident in US society. The values of individualism would prevail in the new order as was the case, the Tofflers claim, before industrialisation. There are strong echoes of Margaret Thatcher's declared intention to 'get rid of Socialism' (quoted in the *Financial Times*, 19 November 1986). President Reagan's mission is worldwide, destroying democracy in Chile, Nicaragua and wherever it opposes market interests. Ideas are shared internationally, no doubt, at official meetings, but there are also intellectual networks and conferences such as those of the Mont Pelerin society which we describe in Chapter 9. It is important to ensure that objective descriptions of the symptoms of British society's malaise, such as the health divide, are properly presented by politicians and the press. It is equally important that information about the causes of the malaise, in the operations of the international market and through decisions of political enthusiasts for the free market, are fully available.

David Walker posed a question in *New Society* on 20 March 1987: 'one is left groping for the reasons (ideological, personal) why the Thatcher government should have expended so much of its energy on successive grant regimes in local government.' We argue here that the curtailment of democratic rights, in the years after 1979, which included restraints on local democracy and local government, was a direct outcome of the means by which the Conservative government chose to tackle Britain's problems. An illustration of how far attitudes changed in less than a decade can be seen from the words of Lord Whitelaw, Deputy Leader of the Conservative Party in 1978, who would be very unpopular with his party leadership if he displayed such sentiments in the second half of the 1980s. On 27 February 1978 he stated:

. . . if boys and girls do not obtain jobs when they leave school they feel that society has no need of them. If they feel that, they do not see any reason why they should take part in that society and comply with its rules.

This old-fashioned Tory insistence on social interdependence understood the need for collective responsibility and support. For formerly 'one-nation' Tories, however, commitment to 'decency' was a sleight of hand to achieve maintenance of an inequitable status quo – one nation to be achieved by a combination of paternalism and deference. For democrats a stable social order has to be achieved by political institutions and practices in which people can actively engage in changing society where they live and work. Margaret Thatcher rejected traditional Tory values, as well as the democratic alternative, in using her parliamentary majority to impose authoritarian solutions.

As long as 80 per cent of those seeking work could find employment, the Conservative plan for economic and social reconstruction could proceed without the danger of wholesale upheaval. Instead of answers to genuine problems there would be the steady erosion of freedoms in order to control the disaffection and disorder which results from increasing inequality and disillusionment among those who experience its worst effects. In such circumstances, conflict and fear would undermine democratic attempts to tackle the problems which British people face at home and abroad, and to take hold of the opportunities which present themselves for creating a more humane way of life. Recognising this, local politics in some of the areas suffering the most severe consequences of economic and political failure over the last two decades, presented an alternative framework for political action. It reasserted more vigorously the traditions of democracy and collective activity from which it has grown. We shall demonstrate that local politics has offered the British people a future in which their place in the world is justified by the kind of society they build, not by economic institutions and political attitudes which can only be justified by an empire now past. This has led to a confrontation between Westminster and localities not merely about the extent and cost of services that should be provided by local government, but about the values that should inform politics in British society.

2

The Roots of Active Local Government

Since Britain became an industrial society local government has occupied a key place in the developing democratic order. On the one hand, it has exerted a political influence, initiating and shaping policies of both local and national significance. On the other, it has been the administrative agent needed to carry out national policies at local level, adapting them to local requirements. We shall show here how this combination of functions has produced a tradition of active local democracy which has come to the fore at regular intervals, alongside the more routine and bureaucratic forms of local government.

During the last 200 years the practice of democracy in Britain has been extended on many fronts. There has been a steady expansion of the right to vote for national and local governments. Freedom of association and the right to free speech have been won, often at great personal cost to those who fought to achieve them. Political parties, trade unions, employers' associations, pressure groups and voluntary organisations have gained a place within the political process as a result. The concept of democracy has also come to include 'personal politics': people claim a freedom to think and act outside stereotypes imposed by others, breaking out of a domination, often complex and subtle, imposed by language, social attitudes and behaviour. Women, young people, the black population and, increasingly, the elderly have made important contributions to extending democracy in this way over the last few decades.

In our view, it is in local communities that the strengths of this democratic pattern are experienced and deployed with greatest intensity. Our concern is not so much with local government, narrowly defined, as with local politics – a combination of both collective voluntary activity and representation of the people by election. From this standpoint it might be said that local politics and democratic rights have advanced hand in hand.

No system of democracy is perfect or simple. There is a strong tendency to speak of British parliamentary democracy as though it were woven from a single thread. In fact, we should talk about different aspects of democracy within the British system as a whole, making up its true strength, actual and potential.

Local councils do not have power in the same way as the House of Commons. Local authorities have no sovereignty. Those who have watched the weaving and fencing between elected councillors and appointed officers during the period when councils were set on confrontation with government over the Rates Act in 1984 became sharply aware of the way in which officers were faced with the contradictions of being part of a legally defined local authority as well as the servants of democratically elected politicians.

Any useful political analysis must begin by defining where power lies; in this country today it lies in the sovereign body of the nation state. But constitutional legality does not totally define the political order, especially in an unwritten constitution where conventions of freedom as well as conventions of power need continually to be reaffirmed and new positions have to be won. In our local communities within the nation state, councillors and officers are part of a political process as well as a legal system, and it is important for the electorate that this is seen to be so. Since the Industrial Revolution, local government, in its attempts to meet the developing needs of the nation, has often pressed its claims on Parliament, not the other way round.

In order to understand local politics in the 1980s we must examine the active democratic practices which have developed over the last couple of centuries. These practices contrast strongly with the more detached concept of representation in parliamentary democracy.

The limitations of Parliament

Although the institution of local government goes back to 1601, local politics as we see them today are creatures of modern industrial society. Parliamentary democracy, by contrast, retains many features of an elite tradition, being based on a limited and remote notion of representative politics which predates the

Industrial Revolution. Local government has been built by a more positive, involved kind of democracy. Recognising this difference between local government and national parliament is a valuable starting point for understanding the contribution made by local politics to British political life.

The basic shape of Parliament was fashioned during the expansion of the British Empire, which witnessed piracy, conquest and slavery abroad and, for our purposes, the rise of the House of Commons at home. In the sixteenth and seventeenth centuries landowners and the new commercial and financial middle class successfully shackled the monarchy and established once and for all the principle of 'no taxation without representation'. That principle lies at the heart of the national parliamentary system and has dominated its development, leading to serious weaknesses. Parliament remains a form of democracy in which people give up power to be exercised by others on their behalf, often for quite long periods, with little contact and opportunity of recall by the voters. Any system which leads to such a remote exercise of power has dangers of becoming an elective tyranny.

Certainly the British arrangements for electing MPs exaggerate the consequences of this tradition. The 'first past the post' principle leads to a very crude representation of the whole voting population. It has led for most of the modern period to the domination of British politics by two major parties, and since 1945 the ruling party in the House of Commons has commonly held a minority of the national vote. The losing Labour Party in 1951 polled its highest-ever percentage of the national vote (48·8 per cent). Between 1979 and 1983 the Conservative Party actually lost 686,771 votes, but gained 58 seats. The following table shows the full details:

The general elections of 1979 and 1983

	Seats		No. of votes received		Percentage of votes cast	
	1979	1983	1979	1983	1979	1983
Conservative	339	397	13,697,932	13,012,315	43·9	42·4
Labour	269	209	11,532,218	8,456,934	37·0	27·6
Liberal/SDP	11	23	4,313,804	7,780,949	13·8	25·4
Others	16	21	1,697,503	1,420,938	5·3	4·6

Two-party domination and the failure of the system to represent large minorities has led to growing demand for proportional representation. Both major parties in Britain are opposed to PR, partly because they would lose their former cosy duopoly of power. More weighty political arguments include the claim that the British system brings stability and that voting should not be purely for individuals but for policies which can expect to be effectively implemented by a government that has a clear majority in Parliament. MPs also hold the view that they represent a constituency, an actual area, a real group of people, not an arbitrary proportion of the population, and they insist that this tradition be upheld.

Nevertheless, without proportional representation, the problem of distorted representation has grown more extreme in the 1980s. The continued existence of the 'first past the post' system and the radical nature of the Conservative government's policies (using their parliamentary majority to push through legislation against all opposition, despite their minority popular vote) puts increasing stress on the checks and balances to parliamentary power which exist in British democracy as a whole. Parliamentarism, which rides roughshod over the wider democratic processes is moving down the road to authoritarianism, whether a majority can be claimed in the House of Commons or not. An important feature of local democracy is that it can provide some kind of check on this aspect of national politics because it combines local representation with local collective voluntary action.

The roots of local politics

Local government has often been thought of as a creation of central government, an agent for putting its policies into practice. However, it is rooted also in people's need to organise their own communities, particularly since the Industrial Revolution. At first local politics was under the control of the new industrial middle class rather than the people as a whole. The merchants and new industrialists who created the modern House of Commons in the nineteenth century began to govern alongside the landowners in their own local areas also. Initially they proceeded to do this through collective voluntary action rather than election. As Sidney and Beatrice Webb tell us, the new industrialists designed voluntary associations – 'Associations of Consumers' – for the purpose of carrying out work that would eventually be seen as a government function.

Sometimes the association was transient only and merely voluntary, as when the leading parishioners of the little town of Ashford in Kent subscribed, once for all, the necessary sum to pave the principal streets. More frequently, the association was that of the owners and occupiers of a district – in some cases those of a particular 'square' in a Metropolitan Parish – who joined together to provide the lamps or the watchmen, the pavement or the sweeping necessary for their own comfort.[1]

When this work could no longer be done on a wholly voluntary basis, associations turned to parliament for a local act to compel inhabitants to pay – thus local, voluntary activity was followed by central legislation.

The new middle class had often sought to defend their property against the 'mob'. But as the Industrial Revolution got under way the great constructive enterprises required to underpin its growth – canals, roads, pavements, street lighting, public buildings – became a matter of local urgency. This was something more than 'no taxation without representation', it was government through the collective action of one section of the population, often in the interest of the whole community as well as their own. Sometimes the law had to be pushed and pulled into new shapes. The business classes who ran the new towns' economies had major problems to contend with, partly created by their own treatment of the men, women and children on whom their enterprises depended. The solution to these new urban problems formed the basis of modern local government.

Until the 1880s the middle classes stayed firmly in the lead everywhere,[2] even in towns like Sheffield, where by 1869 it was calculated that working-class voters were in the majority at local elections. In many places the power of the middle class remained unchallenged. At the end of the century, Robert Tressell's novel *The Ragged Trousered Philanthropists* lambasted the working people of 'Mugsborough', a fictional representation of Hastings intended to symbolise a common situation, for 'electing the same old crew time after time'. 'In the opinion of the inhabitants of Mugsborough,' Tressell states, 'the fact that a man had succeeded in accumulating money in business was a clear demonstration of his fitness to be entrusted with the business of the town.'[3] Despite this, not all businessmen were what Tressell calls brigands, feathering their own nests. They recognised the gains that active and involved local politics could bring to the community as a whole, even if their perspective was often shaped by the needs of business interests for orderly local administration. Joseph Chamberlain in Birmingham clearly recognised the political significance of active local government:

For my part I am convinced that the most fruitful field before reformers at the present time is to be found in an extension of the functions and authority of local government. Local government is near the people. Local government will bring you into contact with the masses. By its means you will be able to increase their comforts, to secure their health, to multiply the luxuries which they may enjoy in common, to carry out a vast cooperative system for mutual aid and support, to lessen the inequalities of our social system and to raise the standard of all classes in the community.[4]

For the last 100 years or so, in successive waves, generations of local politicians have carried on this positive tradition. And despite business and professional domination of council membership for much of that time, the working class finally pressed forward, adding the urgency of its own needs to the arguments of rational business reformers. In those towns where working-class organisation advanced most rapidly a new level of active democracy took up the traditions and responsibilities of local government.

Local politics and the needs of the British people

Where the middle-class businessmen in Chamberlain's mould pursued the general interests of local communities, including those of commerce, but not their own personal profits, they often came to some disturbing conclusions: democratic collective provision was more effective than private enterprise. This was true above all for the universal need of a pure water supply and the increasingly basic modern fuels, first gas and then electricity. In this sense, the interests of the middle classes, wisely perceived, were the same as those of the whole community. Sheffield provides many examples of policies resulting from this understanding.

In 1870 the Mayor of Sheffield referred to the water and gas companies as 'the two huge monopolies with which Sheffield is weighted'.[5] Much of local politics in the second half of the nineteenth century in that city, as elsewhere, was dominated by

2   A private water industry: the tragic Sheffield flood (1864), when a reservoir burst its banks, destroying lives and homes, and the owners passed on costs to the consumer to keep up profit levels.

the effort to gain democratic control of these monopolies. It was not achieved without a struggle, and parliament was often on the side of the profit-maker rather than the community. Sheffield's experience illustrates what was happening in many cities and communities across the country.

Water is so obviously a public utility that we need reminding that local councils actually had to decide that it should be so. During the nineteenth century they promoted local acts of parliament to take over the water supply – sometimes after disasters resulting from private control.[6] After the 1864 Sheffield flood, when the Dale Dyke Dam burst drowning 270 people, destroying 798 houses and flooding 4,357 more, the local water company did not dispute their liability and paid £370,000 in compensation – but they passed it all on to the public, putting up the price of water by 25 per cent.

Sheffield City Council immediately gave notice of a parliamentary bill enabling them to buy out the company. Parliament refused – only granting the company a Water Act to implement the increased price. For over 20 years the council fought the company over this and other abuses of the monopoly. Pressure was often low and the company tried continually to put the cost of fittings and apparatus on to the consumer in order to maximise their direct profit from owning the supply of a natural resource. Even when the House of Lords finally agreed in 1888 to public takeover of water, it was on the condition that the price for the company was 'fair and reasonable' – after the water company had made a satisfactory profit for half a century out of the most basic human need.

Political effort to obtain collective control of the gas monopoly was even harder, often again with the strong opposition of parliament. Despite continual battles, Sheffield gas stayed in private hands until nationalisation in 1945. Parliamentary insistence on paying a 'fair compensation' had continually alerted many councillors to the more mercenary side of municipalisation. At the last attempt, in 1919, permission to take over the gas undertaking was only granted on condition of paying company shareholders an annuity of 5 per cent on the capital value of the undertaking, although, as Labour councillors noted, the dividend had recently been reduced to 3·5 per cent.[7]

Nevertheless, many councils were willing to pay the enormous prices Parliament demanded for gasworks, because it was in the public interest to bring monopolies under democratic control, although this was often only possible through loans which involved the additional expense of interest payments.[8] By 1888, half the gas consumers in the UK were supplied by public gasworks in 168 separate localities.[9]

Electricity became a city council undertaking in 1899 in Sheffield after only ten years of private enterprise. The negotiations were tense, since, as is so often the case, some councillors were interested parties, and eventually the terms were very favourable to the private company. Noting this, a leader in the *Sheffield Independent* in 1899 complained about the deal, but recognised that the corporation did have to sacrifice a lot in order to gain control of a fuel that would have enormous future possibilities for its citizens.

Throughout Britain in the late nineteenth and early twentieth centuries, democratic control of the basic monopolies was pressed forward by Conservative and Liberal councillors – businessmen responding to the progressive ideas of the time. Municipal gas, electricity and trains were seen as a contribution to progress and prosperity.[10]

Sheffield's foresight was shared by many other authorities. In 1905 there were 334 municipal electricity works in the UK, compared with only 260 works in the longer-established gas industry (although, as has been shown, Parliament showed great favouritism towards 'the gas lobby' which probably influenced these figures). Significant portions of the two other major utility industries were also in public hands by 1905 – 1,050 municipal waterworks and 162 municipal tramways.[11]

Loud arguments about the respective merits of public ownership and private enterprise were soon to be heard. A Liberty of Property Defence League was formed to resist the challenge by democracy to the free market. Objectors turned to the courts to 'defend' free enterprise. Manchester Corporation was ruled not to have power to act as a general carrier of goods, despite the power to carry parcels on trams. Fulham failed to be allowed to run a laundry. Legal costs deterred many authorities from fighting in the courts, as did the risk of approaching Parliament who had so often imposed punitive compensatory costs.

Municipal trading gained support from both middle-class businessmen and from new Fabian socialists. Bernard Shaw contributed with his pamphlet 'The Commonsense of Municipal Trading' in 1904. When Sidney and Beatrice Webb wrote their 'Constitution for a Socialist Commonwealth of Great Britain', in 1920, they came down on the side of social ownership at the local level, not nationalisation, because in local collective enterprises producer and consumer were part of the same community – community feeling, not private profit, would provide the incentive for efficiency. The Birmingham local government movement, writes one historian, lies 'at the root of the major developments in modern British history . . . as a form of collectivism'.[12] It did not stop at municipal trading. Chamberlain himself was quite explicit:

. . . private charity is powerless, religious organisation can do nothing to remedy the evils, which are so deep-seated in our social system . . . I venture to say that it is only the community acting as a whole that can possibly deal with evils so deep-seated as those to which I have referred . . . It is our business to extend its functions and to see in what way its operations can usefully be enlarged.

Let me make one single illustration. I venture to say that of all the legislation which this generation or century has seen, the most important, the most far-reaching and the most beneficial is the socialistic organisation of state education . . .[13]

Where education and housing were concerned the failure of the private enterprise system to meet people's needs was even more evident than in the case of the 'great monopolies'. In central legislation the emphasis was always on a minimal standard of public health and education necessary to produce a reasonable workforce for the nation's industries. Local activists refused to be satisfied with this, particularly when working-class representation and the growth of trade unions made inroads against business control of local government. After the 1870 Education Act, working-class representatives fought to defend the work of the new locally controlled state schools against Tories and churchmen.[14] Their work is recorded in reports to trades councils, who from the earliest days played an active part in local government. Although these activists remained in a minority for some time, they became increasingly vocal, organised and successful as socialist parties emerged. Campaigning for free education and free books, they gave the words of Joseph Chamberlain a fuller meaning. Although sometimes uncertain about handing education over to the state, they pushed for a wide and humane view of education, the only justification in their eyes for exposing children to the dangers of state regimentation.

The 1870 Education Act itself provided opportunities for increased local democracy through the creation of local, directly elected school boards. From the early days working people took a considerable interest. In Sheffield at the school board election of 1879 voting hours were extended from 12 noon to 7 p.m., making it easier for working-class electors to cast their votes. Organisations like the Sheffield Labour Association began to challenge the existing parties; its candidate, W. H. Smith, was elected to the board in 1885.

The activities of the boards went beyond education alone. Clerks to the boards reported on poverty and general material conditions. In Sheffield the board began to act as a voluntary association to collect clothing for poor children, introduced regular medical inspections from 1873, encouraged penny banks in schools, and in 1884 established that 'first schools might provide "penny dinners" for poor children for one or two days per week'.[15]

In the 1880s Annie Besant promoted an inquiry which identified 43,000 underfed children in London alone, her work leading to George Lansbury's claim that school meals were one of the most important social reforms of the period. In the 1890s, Margaret Macmillan, a socialist, used her position on the Bradford school board to fight for poor children so successfully that she roused support across the country for a campaign against the 'half-time system' whereby children were expected to work as well as go to school, and spread the word at mass rallies and through intensive lobbying.[16] School boards not only campaigned, they involved the people in a wide range of issues. Their minutes were made publicly available in libraries; times of meetings were convenient; schools were opened up freely for public meetings.

In the industrial cities, school boards made secondary and technical education available in 'central' or 'higher-grade' schools to working-class children long before national legislation brought this in throughout the country. Schools began in Sheffield and soon followed in Bradford, Nottingham, Halifax, Manchester, Leeds and Birmingham. In the words of the Report of the Royal Commission on Secondary Education in 1895, 'This higher-grade school represents a new educational movement from below, and a demand from new classes of the population for secondary education which has sprung up in a few years.'

Thus, as the nineteenth century progressed, working-class and socialist organisations took up the opportunities of active local government politics and extended it in important ways. The early 'association of consumers' was described by the Webbs as having no connection with, and practically no consciousness of, the producers of services. The new activists of the late nineteenth century did not make distinctions between consumer and pro-ducer, between the voters and those who provided the service; they knew that if the interests of both were not met the service would be inadequate. Many school boards therefore took up trade union campaigns for a standard minimum wage, ensuring that contracts for work to be done on the schools would only be given to firms who paid 'fair wages'. Their educational policies recognised that effective public service requires decent condi-tions for producers as well as consumers.

Like water, gas and electricity, housing could no longer be left to the free market. On the one hand, the council began to act as a consumer on behalf of the community, distributing housing more fairly between individuals than the market could. This work gradually developed into the local authority housing service. On the other, the council became the base for collective production, replacing the private system in building and in maintaining a housing stock – organising what are now called direct labour organisations or direct works departments. After the 1888 Local Government Act had set up the major municipal authorities and the 1890 and 1900 Housing of the Working Classes Acts had given them powers to build and subsidise housing, the local ballot box and local activism became a major force for decent housing.

The fight for council housing was based on very close links between voluntary organisations and pressure groups, trade unionists with a political perspective wider than wage bargaining, and radical local councillors. In 1889 a conference on housing the poor was convened in Sheffield, attended largely by ministers of religion and working men. Working-class reformers like Charles Hobson and Tom Shore were both delegates from the Association to housing conferences in Liverpool and Port Sunlight in 1902 and 1909. The Sheffield Federation of Trades Councils, the Independent Labour Party, the Labour Representation Committee and cooperative organisations were all actively engaged in pressing for new policies. By 1912 the pioneer town planner, Abercrombie, commented, 'The Sheffield of today is doing fine work and in many ways is taking the lead of big manufacturing cities in the application of town planning principles.'[17]

Getting rid of the worst slums was one thing, building better houses was another. London County Council, Liverpool and Sheffield councils were among the first to move, in the late 1890s. The first council houses in Sheffield were in the inner city, but a wider vision informed other schemes – the Sheffield Association for the Better Housing of the Poor drew on the ideas of the emerging garden-city movement. Trams, under municipal control, provided cheap and regular public transport so that housing for working people could stand alongside that of wealthier citizens in the suburbs. In 1906 High Wincobank estate was built for a model cottage exhibition and won much praise from the garden-city movement. This was going too far for the *Sheffield Telegraph*. In 1899 its editor had declared at the Conference on Housing the Poor that the jerry builder should be curbed and that 'rotten houses and homes falling into decay should be taken by the local authority and demolished without compensation'.[18] Sheffield's council housing, the *Telegraph* now declared, was blatant socialism with its provision of 'trim and dainty villas for well-paid artisans'.[19] Half a century later Aneurin Bevan, then Minister of Health, would have been delighted with such criticism when he insisted that council housing should be good enough for anyone – not merely the poor.

3 Democratic public enterprise: (a) an early Sheffield Corporation tram *c*. 1900; (b) trams being rebuilt in the body shop, Queen's Road, 1913.

The construction industry and the conditions of its workers were to come under the same democratic scrutiny as had the new education services. London took the lead. The Metropolitan Board of Works, forerunner of the London County Council, was exposed in 1898 for its corrupt dealings with private contractors. John Burns summed up the policy of his progressive group when they took control of the LCC in that year:

The establishment of a Works Department by the County Council was inevitable. It was forced upon us by contractors themselves. It owed its inception more to the faults and failure of the contractors, their with-drawing of tenders, and their systematic cornering of the Council, than to any initiative on the part of the Labour members. The new Depart-ment has completely revolutionised the old corrupt order of things. It has made the County Council independent in its public works. Immedi-ately the Department disappears, back comes the old system. In fact, signs are not wanting of its coming today. Contractors see the moderate policy of wrecking the Department partially successful, and we see them beginning their old tricks again. They want the whole conditions of contract removed entirely so that they can have a free hand to plunder London at will . . . the tenders have gone up thousands of pounds. And why? Simply because the contractors are getting emboldened by the Moderate enmity against direct labour.[20]

In Sheffield a works construction department was set up, dis-banded, and then on 27 January 1904 resuscitated by 30 votes to 27.[21] Then as now, direct works – i.e. work carried out by the council itself, not by private contractors – fundamentally chal-lenged the whole system of private enterprise.

The early decades of the Labour Party, in its local branches, were strongly influenced by the fight for decent housing and by battles against private landlords. Independent Labour Party activists, like Glasgow's Wheatley, fought above all on this issue, taking it through into their parliamentary careers. As a govern-ment minister, Wheatley himself did much to ensure that council housing became a major opportunity for working people to obtain a decent home. The way in which many succeeding governments have used council housing as a tool in national economic policy, forcing local authorities (willing and unwilling) to create modern slums, cannot change the fact that at its best council housing has provided some of the finest and most popular rented housing for those who cannot compete in the private market.

In reviewing local government's contribution to collective

services from water and gas to education and housing, we have shown that new developments stemmed from an active tradition in local politics. In this tradition of local government, politicians seek to achieve direct results, not merely to debate policies. They are in close contact with the constituents who elect them and complain to them. They have developed a personal knowledge of the services for which they are responsible, along with professional officers and other workers. It is difficult to see the same involvement and understanding in the nationally administered public services. The National Health Service, for all its sophistication and success, has never achieved the same combination of local accountability, sensitivity and innovation as local government services.

Local politics cannot therefore be seen simply in terms of its limited legal powers by comparison with national government, nor just as a platform for aspiring national politicians. A study which covered five countries, published in 1963, found that people related to local government more closely than to national government because of its 'greater immediacy, accessibility and familiarity'.[22] In Britain, at least, this follows not merely from the town hall being closer at hand than Westminster, but from the way in which active local politics has extended and developed democracy, enabling new social movements to shape policies and influence their implementation.

3

1945: Labour Rejects Local Politics

'Modern Poplarism is the most acute problem we face,' said William Waldegrave, Parliamentary Undersecretary at the Department of the Environment, in January 1984. He might just as well have declared that the most acute problem we face is modern suffragettes or Tolpuddle martyrs, or any other group which has borne the cost of fighting for democracy. 'Poplarism' became a household word in the 1920s when the East End of London fought to protect itself against unemployment, poverty and totally inadequate government policies towards them. In September 1921 the mayor and 21 councillors of the London Metropolitan Borough of Poplar were imprisoned at a time of widespread demonstrations over unemployment. The boundaries of Poplar Council and the poor law union (both separately elected local bodies) coincided and membership of the two bodies overlapped. Local politics demonstrated a remarkable vigour.

The councillors were rejecting the punitive nature of poor law relief, the workhouse and the stigma of being 'on the parish' which had shaped generations of attitudes towards community support. Poplar Council and the poor law board wished to use what powers they had to develop a new policy to treat the poor and unemployed more like citizens. In their 1921 financial estimates for the borough they more than doubled the amount to be paid in relief for the poor. They approved a London trades council and London Labour Party resolution demanding maintenance at the rate of 40s. for an unemployed man, plus dependants' allowance. Finally, they refused to include in the borough council estimates the prevailing precepts of the LCC, the Metropolitan Police, the Asylum Board and the Water Board, demanding greater rate equalisation across London in order to share the burden of public finance between rich and poor areas.

This was the most dramatic incident in a battle between many local boards and central government which was trying, in the words of a Cabinet memorandum by Neville Chamberlain, Minister of Health, to bring about 'a reversion to the Elizabethan poor law' – amazing as this putting back the clock might seem.[1] In particular, Chamberlain was concerned about the high scale of relief payments, the failure to apply stringent means tests and failure to apply the doctrine of 'less eligibility' whereby only those below local minimum wages could receive relief.

Poplar was important because this stand grew out of a long period of local political activity which had started in the last two decades of the nineteenth century. Those involved had recognised the way in which local government could act in the interests of the working class during a period when they had little control over national government policies which were still wedded to the worst features of traditional capitalism. As on the school boards, so on the boards of guardians they challenged the attitudes and decisions of the middle classes who had so far dominated local government. They were led to confrontation not by foolhardiness or exaggerated notions of what they could achieve through martyrdom, but by the driving force of the democratic politics in which they were engaged. There are a number of features which stand out clearly. First, there was imagination and ingenuity rather than the dogmatic application of first principles. From the early days they saw that the poor law was nothing more than a 'way to keep working people in the labour market',[2] but they also realised that the poor law could be won for local control in a way that the county councils could not. With that control something could be done to shift resources and point the way forward. The local borough council started a public works programme, supplementing the activities of the board of guardians, and many similar ideas were tried and tested. Secondly, there was a continual pursuit of local interests by the maximum extension of powers embodied in legislation and government circulars. Election campaigns were fought on a liberal interpretation of the regulations whereby people could receive 'outdoor relief' rather than being forced into the workhouse; helpful guidelines from the local government board, such as more generous relief for the aged suggested in 1900, were picked up sharply. Thirdly, local politics in Poplar was quite clearly more than a series of local election campaigns, with periods of regular administration in between. Continual contact between councillors, unemployed groups and other organisations was the driving power. These engagements were not always predictable or controllable. In 1922 there were riots outside the board's offices when the guardians seemed unprepared to challenge the new (somewhat more generous but still inadequate) board scale of outdoor relief, laid down by the government.

Furthermore, the dynamic quality of local politics made it much more difficult to retreat into the technicalities of local government. Willingness to defend policies on ideological grounds was a striking feature of the Poplar struggle. 'If people starve on wages, there is no reason why they should starve on relief,' said George Lansbury.[3] Lansbury was a national figure, an MP and editor of the *Daily Herald*, but it was local politics that gave him the base to write, along with his colleagues, a rousing pamphlet 'Guilty and Proud of It'. This was their reply to one of the many savage attacks on Poplar's policies in a government report of 1922.

Finally, of course, there was the courage of the Poplar councillors in standing up against national government for policies which clearly had the support of local people and were in their interest. Poplar is famous because this courage took councillors to prison, but it has been a feature of local political pressure on government even when the conclusion has not been so dramatic. As we can see in the 1980s, holding the line against national policies presented with all the weight of government propaganda, largely backed by the press, radio and television, requires a steady nerve and firm local support.

Poplar was the most radical direct opposition to Westminster from local politics in the 1920s. But other poor law boards adopted similar policies which for years the government found difficult to handle. Government refusal to grant loans to boards, leaving district auditors to handle the situation through surcharge and disallowing members, led to yet more direct confrontation. Eventually the Board of Guardians (Default) Act of July 1926 gave the minister power to suspend boards and send in a commissioner, as was done later in West Ham, Chester le Street and Bedwellty.

Other poor law unions continued to provide opposition, particularly by stretching the principles of the poor law to give additional relief to the unemployed. After 1931, when public assistance committees were set up, composed of both elected councillors and co-opted members in an effort to reduce militancy, resistance continued. Among the first to be warned for 'illegal payments' by refusing to apply the tests rigorously were Durham County, Glamorgan County, Rotherham and Barnsley. Eventually disciplinary action was taken. At the end of 1932, Rotherham and Durham County committees were replaced by government commissioners.[4] The other poor law unions drew back from open confrontation but continued to try to get round the tests in various ways. Local politics in the 1920s and 1930s has to be judged in the long term, rather than through an assessment of immediate 'successes' and 'failures':

For many years, the word 'Poplarism' which still appears in the Addendum to the *Shorter Oxford English Dictionary* was defined censoriously as the 'policy of giving out relief on a generous or extravagant scale practised by the board of guardians about 1919 and later any similar policy which laid a heavy burden on the rate-payers.'

Later the definition was significantly modified and now reads: 'the policy of giving generous or (as was alleged) extravagant outdoor relief, like that practised by the board of guardians at Poplar in 1919 or later.' There was good reason for the alteration. For most of the immediate gains for which Poplar councillors and guardians fought and for which they were denounced as Bolshevik extremists have long since been officially recognised as desirable. At the time their attitudes were thought to offer a threat to society. But now society has to some extent adopted these attitudes, or at least claims to do so.[5]

Creating alternative policies

The commitment and energy which drove such direct opposition took other forms. People in the United States who look back at the Great Depression for the way in which democratic politics offered an alternative to the misery experienced by millions can give some credit to the Roosevelt administration in the White House for its New Deal. In Britain they would find the equivalent not in Westminster, but in the cities. Two examples are outstanding, and their historical significance was recognised even at the time. They are properly understood not in isolation but as part of a movement under way in many localities.

Arthur Greenwood, Health Minister in the Labour government of 1929 to 1931, wrote a foreword to a booklet, 'Six Years of Labour Rule in Sheffield, 1926 to 1932'. Sheffield was the first major city to elect a solid Labour administration dedicated to achieving substantial gains through local politics. Greenwood summed up the achievements: 'If the citizens of Sheffield will look at the record and compare it with any other six years of administration I am satisfied that they will come to the conclusion that at no time were the people of the city better served.'[6] In the booklet the council described how the 'mainspring has been wherever possible to use the great municipal machine for the improvement of the city and bring the greatest health, educational and cultural benefits to the people.'[7] Collective policies were set against the forces of the free market in a remarkable range of ways.

For the unemployed, as elsewhere, the poor law was stretched to its limits in providing assistance. In the past there had been pointless task work for the unemployed – 'One instance where a field was repeatedly dug over for no purpose whatever, created disgust among the onlookers and shame amongst those who were compelled to indulge in this futile work.'[8] The council now engaged in a programme of public works to improve the city infrastructure and expand its amenities. There were housing schemes, new roads, miles of additional tram tracks, open-air baths, markets, an abattoir, libraries and schools. A magnificent new city hall was built as a cultural and entertainment centre, providing 120,000 'man days' of work.

A second major amenity, the central library and art gallery, was built by direct labour with a standard of workmanship remarked on to this day. Direct labour was expanded largely because of the low standard of work on houses built by private enterprise (in one year £48,000 was required to repair houses alone); wages and conditions were improved as well as the end product. Trams were built better and cheaper through public enterprise: 'On the last competitive tender the local firm which had built the city's trams previously, quoted a price £580 per car more than the cost of building by direct labour.'[9] The first municipal printing department was set up in 1927 to supply the needs of the whole corporation. It was a product typical of active local politics where imagination in politicians releases the same in officers. Success was 'in no small measure due to Dr Percival Sharp' who, as Director of Education, 'with a fine display of public spirit for four years voluntarily supervised and directed this great undertaking'.[10] Efficient and cost-effective, it soon provided a model for other authorities, including Bristol and Smethwick.

Among the more far-sighted policies were attempts to place the city's finances on a basis which could deal with the economic circumstances. Powers were achieved to set up a land fund which could promptly purchase land without saddling the city with long-standing interest and debt repayments. The Finance Committee set up its own insurance scheme for corporation employees. A major innovation to institute a municipal bank was blocked by a House of Lords refusal to agree to the necessary parliamentary powers.

In more conventional areas of local government Sheffield showed the same imagination and inventiveness. Educational policy anticipated the Hadow Report of 1933. The new administration was determined to bring a new spirit into public health. The first step was to coordinate activities under an enlarged health committee. On this basis health policy was seen in the round: sanitation, maternity and child welfare, food purity, hospitals, baths and wash-houses and the treatment of infectious diseases like tuberculosis.

These policies provided a different kind of challenge to the government of the day from that symbolised by Poplar. Yet the politics from which they grew were the same. Unemployed groups, trade unions and local political parties were bringing pressure and building the ideas. In their own words, 'Men from the Mine, Bench, Lathe, School, Footplate, Bricklayers, Silversmiths, Trade Union Officials and women from the homes, have banded together with vision before them.'[11]

All these policies pointed to the future; they combined local initiative, enterprise and effective administration under political leadership. The other political advance at local level of recognised national significance placed most emphasis on sound administration.[12] Labour's victory under Herbert Morrison in the 1934 elections for the London County Council was important in reviving the fortunes of the Labour Party nationally. It also reinforced the position of Morrison, General Secretary of the London Labour Party since the First World War. Morrison was a moderate, the darling of the Fabians, and an opponent of Poplar. Michael Ward, a leading member of the GLC administration in the 1980s, has reminded us how mild the election manifesto of 1934 was: mainly pledging to expand house building and to improve the administration of education, hospitals and the poor law. Yet, he notes, its firm commitment to public spending through the rates – 'money raised by the rates and spent on social services may be the truest economy' – still brought the accusation of extremism from opponents. Nor was the Morrison administration without courage, banning warlike activities like the cadet corps and visits to military establishments from the schools: 'The council treats the training of the coming generation as a sacred trust, and not an opportunity for disguising the beastliness of war as a pageant or game.'[13]

The programme of public works adopted by the London County Council was less wide-ranging than that undertaken in Sheffield. Resources were concentrated on attacking a social evil that was particularly acute in London – slum landlordism. Between 1934 and 1939 the slum clearance and rehousing programme in London rehoused 82,999 people and demolished 12,652 slum houses.[14]

However, the LCC's housing policy was a field of frequent conflict resulting from the clash between the fiscally conservative assumptions of council officers and the aims of Labour councillors, both in the 1930s and after. The dominant 'Morrison' faction in the London Labour Party shared some of these conservative assumptions and their suspicion of 'Poplarism' prevented them from encouraging mass demonstrations of popular grievance which could have been an effective pressure for an extension of the housing programme.[15] The undoubted successes of the 30 years of Labour administration of the LCC (1934–64) were unfortunately tempered by a distrust of the traditions of participative democracy and public accountability that may be found in the tradition of local politics.

Another major plank of the Labour Party's LCC 1934 election platform was a municipal health service (all the council's hospitals were rapidly removed from the control of the poor law authorities after the election). Increased numbers of medical and nursing staff were recruited and a special emphasis was placed on maternity provision. The figures in the following table show both the increased use of the new maternity facilities in London in the 1930s and their beneficial effects.[16]

	1932	1939
Confinements in LCC hospitals	11,239	19,614
Antenatal attendances in outpatient clinics	148,618	132,270
Maternal death rate per 1,000 births	7·2	2·49

Above all, Morrison was dominated by the idea of proving that Labour was fit to govern:

> You will wonder whether I am talking about running a government or a municipality. It is a municipality, but so large that it is bound to resemble a government. I believe the London County Council is, in many respects, a model of public administration, it is clean, it is upright, and the machine works with precision, good sense and humanity. Whenever I go over Westminster Bridge, I can almost hear it ticking.[17]

These are essential qualities in local politics. But Morrison over-emphasised the smooth running of the machine. His limited vision of the true significance of local politics had serious consequences after 1945.

The councils of a number of other major British cities were not controlled by the Labour Party between the world wars and the ruling alliances of independents, Conservatives and Liberals on these councils were correspondingly more cautious, if not simply opposed to these ways of meeting the needs of all citizens within their jurisdiction rather than a favoured minority. Even so, the same reforming tradition of social service which had characterised Victorian local government was still evident, for example in housing policy, both before and after the second Labour government's 1930 Slum Clearance Act.

	Population in 1937	Total number of council dwellings built 1919–37	Number of dwellings for slum clearance 1930–37
Birmingham	1,038,000	47,265	6,708
Liverpool	867,110	32,317	3,913
Nottingham	283,030	15,092	2,686
Manchester	766,311	27,426	5,705

Source: *Municipal Year Book*, 1937.

Yet the 1930s also saw the beginning of what many writers have called 'the decline' of local government and have traced down to the present day.[18] The nature of the decline and its specific manifestations in public policy can be summarised as follows:

General trend	Specific policies
Loss of functions	Trunk roads, hospitals, public assistance, water, electricity and gas supply and recently passenger road services.
Failure to attract new functions	New town boards, countryside commissions, regional planning boards.
Loss of financial independence	Rate support grants valuation.
Increased central control	All the above plus the recent Local Government Finance Acts and Rates Act.

Labour's great mistake

In 1945 Labour was presented with a massive parliamentary majority and a tremendous opportunity. The armed services and their families at home had been fighting against the fascist destruction of civilisation, and many of them, both middle class and working class, saw the victory as a launching pad for further advances in democracy at home. Democracy and citizenship were to be defined in terms of economic and social opportunity as well as universal suffrage and freedom of speech. Citizens, it was argued, should play an active role in creating the new order. Many influential new Labour parliamentarians, Herbert Morrison and Aneurin Bevan, from the 'Right' and 'Left' of the Party, had been active in local government. Local government and local politics had for long provided examples of the way forward. Yet the party turned largely to nationalisation, not local control, and to national rather than local administration as it set out to build some advance positions for democracy in a capitalist state. Why this tragic mistake?

The matter was by no means cut and dried, as we can see from the part played by a central figure, Aneurin Bevan at the Ministry of Health. Michael Foot has pointed out that

Within a few months of taking office on some matters in the first weeks he made a few decisions which governed the whole of his housing policy. What was to be the instrument for executing the housing programme? That was the crucial question. Right from the start Bevan placed almost the entire responsibility, under his direction, on the 1,700-odd local authorities, county boroughs, and urban and rural district councils.[19]

He fought off the civil servants and some experts in the Labour Party itself, who wanted to put the vast enterprise into a new Ministry of Housing which would be developed into a gigantic Housing Corporation. In his view 'the giant would be muscle-bound', and the officials who canvassed it at the Ministry of Works were too much at the mercy of big business and the building contractors. Local pressure would be powerful in their areas. Councillors might not be experts but they had a more important qualification: 'they spoke for the homeless and needed their votes. Housing called for a *democratic* organisation.'[20] (Foot's emphasis.)

More robustly, Bevan fought off the Tories, who wanted to promote the interests of the private builders. He wanted a plan, and 'the speculative builder by his very nature is not a plannable instrument'.[21] He even refused to give the same subsidies to private builders of houses for sale as to the local authorities when civil servants wanted to offer the building industry a sop. 'The only remedy the Tories have for every problem,' he said bluntly, 'is to enable private enterprise to suck at the teat of the state.' He set out to overcome all doubts about local politics taking on housing by vigorously enlisting local authority enthusiasm. A national programme was achieved through central approval of schemes and financial carrots but also leaving the initiative with the local councils. The best responded with some very good council houses indeed and it is neither their fault, nor Bevan's, that the Labour resolution to plan and allocate resources for good standard housing was followed by a Tory and Labour reversal to free-market philosophies in varying degrees from 1951 onwards, with disastrous consequences for the reputation of council houses through many deplorable schemes in which 'homes were like an unsavoury silo, places to store people rather than house them.'[22]

Why then did Bevan not go the same way with health? The nationalisation of the health service has often been seen as a serious reversal for democratic public administration led by local government. Here Bevan was soon accused of treating the local authorities badly, Herbert Morrison, an ex-LCC man, being represented as their champion. In 1944 the then Minister of Health, Henry Williams, had produced a White Paper in which local authorities retained their place in the health service, working as groups in regional boards. In this case Bevan decided that the local authority was not the appropriate instrument, not because their democracy was ineffective, but because their prestige was low with that most elite of all the professions, the consultant doctors. Local democracy was overridden by the political clout of senior hospital doctors. General practitioners also succeeded in objecting to a salaried service. In Bevan's mind, health centres, to be provided by local authorities, would be the linchpin of general practice but they developed slowly partly because he gave in to the GPs' objections.

It remains a pity, however, that Aneurin Bevan never pursued his vision of what local authorities could do to its conclusion. In 1954 he wrote an article in the *Municipal Journal* in which he drew on plans earlier left in the files of the Ministry of Health, for the reform of local government which he felt was essential if the welfare state was to be properly democratic and responsible to the public.

We should wish to revive and maintain local government as a form of government which is truly local and which is so near the people as to ignite and keep their interest.

This interest by the public is important as a spur and refreshment to the governing bodies themselves and for the creation of an intelligent and educated democracy inspired with civic spirit. Quite apart from its value to the individual citizen, it is of incalculable value to the community in any kind of crisis.[23]

The article explores the possibilities of administrative efficiency and creativity in the best spirit of the local political tradition. 'His scheme never saw the light of day,' Foot tells us, 'he knew there was no immediate political advantage to be gained by it and probably he did not press the matter strongly in Cabinet.'[24] Westminster displayed its traditional limitations. Despite this, councils continued to develop public health policies within their political and administrative powers. Sheffield was among the most purposeful lobbyists for the Clean Air Act of 1955 and the most assiduous in implementing its provisions. The following graph showing the success of its health policies indicates the value to Sheffield's people of the reputation the city gained for being the cleanest industrial city in Europe.

A number of reasons, besides parliamentary blinkers, can be suggested for Labour's failure to put services under local democratic control. Wartime mobilisation had been a centralised task, so it seemed appropriate to plan and organise centrally for postwar reconstruction. Many Whitehall civil servants have little

Pollution and Health in Sheffield

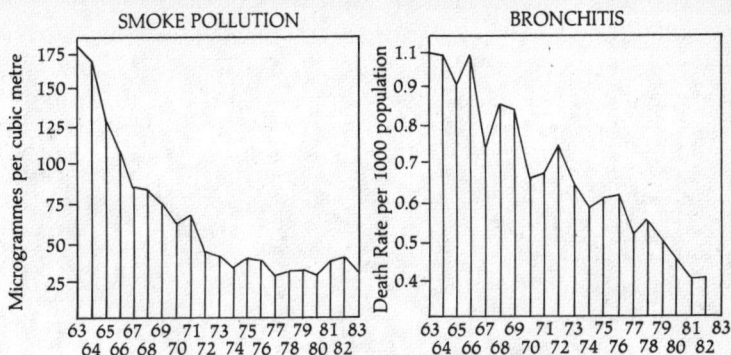

SMOKE POLLUTION   BRONCHITIS

Source: G. Green. *Working Towards a Budget Strategy.*
Working Paper No 3. Sheffield City Council 1984.

respect for local government and they are always a strong
influence on ministers. Above all there was the immensity of the
political task and the need for the government to use their large
parliamentary majority to act as quickly as possible. Whatever the
precise reasons, local authorities lost many functions during the
1945–51 Labour administration. In the process the country missed a great opportunity. Democratic socialism became associated
with the practice of large national organisations. Now, when the
values and practices of democracy and collective political
organisation need defending against exponents of free-market
economics more strongly than they have for a generation, it is
important to demonstrate that they are not synonymous with
centralised bureaucracy.

In 1918, at the conference which shaped the constitution of the
modern Labour Party, a resolution on local government was
moved by F. W. Jowett, MP, and John McGurk of the Miners'
Federation of Great Britain. It was put to the vote and agreed as
follows:

That in order to avoid the evils of centralisation and the drawbacks of
bureaucracy, the Conference suggests that the fullest possible scope
should be given, in all branches of social reconstruction, to the
democratically elected local governing bodies; that whilst the central
Government Department should assist with information and grants in
aid, the local authorities should be given a free hand to develop their
own services, over and above the prescribed national minimum, in

4 (a) and (b) Sheffield's health policies: contrasting views of the Don Valley, Sheffield's heavy industry centre, from Wincobank Hill, before and after the clean air policy, 1948 and 1985.

whatever way they choose; that they should be empowered to obtain capital from the Government at cost price, and to acquire land cheaply and expeditiously, for any of the functions with which they are entrusted. The Conference holds, moreover, that the Municipalities and County Councils should not confine themselves to the necessarily costly services of education, sanitation, and police, . . . nor yet rest content with acquiring control of the local water, gas, electricity, and tramways, but that they should greatly extend their enterprises in housing and town planning, parks, and public libraries, the provision of music and the organisation of popular recreation, and also that they should be empowered to undertake, not only the retailing of coal, but also other services of common utility.

Our argument is that this position remains a correct one, taking into account contemporary circumstances, and that putting it into practice is a matter of urgency for the future of democracy in this country.

In examining the quality of local government we have shown that it is not merely an agent of central government; it has its own political base. Local councils counterbalance the power of Parliament when it fails to represent important sections of the population. Its origins and development have emphasised active democracy along with representation through the ballot box. During important periods of social and economic change, local politics has moved in advance of Parliament in the most active towns and cities where interests and groups within the community have recognised the possibilities for action. The qualities of public enterprise and initiative are needed to ensure that the problems facing Britain now become the opportunity for an extension of democracy rather than an excuse for its curtailment. Against mounting odds, there have been significant attempts to demonstrate that this is so in local government during the 1980s.

4

Public Transport: Community, Freedom and Choice

In the history of human civilisation new methods of transport have been turning points – the domestication of the horse, the invention of the wheel and sailing vessels, the steam locomotive, the motor car and the aeroplane. Today people want to travel to work or on business, to meet friends and families, to pick up their pensions, to shop and to enjoy a day out. How to organise the best transport for everyone, given the mechanical means available, is a decisive political question which affects our basic quality of life. Local politics has addressed the question through the age of the tram, the bus, overground and underground light railways and the motor car. For those who have the means the motor car apparently provides maximum freedom and choice, but for many car ownership is still not available equally to all members of the family at all times, and some individuals or families do not have a car at all. There are also very heavy social costs, in providing roads, and through pollution and accidents. If the benefits of good transport are to be distributed more equally and the costs reduced, collective provision is essential, as we now intend to demonstrate. The importance of transport in human society points up the significance of democratically accountable, collectively financed and organised economic activity for many other areas of life.

In 1981 London's 'Fares Fair' public transport policy caught the national imagination. Unfortunately the policy had such a short life that its long-term benefits could not be measured. South Yorkshire County Council's cheap fares policy was maintained for over a decade, eventually defeated by the combined effects of rate-capping, abolition and the 1985 Transport Act. It had implications beyond transport, indicating the lead which local government and local politics was increasingly taking by putting forward policies to unify rather than divide the nation. Attention to collective needs was shown to be no ideological diversion but a practical contribution to the social and economic life of the community which held the support of the people of the area because they could see that it worked for their benefit.

December 1972 was an important month for South Yorkshire politics. On a cold wet evening in Rotherham a group of South Yorkshire politicians put the finishing touches to a document which started a train of events leading to confrontation between the Greater London Council and the House of Lords.[1] At this meeting the Labour Party's Manifesto Working Group for the new metropolitan county elections recommended:

The aim of the County Council, under Labour control, will be to provide, in consultation with the district councils, free public transport for the elderly, the handicapped and the disabled as an immediate objective.

This will be regarded as a first step towards the ultimate provision of free public transport for all.

A policy so clearly determined by political priorities was something that administrators were not used to. Their response between 1972 and 1974 was to produce a flood of technical and other information which threatened to overwhelm the politicians as they tried to hold fast to their political line. Reorganisation of transport under the county council, newly created by local government reorganisation in 1975, meant that different local district fares had to be brought into line. The technical requirement of 'rationalising' often produces a defensive twitch among politicians. This time it was seen as a political opportunity. By setting fares at the level of one of the cheaper districts and later deciding to freeze at that level, South Yorkshire took a major step towards a free public transport system as inflation reduced the real price over the next decade.

Local politicians were responding to their party and local community groups who wanted a democratically controlled, publicly accountable transport system. They refused to leave transport to private enterprise. South Yorkshire County Council placed subsidised cheap fares at the centre of its policy. Frequently attacked as irresponsible by local and national champions of the free market, the policy had to be defended against both Labour and Conservative governments. Majority support in the community was regularly demonstrated since the policy was highlighted at elections for over a decade.

At the 1975 Labour Party Conference Shirley Williams answered the transport debate from the platform not by supporting the transport case but by asserting a monetarist policy. Bill Rodgers, a little-known figure at the time, who gained prominence by joining Shirley Williams in the 'Gang of Four', swept into action as Minister of Transport and set a later precedent for Michael Heseltine by penalising the county council for its refusal to treat transport as a commercial undertaking. The amount saved to the nation by reducing the transport supplementary grant to South Yorkshire was a mere £300,000 in 1977–8 – absurdly small compared to the amounts spent annually on highway building and private transport expansion. For South Yorkshire such a reduction was a severe blow, but the result was to strengthen the political will of those committed to the policy.

The period leading up to the 1981 county elections saw increasing national interest in the success of South Yorkshire's transport policy. The metropolitan counties, particularly those who had experienced Conservative control, had seen for themselves the results of raising fares to reduce subsidies. The South Yorkshire subsidy was 75 per cent of operating costs in 1983, yet the long-term effects of a cheap fares policy could be to reduce the subsidy needed per passenger journey as we shall show (see table, page 75).

Meetings took place with the Shadow Spokesman on Transport and representatives of the GLC and metropolitan authorities at the Labour Party Local Government Conference in 1981. Policies for reducing fares and a consequent commitment to supplementary rate increases by the GLC, West Midlands and Merseyside authorities were agreed.

National attention focused on the collision between the GLC and the government.[2] In South Yorkshire local pressure prevented the county council being panicked into taking a backward step by these events. The battle was fought on the different legal position outside London.[3] There was a demonstration 'stoppage' of public transport in Sheffield, supported by engineering and steel workers on 25 January 1982. A campaign produced thousands of leaflets, stickers and badges. In just over a week 100,000 signatures had been obtained for a petition which quickly reached its target of a quarter of a million.

On 17 February, a favourable divisional court judgement on Merseyside's reduction of fares[4] lifted South Yorkshire's spirits. On 1 March the County Labour Party firmed up their resistance.

Sheffield Newspapers Ltd.

5   Defending effective local transport: South Yorkshire Passenger Transport Executive buses in procession on High Street, Sheffield, as part of Transport Action week (November 1986).

A highly successful 'invasion' of London took place when a convoy of double-decker buses cruised down the motorway to present the petition. Finally, the council meeting of 4 March decided that fare levels were to be held and the transport policy sustained. Above all, success was obtained by massive public support.

This is not simply a story of local commitment. It is a tale of local democracy in action, an alternative to market economics and private self-interest which Tories and Social Democrats alike could not tolerate. The policy was popular and successful – a practical as well as an ideological threat to its political opponents. For the people of the area cheap public transport had brought freedom and choice. While passenger mileage fell around the country – a 30 per cent decline in urban areas between 1974 and 1984 – bus travel in South Yorkshire increased by 7 per cent in the same period.[5] During 1982–3 more passengers boarded per mile in South Yorkshire than anywhere else in the country.[6] The most obvious to benefit were transport-dependent groups – the less wealthy (49·6 per cent of the South Yorkshire population have no cars, according to the 1981 census); the 'other' member of a one-car family, often a woman; the unemployed who, by October 1986, comprised 16·20 per cent of the population; pensioners

(17·3 per cent of the county's population); and young people. A full review of the policy shows how the whole community gained.

In 1985 adults could still ride six miles to town or countryside for 10p; children for 2p, the disabled travelled free, as did pensioners outside peak hours. The six-mile bus fare compared with 58p in Manchester, 55p in London and 50p in Leeds. A 'City Clipper' service, incorporating the innovative 'Bendibuses' – an articulated single decker – operated in Sheffield city centre, linking bus and rail stations with shops and offices. Passengers travelled free on the City Clipper, which meant they could board and alight at any of the three passenger-operated doors. The speed of the service in heavy traffic was increased as the bus was stationary for short periods only.[7]

Cheap fares on their own are not enough: a comprehensive transport network must exist, with regular and reliable services. By reversing the declining demand for public transport, the South Yorkshire policy led to an expansion of the network in contrast to the national system. South Yorkshire buses operated within a diameter of 80 miles, from Goole in the east to Manchester in the west. No other passenger transport executive had a larger operating area, even though Birmingham and Manchester are larger conurbations. South Yorkshire also pioneered integrated services with British Rail. Suburban trains were subsidised by the council and the fares frozen in 1977, joint rail/bus passes were developed and rail stations, such as Chapeltown, relocated closer to bus termini, shops and centres of employment. Finance for these projects was provided by South Yorkshire County Council.[8]

Despite the growing recession, revenue from fares was maintained. While in 1979, Manchester transport committee decided to make 2,400 redundant from a workforce of 7,000, South Yorkshire was making plans to create 800 new jobs and increase its bus fleet (from 949 buses in 1975 to 1,200 by 1985). In the long run a cheap fares policy is cost-effective. An expanding network utilises economies of scale. Raising fares causes the network to contract and leads to subsidies on routes which are socially necessary but carry few passengers due to high fares – hospital routes, for example. A large and busy bus maintenance garage is more efficient than a half-full one.

The following table compares the South Yorkshire subsidy with other metropolitan counties in 1977 and should be read alongside the facts about scale and expansion of the service:

	Annual bus subsidy	Fare per 2½-mile journey
South Yorkshire	£48·9m.	7p (reduced to 5p in 1984)
West Yorkshire	£48·3m.	36p
Greater Manchester	£43m.	28p
Tyne and Wear	£40m.	30p
Merseyside	£33·5m.	27p
West Midlands	£9·6m.	20p

The most comprehensive review of world public transport, *Jane's Urban Transport Systems*, places South Yorkshire's policy in an international context:

A casual observer may feel that the apparently obvious solution to the nose-to-tail traffic snarl-up on a peak-hour radial route must be provision of additional road capacity. But this is no solution at all; for if the problem of arterial thrombosis has been created by the 20 per cent who choose to travel by car, the lure of more road space needs only to attract another 2 per cent for traffic flow to revert to its former congested state.

Public transport provision and financing is part of the role of a naturally defined conurbation-wide administrative unit, and nothing has happened over the past year to change the persuasiveness of that view.[9]

The economic benefits of South Yorkshire's policy have been many-sided: for personal income, commerce and manufacturing. Calculate the cost of the journey to and from work, five days per week, for one person in Sheffield and Manchester:

	Distance to work	Fare per journey	Weekly cost per person
Manchester	5 miles	58p	£5.80
Sheffield	5 miles	10p	£1.00
	Weekly saving for Sheffield worker: £4.80		

Add one journey per day, to school, shops or for recreation, for every member of an average household of four, and the increased disposable income within the local economy is evident, raising the value of local wages and the turnover of local shops.

The consequences for manufacturing are equally important. Controversy was generated by the possibility of British Leyland passing into foreign control in the early months of 1986. The viability of the bus and truck division of the firm was crucial to takeover discussions. By that stage government policies to cut back public transport systems, through a withdrawal of the bus grant subsidy and limits on local authority spending, had caused British Leyland to close two body plants and one chassis plant. An important aspect of British Leyland operations is the nature of the bus market which depends on the demand from mainstream local passenger transport operations, as this British Leyland report makes clear:

Currently over 95 per cent of the stage carriage services are provided by the public operators. The vehicles they use to provide this service are all *purpose*-designed and manufactured to precisely meet the exacting demands of that particular market. Both double- and single-deck types have been carefully developed over many years to ensure that they provide a safe, reliable and economically sound answer to the problems of mass movement and fluctuating demands for travelling public which includes: the elderly, the disabled, shoppers, etc. . . . This has produced essential parameters for this kind of vehicle such as:
  * low, flat floors
  * wide, easy-access entry
  * good handrail provision
  * low-access platform
  * wide, easy-access seating
  * single-step boarding
  * driver control of entry and exit[10]

Vehicles like these are not the cheapest available at initial cost, but they are an extremely good investment for their 15–18-year life cycle. Private operators pay less initial cost but offer a much poorer product. South Yorkshire was seeking maximum value for public money. In 1984 the passenger transport executive described the life of an average single bus, which lasted approximately 12 years and included the following stages:

First year	416,000 miles
Second year	2 million passengers
Third year	Repainted twice
Fourth year	Two new engines
Sixth year	Four new gearboxes
Eighth year	Ten new sets of tyres
Tenth year	Two new axles
Twelfth year	Scrapped after 18 million passengers

Only a planned service can provide the workshops, skilled workers and organisation to achieve this value from each investment in stock. The vehicle which results from this policy is a clear example of what has been called a socially useful product. It is the outcome of a democratically accountable system of effective distribution to users. This distinguishes it from a purely commercial commodity whose value is decided from the profit it brings through distribution in the market.

It might be said that councils could provide the bus service but private business could do the servicing. However, small contractors could not lay out sufficient capital to do the job properly on the scale and with the quality required. Or large investment costs would lead to concentration of ownership, as we have seen with the merger between Hawley/Pritchards, who are major providers of public services. Such international private monopolies do not have the accountability of democratically elected bodies.

Deregulation and privatisation in the 1980s eventually brought older buses and vehicles, unsuitable for the full range of public requirements, onto the roads, with a general reduction in reliability, comfort and quality. Excellent maintenance and training workshops created by public investment were reduced to the level of private operators in an effort to cut costs, despite the consequent reduction in real efficiency and effectiveness for the public.

London Transport's experience also illustrated the benefit of maintaining garages and maintenance staff. Their characteristic open-doored 'Routemasters' were designed specifically for London and built at a British Leyland production plant at Park Royal and Southall in the 1950s and 1960s. By 1970 London Transport had been converted to the introduction of 'one-person-operated', 'pay-as-you-enter' buses to save wage costs. BL closed Park Royal and Southall in 1979. Two thousand six hundred 'Fleetline' buses were bought in 1970 and Routemasters were phased out. By 1977 only 200 Fleetliners were still working, all the others had broken down.[11] Routemasters were reintroduced, many still working perfectly today after 30 years' service. The Fleetline buses were bought as single units and could not cope with London's heavy traffic which involved much stopping and starting. The Routemasters' secret is that they are built like meccano models: if one component fails it can easily be replaced. Body and chassis are interchangeable. As LT have tried to save money, they have increased inefficiency and in some cases increased costs.

Without a general application of these transport policies, a declining demand for buses affects heavy industry. The British Steel Corporation closed Tinsley Park steelworks in 1985. One thousand one hundred and fourteen jobs were lost and 75 local suppliers who rely on Tinsley Park for orders were threatened.[12] This was the largest single factory closure in Sheffield since 1979. An important element in BSC's reasons for closure was declining national demand for special steels from commercial vehicle manufacturers. Every Leyland bus contained 25 tons of Sheffield special steel.

Proposals for reversing the long-term decline in the British share of world manufactured exports are dominated by exhortations to improve competitiveness in the private sector – 'Sell to survive'. Not enough attention is given to the way in which public-sector purchasing for specific needs at home can provide the industrial base for developing exports which meet customer requirements. There is an expanding market for urban transport in developing countries. (France, for example, has won contracts to build underground systems in major cities such as Mexico City.) Buses are modified for the hilly conditions of South Yorkshire and for the special traffic conditions in London. These public-sector specifications create the conditions for specialised exports geared to varying conditions found throughout the world.

When he moved from Plymouth City Council to become Commercial Director on the South Yorkshire Passenger Transport Executive in 1984, Peter Sephton (later Managing Director of South Yorkshire Transport Ltd) recognised the intention of South Yorkshire's politicians:

Everything in this country is geared to the motor car, yet the whole of Europe and now America has recognised the value of a good public transport system. Eventually this country will have to appreciate the importance of public transport.[13]

His judgement was based not only on 'social' arguments in favour of the disadvantaged, but also on the recognition of its place in the whole economy. Cheap fares and a viable public transport system were vital to the county structure plan. They made sense of the regional strategy for work, housing, leisure or recreational facilities. Public convenience, health and safety were increased through less road congestion. (After the GLC cut fares by 25 per cent in 1983 it was estimated that there were at least 3,000 fewer accidents each year, with all the saving in personal and social cost which that implies.) The saving of high-cost oil was also an important feature in South Yorkshire's stand for public energy policies.

The cheap fares strategy refused to separate economic from social and indeed cultural policy. At the hub of its approach was a challenge to the myth that there is a necessary separation between wealth creation, the domain of private industry, and wealth distribution (the Right call it 'dissipation') through the provision of public services. According to this myth, private insurance is economically good, public insurance not affordable; space games good, wheelchairs socially desirable but not economically viable; home 'angels' provided by private companies a valuable social enterprise which creates wealth, home helps the essence of profligate local government spending; private funding for theme parks and shopping complexes is praiseworthy, but public support of recreation facilities or the refurbishing of houses is a drain on funds. Challenging these myths is vital if there is to be a popular movement against recent policies.

After the Transport Act 1985 had received royal assent, Nicholas Ridley, Secretary of State for Transport, said:

There is a great talent for innovation in this country. We have now given entrepreneurs the freedom to use that talent.

There can, of course, be no guarantee of the future profitability or success of individual operators. But it is a safe bet that an industry which is striving more to serve the customer will expand its market and do better *overall*. That means more security for those involved in the industry.

Local authorities will continue to be able to subsidise services. In future they will be required to go out to open tender for those services. This will allow the public to see exactly where their money is spent, will take advantage of competition between operators, and will get better value for money.[14]

South Yorkshire has shown that there is a talent for innovation in Britain and that 'public entrepreneurs' have succeeded in serving the customer and expanding a home market by not allowing immediate profit on each journey to determine the production and distribution of their service. Competition for immediate profit produces badly maintained buses, infrequent and poorly integrated services, and little coherent long-term investment.

Nicholas Ridley said what he really meant at the Bus and Coach Council's Annual Dinner in February 1986: 'You are now free to run your businesses without the constraints of a social conscience.'[15]

The South Yorkshire cheap fares policy lasted for 12 years. Its opponents had hoped in vain that the Law Lords' ruling against the GLC would damage similar policies elsewhere. Neither were grant reductions successful, as local people were prepared to pay the necessary rates. It finally fell victim to national legislation embodied in the Transport Act 1985, the Rates Act and abolition legislation.

Abolition of South Yorkshire County Council in 1986 itself did not kill the policy. It was the designation under the Rates Act of the successor joint board which empowered the government arbitrarily to fix expenditure levels for the new transport authorities and to impose a precept limitation so that successor authorities could not raise revenues to continue a policy of subsidy. Finally, the Transport Act 1985 brought the structural changes of deregulation in autumn 1986, opening up public transport to private enterprise, and an integrated public transport network based on low fares became not only impossible but even illegal.

The government's recognition of the challenge which South Yorkshire and other cheap fares policies posed to its own free-market ideology is reflected in the punitive element they included in the expenditure levels (E.L.) which they forced on the new joint boards, as shown in this table.

	Expenditure 1985/6 £m.	Proposed EL 1986/7 £m.	Per cent change
South Yorkshire	78	50·5	−35
Merseyside	88	75·2	−15
Greater Manchester	80	74·3	− 7
West Midlands	54	54·2	+ 1
Tyne and Wear	55	60·0	+ 9
West Yorkshire	47	57·8	+23

Source: Sheffield City Council, *Report to Employment Programme Committee*, 19 November 1985.

On 1 April 1986 a 250 per cent fare increase was put into effect, as follows:

Distance in miles	Old fares	New fares	Off-peak new fares
2	5p	20p	15p
6	10p	40p	35p
9	15p	50p	45p
12	20p	70p	60p
16	25p	80p	70p

A flat fare of 5p was imposed for children, pensioners and for the City Clipper (increasing its journey time). A forecast annual loss of 70 million passenger journeys was the official estimate and the first month's figures showed a 30 per cent drop in passengers by 1 May. A 10 per cent mileage cut was implemented in June 1986. A report prepared for Sheffield City Council in July 1986 outlined some of the initial effects and costs on council departments and Sheffield's people:

* extra travel cost £30,000 for home helps in the social services department;
* works department employees' travel costs will increase from £100,000 to £250,000;
* attendance at day centres for the mentally handicapped fell by 10 per cent;
* attendance at Sheffield's Mappin Art Gallery dropped from 8,000 to 5,000 at a time of year when it normally increases.

The report included interviews with the customers:

'A stark example of the effect of the fare rise on the poorest is given by M. He travels on two buses to attend his YTS scheme. His weekly fare was £2, now it is £8. Out of a YTS wage of £27, 30 per cent now goes on travel costs.'

'You used to be able to go anywhere in Sheffield with £2 in your pocket.'[16]

There were flaws in the conception and implementation of the South Yorkshire transport policy which reflected inadequacies in local government even when it operated in the best traditions. Bus workers suspected throughout the life of the South Yorkshire policy that cheap fares were maintained at the expense of their wages and conditions. There were disagreements about whether job security or high wage levels were more important. As a result, workers were not wholly committed to the policy and were often excluded from discussions about improving and updating the service. More enthusiasm was therefore generated in the community than among workers when the cheap fares policy came under attack.

Problems of bureaucracy and inertia were not always resolved. But these problems are not unique to public services, as anyone knows who tries to complain about products and services to giant private corporations, or even local garages when they are in a sellers' market. Such problems are more capable of being resolved by democratic means than through the profit motive, and we turn in the next chapter to the way in which local politics has been taking steps in the appropriate direction.

Despite such inadequacies, however, the cheap fares policy showed that local politics can provide a fully viable alternative to cutting public services and promoting private enterprise in their stead, a policy which had steadily become the accepted wisdom of parliamentary spokesmen of all parties during the 1970s – Labour as well as Conservative. Margaret Thatcher's Conservatives were able to benefit from Labour's failure to challenge nationally the free-market ideology, declaring in their 1979 manifesto that policies which encouraged individualism and competition were 'going with the grain of human nature'. In their view, that is why the free-market system is morally correct, effective and, indeed, inevitable.

South Yorkshire's transport policy reflected a different view of human nature. Social living – from the tribe to the modern city – has always depended on cooperative behaviour. Popular support for the cheap fares policy came from a recognition that sharing the costs and sharing the benefits was both consistent with good housekeeping and a necessary underpinning to any equitable system of transport. The values of collective living advanced individual freedom more convincingly than the promotion of individualism. During the 1980s, as the consequences of the new Conservative thinking became evident, a number of Labour-controlled authorities realised that defending their communities required a reassertion of these values in wider areas of social and economic policy.

5

Local Politics and the People

In the 1920s and 1930s active local politics had turned confidently to the 'great municipal machine'. The efficient, businesslike town hall was to be its vehicle for change. Creative local politics in the 1980s has had to face the fact that to many people the town hall and all it provides can seem impossibly remote and anonymous, and may sometimes work against their interests. Those who advocate a free-market production of all goods and services divert attention away from the increased centralisation and remoteness of decisions in the private sector by highlighting bureaucracy and paternalism in the state. This sleight of hand promotes the illusion that democracy is extended through 'privatisation'. In this chapter we consider examples of how local politics has started in many ways to demonstrate that the state itself will change if people recognise their own power – it will operate less as a machine and more as an arena for democratic participation in which the people play an active part.

The 1980s have seen a confrontation between two sets of political activists with diametrically opposed ideas. Activism is generally associated with visible shop-floor or community politics; the activism of the boardroom is out of the public eye. Nonetheless, decisions made in the boardroom and the motivation of financiers and transnational decision takers have much more powerful political implications. Boardroom activist organisations of the Right have flourished in recent years. As *The Times* said, in writing about the rightwing organisation, Aims of Industry, on 1 July 1982, 'In the past decade it [the Right] has moved from the fringe of political thinking to the centre of conventional government thinking.' So have the ideas of many others who 'were regarded not so long ago as mere eccentrics'.

The Right's increasing recognition of the need to combine theory and practice has brought them more obviously into the centre of politics. Theorists and businessmen have come together in numerous 'think-tank' organisations.[1] At least £1¾ million was donated to eight organisations of this kind in 1982/3, including the Economic League, the Centre for Policy Studies, the Adam Smith Institute, the Institute of Economic Affairs, and Aims of Industry. Activists have included industrialists like Sir Hector Laing (the construction firm), Lord Cayser (British and Commonwealth Shipping) and Richard Halstead (Beechams), with political columnists such as Ferdinand Mount of the *Daily Telegraph*. *The Times* reported, on 31 March 1983, that Mrs Thatcher was 'a surprisingly keen participant' in the philosophical discussions promoted by these organisations. 'Boardroom activists' have transformed the Conservative position away from 'one-nation' politics to its present divide. They have addressed themselves to the problem of restructuring the British economy to increase profits within a political programme which appeals to people's acquisitive instincts, and exploits their fears and uncertainties under the pressure of change and recession.

That British industry needs restructuring is not in question, but whereas the activists of the Right have seen this in terms of extending the free market, activists in local politics have proposed a restructuring in the people's interests – for labour rather than capital.[2] At the centre of their rethinking is an examination of how the state can help to create a social programme that answers people's real needs, by drawing on their capacity to cooperate and to play a full part in democratic society.

Voices in government and industry give the impression that the dangers of state power are only seen by the Right. Local politics has been ready to take up and respond to critical views of the state which have been expressed in liberal and socialist traditions, recognising its contradictory nature. On the one hand, when the present generation seeks freedom and justice, it finds the machinery of the state as essential as ever. Only a democratic sovereign state can uphold laws which defend the people against powerful elites in society and harness the resources of society for the collective good through taxation. On the other hand, the state is itself a product of this unequal society in a manner which people experience in many direct ways: when property laws protect vast areas of open countryside to be enjoyed as grouse moors by a privileged few; when social security officers can pry into the private lives of people entitled to state benefit; or when police are used on the side of employers in industrial disputes, to name only a few examples. Because local government is responsible for so many services close to people's lives, it also plays a major part in the process whereby the state intrudes into their personal affairs and social relations, in education, social services and housing.

Many people's experience of the public services produced ambivalent attitudes towards the welfare state throughout the 1950s and 1960s, both at national and local level. While there was much that was good about the direct provision of services – opinion polls have shown consistent majority satisfaction – there was also a new professionalisation of decisions which failed to take account of how people wanted to live. Urban renewal swept away close-knit communities where self-help and the extended family had aided survival in the worst of conditions. Awards were proudly displayed for high-rise developments in the years up to the mid-1970s (and structure plans up to the early 1980s) were still being put together around the notion that 'big is beautiful'. The expenditure cutbacks which followed in the mid-1970s further reduced quality by hitting maintenance and improvement work to houses, schools and roads. Bea Campbell in *Wigan Pier Revisited* vividly describes the depths which public housing could reach at its worst, as we noted in Chapter 3. People were increasingly alienated from what was happening in the public arena. Margaret Thatcher took advantage of this to press her own ideological cause.

In the late 1960s and early 1970s two new strands in local government policy were woven together to increase efficiency. They can be summarised as 'corporate management' and 'community development'. The former involved adopting the methods of big business in order to tighten control over finance and the workforce. At the same time, policies had to be acceptable to their intended beneficiaries if they were to be effective, and community development involved 'public participation' programmes, better public information systems and support to community organisations. This apparent extension of democratic practices was severely limited, and in the end largely discredited. As a managerial device it was not backed by a political programme that allocated resources to meet heavy demands on the welfare state, particularly in the big cities, which were most affected by urban renewal and economic change. Politicians of all persuasions were also nervous and unsure about participation exercises that seemed to cut across their own direct link with the electorate and led to independent organisations. This was true

even of those Labour councillors who advocated tenant participation and similar exercises.

Community development was partly a way of buying off
pressure from communities organising independently outside
the state. The members of community organisations became
more sharply aware of the contradictions in the state, both its
positive and negative aspects. Although they were not always
conscious of the parallel, they began to emulate the way in which
private business enterprises or bodies like the public schools deal
with the state, only accepting resources so long as the control
over their use could be retained by the organisations themselves:
action groups to defend homes against urban motorways, tenant
groups seeking self-determination, organisations to improve
neighbourhood facilities. Women played an increasingly prominent role in these organisations, asserting their right to organise
in new ways and to place high on the political agenda issues that
particularly affected them, like child care, health, housing, the
environment and transport. Against outright state opposition to
their plans and ideas, little progress could be made by these
groups. However, there were some successes and increased
activity brought greater political awareness and effectiveness,
both locally and nationally. The 'community movement' of this
period was part of an international realisation that people might
be able to play a more direct part in democracy, using their own
talents and energies.

Organisation to resist the Housing Finance Act in the early
1970s gave tenants' organisations political experience and added
momentum to their desire for a political voice. The voluntary
sector developed throughout the 1970s and early 1980s, both in
its traditional charitable role, often associated with the National
Council for Voluntary Organisations, and in new political pressure groups, single-issue campaigns and local self-help and
campaigning organisations. These included, for example,
tenants' and residents' groups, pensioners' action groups and
amenity organisations, the local activities of Shelter, and anti-
racism campaigns. Trade unions and community projects
established joint resource and research centres, as in
Birmingham, Newcastle and Coventry. These alliances between
local government, the community, environmental and recreational groups and trade union organisations added momentum
to wider democratic participation.

At work, new forms of trade union activity developed as

industrial restructuring gathered pace through amalgamations and rationalisations. Work-ins and occupations led to less defensive, creative attitudes to the production process. Clydeside, Merseyside, South Yorkshire and the West Midlands all witnessed attempts to take over industrial undertakings. When the workers occupied the Upper Clyde Ship Builders during the Heath government, their demands included more than keeping their jobs.

The workers of Britain are getting off their knees, getting on their feet, and asserting their dignity. Asserting their abilities in a determined and disciplined way that they will have a say in the decision making of this country.[3]

The 'Lucas Workers' Corporate Plan' developed this approach further.[4] Lucas Aerospace Shop Stewards' Combine represented workers in a major private company whose market was dominated by public-sector defence contracts. The plan outlined proposals for the manufacture of rail buses, heat pumps and kidney machines rather than components for nuclear missiles. Workers showed in detail how their skills, the necessary materials and technology could be combined for people's needs. Public-sector unions responded in similar fashion, taking the lead against monetarist-inspired cuts in public expenditure from the mid-1970s, and deploying members' experience and imagination to produce proposals for public service improvements. In 1975, following government cuts, NUPE, for example, produced a school meals charter, not just arguing for better pay and conditions for their members, but also detailing ways to improve and extend the service. This was subsequently developed in Haringey, for example, through cooperation between workforce and council, as we outline in Chapter 6.

Community politics

The Labour Party was initially slow to respond to new forms of community politics. The Liberal Party, at the beginning of its electoral revival in the early 1970s, seized the opportunity. Liberal 'community politics' took up the 'community movement' and used it as the means for gaining a political presence in local government by focusing on immediate grievances – cracked paving stones, local planning policies and the like – notably in Liverpool among the big cities. However, Liberal activists had no coherent perspective from their party on how local government could present long-term alternative solutions to the crisis in British cities. Liverpool's Liberals demonstrated an opportunistic type of 'community politics'. Their contribution to local government was, with Tory collusion, to make a mess of administering Liverpool, and to leave the city's finances in disarray, thus building a platform for the local Labour Party in the 1980s. They failed, in any constructive way, to focus national attention on the economic collapse of Merseyside.

During the same period, many Labour Party members felt disenchanted with the 1974–9 Labour government. The IMF-inspired cuts, and the 1978/9 'Winter of Discontent' had been bitter pills to swallow. Victory for Margaret Thatcher's Conservatives increasingly focused attention on local politics as a base for opposition. A realisation developed in local Labour parties that local government might develop, once again, into the tool for change which had been so effective in the late nineteenth and early twentieth centuries, as we have already seen.

Elected councillors convinced of the need for a new approach to public services became prominent in local government. People who had been part of the community projects and local experiments of the late 1960s and 1970s began to work as council officers with local authorities, as politicians sought to put their ideas into practice. People with experience in workers' plans, innovation and democratic practices in industry were recruited into a number of local authorities. Although the GLC and Sheffield drew most attention at first, a new climate gave many local authority offices and workers the opportunity to break with the limitations of traditional practices.

Local government thus became a field where new ideas and policies in democratic public administration could be put into practice. Despite mistakes and some diversionary forays, a new relationship between local society and the state began to seem a possibility. This can be illustrated by looking at four areas of local political activity: the relationship between voluntary activity and local government; the opening out of local government through decentralisation; how the community can contribute to health care as a major public service; and how local politics can improve the general quality of life.

The state and the voluntary sector

In recent years voluntary organisations without formal political affiliation have played a more significant part in local politics than at any time since 1945. In the post-1945 era, people, having cooperated in the war effort, were ready to join together in building peace. But they were never given a proper active role in building their own welfare state. 'Statist' Labour politicians regarded voluntary organisations, the 'voluntary sector', as a relic of private philanthropy from rich to poor. They forgot the working-class voluntary movement which has provided local support and help to people in difficulty, and brought them together for recreation and celebration, ever since the days of the Goose and Burial Clubs and Friendly Societies in the early nineteenth century. The vitality of working-class traditions of community support was seen again in the 1980s in the Women Against Pit Closures movement and the immense range of support groups which sprang up in the mining areas to feed and organise the pit communities.[5] It is towards this view of the voluntary sector that local politics has turned the local state, so that people's initiative and ideas can be seen to be as legitimate and significant a part of democracy as the act of putting a cross at local and national election times.

The 'voluntary sector' of the 1940s is barely recognisable today. No longer dominated by traditional councils of social service and local branches of national philanthropic organisations, the community movement has made locally rooted groups more assertive and confident.[6] Often they join hands with more formally established organisations and pressure groups: Age Concern, Child Poverty Action Group, Friends of the Earth. They have also set up new regional or national organisations such as the Federation of Women's Aid and the Federation of Law Centres, and federations of Pensioners' Action Groups. Their significance extends beyond their influence on the single issues with which they may be concerned.

Linking local authority policies with voluntary organisations has been one important way of responding to the demands for equality made by women. By 1984, 12 major authorities had women's committees and more had appointed officers to work with women's groups. Women, who form 52 per cent of the population and 40 per cent of the paid labour force, play the most important part in caring for children and dependants. Three out of every four carers of this kind are women and, according to the 1983 census of women and employment, over 3·25 million women provide essential *full-time* care to a disabled or elderly dependant. As many as 6 million people – women and men – now provide regular essential support, full- or part-time, to dependent relatives or friends. In these circumstances, respite care to allow short breaks to alleviate stress and strain is an essential part of local authority support services.

Women are poorly represented in decision-making and discriminated against through low pay, poor conditions, lack of recognition of practical qualifications and opportunities for promotion. For local politics to improve their position there will have to be great advances in the mainline services of housing, transport and education and major changes in economic policy, since, as Bea Campbell noted it is 'the massive increase of employment among married women in peacetime which has changed the culture we all inhabit and the legal rights of women'. When the local state responds to voluntary activity, however, community organisations that deal with the concerns of home and neighbourhood also give a voice to many women who might not participate in more explicitly feminist organisations, as was demonstrated by the hundreds drawn together for a Women's Day in 1987 by the Centre against Unemployment in Sheffield, to spell out their needs to the authorities.

Grants have been given to voluntary organisations for decades. Some local politicians have encouraged private benevolence at the expense of public rights in this way, others have seen it merely as a cheap substitute for state provision. Involving voluntary groups in the actual policies which involve grants of state resources is a new element in a political rationale which seeks to extend the democratic process. The black community has made an increasingly significant contribution to local politics in the form of, for example, independent West Indian and Asian community associations, educational groups, cultural organisations and employment projects. Black organisations do not want help that is dependent on political 'respectability' – they want recognition as a political right and the freedom to negotiate independently. In order to influence local authorities themselves, there has been a move to co-opt such groups on to the structures of the council much more than before. The GLC took the lead, welding together a grants policy which gave particular support to black voluntary organisations; an equal opportunities

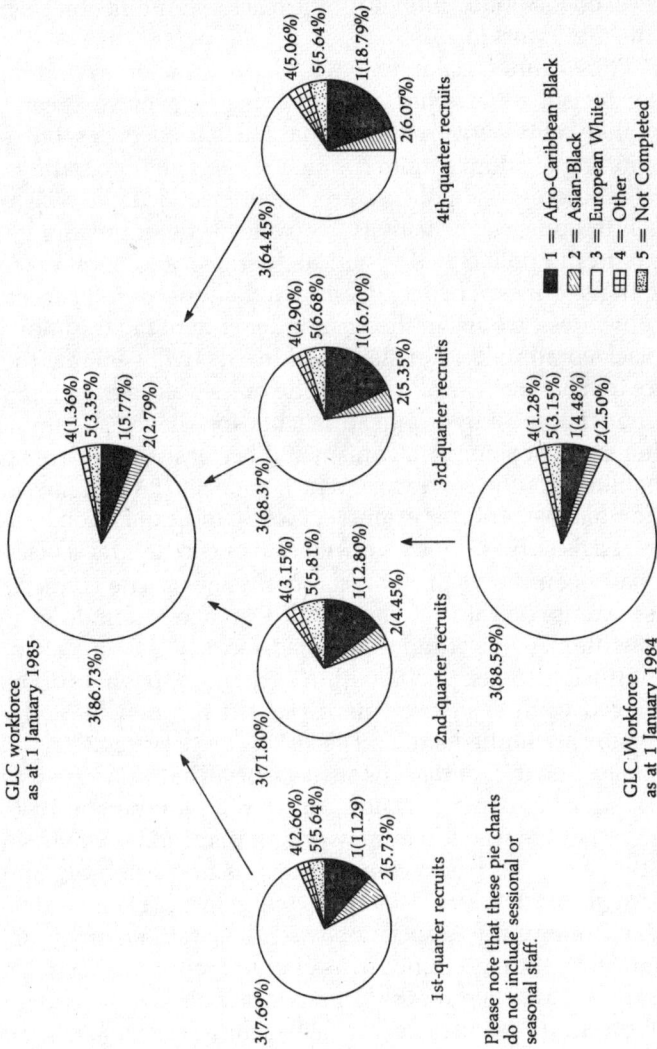

GLC workforce
as at 1 January 1985

4(1.36%)
5(3.35%)
1(5.77%)
2(2.79%)
3(86.73%)

1st-quarter recruits

3(71.80%)
4(2.66%)
5(5.64%)
1(11.29)
2(5.73%)
3(7.69%)

2nd-quarter recruits

3(88.59%)
4(3.15%)
5(5.81%)
1(12.80%)
2(4.45%)
3(68.37%)

3rd-quarter recruits

4(2.90%)
5(6.68%)
1(16.70%)
2(5.35%)
3(64.45%)

4th-quarter recruits

4(5.06%)
5(5.64%)
1(18.79%)
2(6.07%)

GLC Workforce
as at 1 January 1984

4(1.28%)
5(3.15%)
1(4.48%)
2(2.50%)

1 = Afro-Caribbean Black
2 = Asian-Black
3 = European White
4 = Other
5 = Not Completed

Please note that these pie charts
do not include sessional or
seasonal staff.

Summary of the effect of the GLC equal opportunities policy on employment by race
Source: GLC, *Equal Opportunities Monitoring Report*, 1985.

committee to monitor racial discrimination; and a serious attempt to implement positive action in its own recruitment policy. In 1984 alone there was evidence that the combination was having some effect on job opportunities for the black community, at least within the GLC workforce.

Local politics cannot claim to have made a major impact in opposing racism or enabling black people to achieve greater equality. Like central government, it has failed for decades, but is now beginning to adopt a more courageous and definite stand to ensure that necessary policies are developed against racism wherever it appears. Sensitivity as well as determination is required from politicians, political parties and voluntary organisations, but experience has shown that, just as it has been true of powerless groups in the past, independent organisations in the black community, not state institutions, will generate the real force for change in local politics. The press was able to pillory Brent Council's sacking of a head teacher for alleged racism in 1986, thereby provoking antagonism and backlash. There are no such headlines for the solid work which councils have begun, in combating harassment, for example. Newham Council commissioned a Harris survey which showed that one in four local black people had been the victim of racial harassment. The council's response was practical, not rhetorical. Damage to windows is repaired within 24 hours and toughened security glass installed. Racist graffiti is also cleaned off within 24 hours, and where doors are damaged by fire, or excrement pushed through the letter boxes repairs are immediate, and security devices fitted. This all costs money, and it is for reasons such as these that Newham was picked out as a high-spending authority for rate-capping in 1986. All that can be achieved is a framework for democratic activity in which the voice of black communities, Afro-Caribbean and Asian, can be clearly heard. When the Sheffield and District Afro-Caribbean Community Association was joined, after many years of hesitancy, by the city council in its energetic efforts to establish a social and cultural centre, the shift in local politics was evident to all involved. Its facilities near the city centre are extensive and wide-ranging, offering social, educational and training facilities which SADACCA itself decided were needed and for which the local authority was prepared to offer funding and other resources.

Many voluntary groups are volatile and impermanent, nor can they be considered representative in the same way as elected councillors, but they do speak directly on behalf of their members or users, and the important task is to give the energy they represent a permanent and assured place in local politics. Perhaps the clearest and most concrete evidence of the possibilities can be seen where councils fund, support and respond to networks of voluntary advice centres and law centres who campaigned very effectively, for example, to spread information about the Fowler Review of social security during 1985 and 1986. The media has sought to pick on the more contentious voluntary groups in order to discredit a form of political activity which breaks the mould and raises uncomfortable issues, but by engaging with the active politics of the community, local elected representatives and party leaders introduce a richer dialogue into political life.

Without that dialogue it is impossible for politicians to listen to people or to ask them to support their policies. The systematic public debate on its budget conducted by the ILEA in 1984 when it had been rate-capped was only possible because it had recently established a framework for debate. Teachers, parents, students and voluntary organisations were involved in an extensive programme of discussion. As one commentator noted, most people who came to meetings came with 'real fears about the future, insecurities that have developed not simply because of Thatcherism. They bring worries inspired by the way in which ILEA's policies have been represented . . . Does it want to do away with the boy scouts?'[8] Their fears were also real because of the many uncertainties that arise at a time of rapid change. Unless there are ways of publicly debating issues which concern people, they cannot be expected to take a part in shaping change for themselves and for others.

Voluntary organisations concerned with political action are not the only voluntary groups which local politics has to consider. People join voluntary organisations for all sorts of shared interests and recreation – whether angling groups, photographic societies, or gardening and allotments clubs – and their voices can also be heard in a neighbourhood forum or consultation over local planning. By establishing closer relations with all voluntary movements, local government inevitably becomes less parochial. People do not define the limits of their lives according to local government boundaries or indeed national frontiers. The peace movement has been one of the more dramatic examples of pressure-group activity in the 1970s and 1980s. Local authorities have responded in many ways. The 160 councils who are now (in 1986) banded together in the Nuclear-Free Zones Steering Committee do not believe that they can protect the people of their own areas from nuclear disaster, but they are bringing the issue to the fore, joining voluntary movements in ensuring that the debate on nuclear weapons is not dominated by government propaganda. When the Ministry of Defence and the Foreign Office send out material about the possibilities of nuclear survival to schools and voluntary organisations it is important that local authorities make their educational facilities, libraries and community facilities available to ensure that the debate about peace is not one-sided.

Twinning arrangements with overseas towns have for many years provided an opportunity for exchange visits in which ordinary people can break down stereotypes of what life is like elsewhere, and links have been extended as far as China, Eastern Europe and the Third World. Local politics can also build broader economic and political alliances between different countries. A number of European cities have banded together to help with a water project in Nicaragua, part of Sheffield's contribution being to grant leave to council workers who wanted to work directly on the project. In response to the anti-apartheid movement a National Local Authority Anti-Apartheid Steering Committee was established in 1983. The furtherance of peace and justice cannot be left to international statesmen alone, it needs to be part of the politics of everyday life.

Decentralising the town hall

We may be seeing a more active democratic dialogue in local politics, but unless the structure of local politics is altered, people will still have very little say over what is done. There is much evidence that ordinary people are not happy to leave decisions to the politicians alone, even if they support their policies.

Cleveland County's Research and Intelligence Unit have monitored public attitudes to council policies in regular surveys since 1975. In 1983, people were presented with the county council's dilemma: massive unemployment and the need to keep up rather than reduce public spending.[9] The results of the unit's survey showed that most people were prepared to pay more rates to maintain services, but 'fewer than half felt that the council were aware of the problems and wishes of people like themselves, and only a quarter felt that they knew enough about council decisions and what the council did'. In 1981 Walsall Labour Party outlined objectives which were taken up in many other areas over the next few years to deal with this problem:

Walsall Borough Labour Party had a vision of a very different sort of local democracy and community action. . . . Residents are to have a creative permanent input into local government. Rather than distinct divisions into 'the people', 'councillors' and 'the officials', the three are to join and work together.[10]

'Decentralisation' has become the catchword for policies seeking to achieve these ends. Schumacher's phrase, 'Small is Beautiful,' may not point the way for every area of economic activity, but it is valid for important aspects of local administration and politics. Local government reorganisation in 1974 had, moreover, removed many of the accessible local offices and services of the urban and rural district councils when the new district and county structures were created and thus increased the problem of remoteness.

Effective decentralisation policies require a number of changes: shifting the office or worksite to where people live; changing management structures so as to move decision making lower down the line; providing opportunities for people to contribute at regular meetings and by direct contact with managers and workers. Housing services, direct labour organisations and social services have been the chief fields of activity, but 'going local' has also emphasised the need for more coordination between departments over the services they provide, for example, the important gains to be made by integrating recreational provision into neighbourhood schools and colleges. Achieving these ends has required active participation from community organisations like parent-teacher associations, residents' and youth groups and sporting interests, taking different forms according to local circumstances.

Walsall Labour Party took control of the council on 10 May 1981 on a manifesto pledging 25 local offices to serve the 42,000 council tenants. Most of the Labour councillors were themselves council tenants and, with direct experience of a centralised housing administration, moved rapidly to decentralisation. Other councils, like Islington, have proceeded through an extensive consultation process. Hackney tenants were so keen to see manifesto commitments to decentralisation more speedily carried out that they occupied the St John's Area Housing Base in

January 1984 and, with local authority building workers, operated their own repair service. 'The failure of the council to impose change upon the bureaucracy raised, they suggest, the question who actually runs the borough – councillors or senior management?'[11]

Regrettably not all local initiatives have been immediately successful or welcomed by all professional workers, who thus give ammunition to the opponents of public services. There is indeed evidence of problems for white-collar and management workers whose working practices and responsibilities are changed and often made more complex by reorganisation. They must deal more directly with the public than has been customary and this may bring greater stress than sitting in the town hall away from the front line. Some initiatives have been seen as an imposition of area based management, not the introduction of neighbourhood centres in which people would be welcomed. In some authorities there have been largely obstructive wrangles over pay and conditions during the process of decentralisation, which have played havoc with the services it was intended to improve. The only way of responding to this is by giving a clear political lead with the maximum contribution of consumers and their organisations, which means that there has to be time for proper discussion and patient explanation.

There are also gains for workers, however. Decentralisation provides the opportunity for new working relations between white-collar and manual workers (and their unions) and the customer, which leads to more job satisfaction. In the early stages of area-based housing management in Sheffield, the Federation of Residents' and Tenants' Associations, frustrated by what they saw as hasty introduction and implementation, produced their own arguments for reorganisation of the housing service, discussing ideas with white-collar and manual workers.

By the mid-1980s the authority which, apart from Walsall, had progressed furthest in decentralisation was Islington. The structure of a typical decentralised neighbourhood office is shown in the following diagram.

A worker at one of the Islington neighbourhood offices clearly shows his satisfaction with the system. He writes in *Islington News* on the first anniversary of the Upper Street neighbourhood office, 'The key is the way people are made welcome. We are determined people should get what they come in for. Staff have a

'Temporary
attachments'
e.g. architects
working on local
schemes

'Located
functions'
e.g. a library if the
local office is within
it, or a community
centre

'Core functions'
Housing,
Social Services,
Community
Development

'Added
functions'
e.g. planning
applications
at certain
larger offices

'Dependent
functions'
e.g. day nurseries
or playgrounds

'Outposted staff'
e.g. housing estate
managers on larger
estates and caretakers
where local
management
arrangements apply

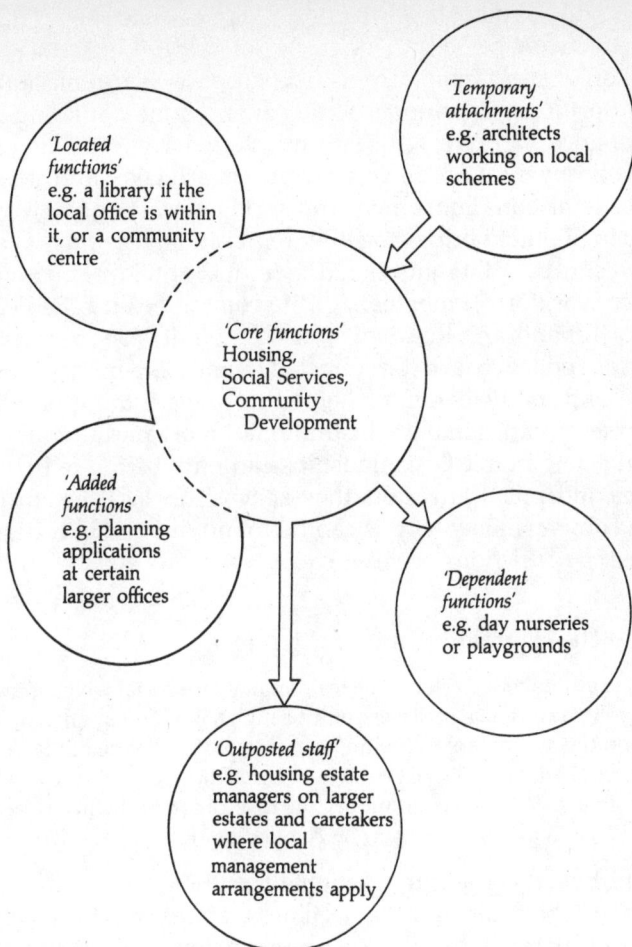

The neighbourhood office – basic framework
Source: Decentralisation Subcommittee, *Committee Report*, London
Borough of Islington, July 1982.

real commitment to consumer service. You can't pass the buck
round a neighbourhood office – it is too small.'[12]

By the beginning of 1985, 11 London boroughs had 'going-
local' policies along with Birmingham, Bradford, Glasgow,
Manchester, Newcastle, Sheffield and others. Decentralisation is
not a substitute for local and national policy making. Services
cannot be improved effectively unless national or local restrictions on resources are removed. Yet even within the constraints

imposed, the opportunity for greater democracy to use resources more effectively has been demonstrated.

One of the most important consequences of decentralisation is the opportunity it presents for tenants, council building and maintenance workers, officers and elected representatives to work collectively at producing a service which takes into account the needs of both consumers and producers. The Joint Works Group in Sheffield brings together representatives of workers in the Direct Labour Organisation (the council's building and maintenance workforce), members of the committee and the Federation of Tenants and Resident's Association. It exists to consider city-wide policy based on direct personal experience of the service and its deliberations helped to prepare the ground for area-based management. Institutional reorganisation is not enough: new political relationships can only be judged by the policies and practical results they achieve. In local health provision some evidence of this can be found in Sheffield, despite increasing restrictions on resources.

The community and health care

Health is a state of complete physical, mental and social well being and not merely the absence of disease or infirmity; it is a fundamental human right and the attainment of the highest possible level of health is a more important worldwide social goal whose realisation requires the action of many other social and economic sectors in addition to the health sector. (World Health Organisation, Alma Ata Declaration, 1978)

A disturbing feature of the National Health Service has been the danger of it becoming a 'national illness service', not the means of achieving positive health. Yet the main reasons for improvements in health over the last century or so are to be found in the prevention of infectious diseases and the institution of public health programmes, not the discovery of expensive new cures and methods of surgery.

In the postwar years, the actions of local authorities through policies for clean air and slum clearance probably did more for the health and wellbeing of people in industrial communities than any other combination of measures. A partnership of local initiative and national resources could be seen working in practice.

The promotion of health is now being taken up in new ways through the integration of voluntary and statutory services. Sheffield's Health Care Strategy Group brings together the city council, the Community Health Council, trade unions and voluntary organisations to forge a policy which emphasises primary preventative health care. Linking personal social services, housing and environmental health for positive social policies together with other services can throw the weight of wider resources into finding solutions. The Food and Health Conference 1984 (organised by the Health Care Strategy Group and the Sheffield City Polytechnic's Health Studies Department) put forward recommendations for the Environmental Health Department to extend its resources in order to develop a food policy for the city, bringing together local authority departments, such as education, with the health authority to examine food production and distribution in the city and to develop a community dietetic service. Similarly, the Health Panel of the Greater London Council was set up in 1982 which, amongst other things, issued a guide to health service resource allocation in London.

A People's Campaign for Health was established with the assistance of the Sheffield Health Care Strategy Group in 1982 which conducted a people's inquiry in the first half of 1984. Following a well-supported rally, local groups met regularly over a six-month period. They examined the performance of the health service and produced concrete recommendations for ways in which the National Health Service might be reconstructed 'upon a new, positive vision of primary health care'. For example, the report looks carefully at the concept of 'community care' and seeks to emphasise the dangers of cost-cutting. Community care should be advocated, 'but only if the standards of care are as high as possible' and as long as 'relatives, neighbours and volunteers are not abused as a source of unpaid care'.[13] Since local politics has little direct influence on the National Health Service, the people's inquiry registered its concern that there should be more democratic control.

In caring for the elderly, the local authority does have responsibility, however, and Sheffield has been introducing a policy of community care whose aim, in the words of the people's inquiry report, 'is to maintain the health – psychological, social and biological – of the individual at the highest standards whilst they are in their own environments, thus retaining the client's independence and preserving as much of the normality of their lives as they are personally able to cope with'.[14] This is quite impossible without new relations between the consumers, the producers, voluntary organisations, neighbours and friends.

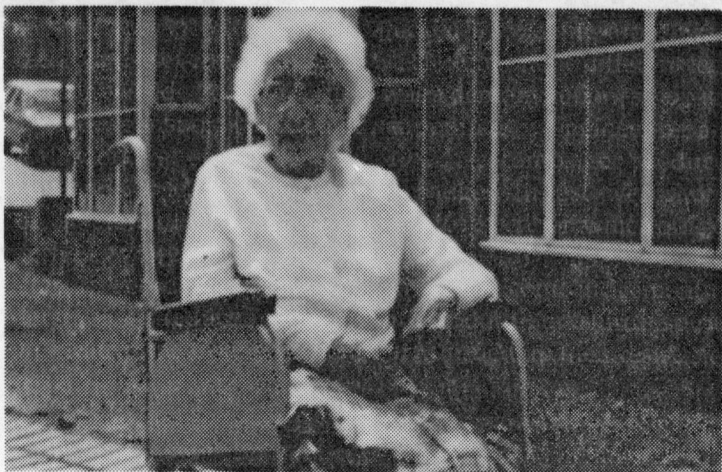

Sheffield City Libraries

6   Control of our lives: Mrs Irene Pass, who took part in the Olympic Games of
     1924, found new vigour with the help of the Elderly Persons Support Unit,
     Ecclesfield, Sheffield.

The proportion of people in the population over retiring age is
increasing and creates major problems for health care. The
market treats the elderly as it does other so-called non-productive
groups – not as people, but as economic and social problems.
Such problems are less acute for those who can afford the best
institutions, or adapt their houses and pay for facilities. A rational
approach to the economy and to collective organisation could
ensure that wealth created during working years is returned over
the whole of one's life. It is not simply a matter of 'caring for the
elderly', but of ensuring that an increasingly active older population can contribute to society and tailoring necessary support
accordingly, as strength and health fails.

A full range of options can only be made available by assessing
the needs of different groups and developing varied forms of
support for rehabilitation, health care and long-term community
or residential care. Innovatory schemes like Sheffield's elderly
persons' support units ensure that key workers like home helps
and wardens, as well as professional organisers and social workers, can contribute their ideas about the needs of different
groups. Primary preventative health care teams help to broaden
this approach which can never be offered in the private sector
other than to the extremely rich. Equally, aids and adaptations

which make independent living possible form an essential part of the support available from the community and illustrate the interrelationship of housing, social services, design services and medical practice. In Sheffield, the elderly person support units also mobilise the voluntary resources of the community along with the statutory provision by the council. The conception, planning and management of these support units incorporates new forms or organisation and close relations with the voluntary sector.

There is no uniform model for these units. Existing residential accommodation, new buildings, adapted buildings and day centres are all involved. In one unit, a luncheon club is so attractive that it brings in people who once preferred meals on wheels in their own homes. There is a launderette, a specially adapted bathroom, a hairdressing room, an advice centre and space for 'messy' activities like painting which are difficult in a small house. Another unit includes a library and facilities for the Tenants' Association. Its design followed months of discussion with local people. New technology is to be introduced to provide an alarm and communication system across the neighbourhood.

The concept of home helps has broadened into one of community support workers. Jobs within a neighbourhood have been expanded – 800 people applied for 21 vacancies in the first unit. Those chosen were mostly local people, not professionals from 'the smart end of the city', as one applicant put it, although this is not to discount the effective professionalism which also made the scheme possible. Pensioners can continue to be involved in their community, when they are still fit and well, they can have entertainment at the centre, or 'it could be that they would just like to go to a football match, so, we'll take them'. Residential beds provide care when needed rather than long-term institutionalisation. At present, the network of units is small, but there is positive evidence of success. A feature for the local paper, 'In Control of Their Lives',[15] points out how the centre had been able in some instances to restore self-respect and dignity.

A foretaste of the future is the experience of the Ecclesfield residents. Just by listening, a support worker discovered that a depressed and very ordinary elderly woman held three world records for swimming in her youth. Now, with the certificates out of brown paper and onto her wall, she is one of the neighbourhood's stars.

There is therefore a way forward which does not depend on the dictates of the 'marketplace'. Services are being integrated into the life of the community, but not as a cheap expedient. This is a coherent approach to social policy in contrast to past departmentalism, in both local and central provision. No such coherence can be expected from private enterprise which provides for individuals and groups only according to their ability to pay and provide profits – encouraged by central government and often supported by public funds.

The lucrative nature of the business is borne out by the country's largest agent for small business, Christie & Co. In a recent report, the company said: 'The care and comfort of our elderly population in long-term nursing and residential homes is no longer just another role for our heavily burdened social services. It is fast becoming big business in the private sector.

'With the number of residents in private nursing and rest homes expected to rise to around 129,000 by 1990, there is growing interest from the commercial and business world.'

A spokesman for Christie's in London said: 'It is a very profitable business and one which has a very healthy future.'[16]

Government funding for the private care for the elderly takes place through the supplementary benefits system which pays for the private care of those elderly residents who cannot afford fees in the mushrooming residential homes in which families are encouraged to place their relatives (estimated recently at 43,000 old people). This can amount to £120 per week in a care home and £170 in a nursing home at 1986 prices, with homes charging above DHSS rates to maximise profits. There is a growing body of opinion that many old people live in pain and humiliation, given little protection by legislation.

'What amazes me is the dramatic change over the last ten years in the type of old people these homes are looking after,' said Dr Hullin. 'There are geriatrics, psychogeriatrics, the incontinent and the forgetful. Ten years ago people who had reached this stage of old age would have been transferred to National Health Service hospitals.

'In a sense there is no choice. It illustrates the general problem that we have not expanded National Health Service facilities on the same scale as the increase in the elderly.'[17]

He could also have pointed out that community support can often prevent the necessity for hospital care, but that underinvestment in both local government and the health service have led to a lack of planning for demographic change. In 'Cinderella' services such as work with the mentally handicapped, the mentally ill or frail and confused elderly, local government has often been the last resort where other help has been denied. Local political debate has focused on these unglamorous areas of health care. Sheffield increased its residential bed provision to 1,800 while the health service were reducing theirs to well below half that number.

Local politics and the quality of life

Local services can be crucially important to people in particular need. They also affect the general quality of local life: the environment, recreation, leisure and transport. The commercialisation of leisure poses serious problems. The video revolution, for example, pushes in the direction of social fragmentation and passivity, as does proposed cable television and the marketing of increasingly cheap home-based leisure goods. Active sports and recreation, if left to free enterprise, are relatively more costly and rationed by their price.

With high unemployment among the young and over-fifties, but relative affluence among the employed, and with people living longer and more active lives, a recent report has noted that 'leisure' is 'a crucible for some of the major social issues facing British society as a whole and, therefore, local government over the next decade and into the next century'.[18] In the creative local authorities which opposed government policies in the 1980s there have been signs that the importance of this issue is recognised, with explorations into new and existing leisure facilities. Their aim has been to make it possible for all groups to engage in collective activities regardless of means or personal circumstances, and in different cultural forms. Popular festivals sponsored by the GLC on the South Bank have reflected the cultural diversity of London's population, young and old, black and white, and not merely the diversions of an elite minority. They were the glamorous tip of an iceberg. In Sheffield, Manchester and other cities, as well as London boroughs, there has been support for local festivals and sporting events and for local publishing in writers' workshops and theatre workshops, in ethnic communities, in mining communities and in the production of local histories and community studies.

Recreation services have opened themselves up as resources available to all, whatever their financial means. Sheffield's 'Passport to Leisure' offers free opportunities, not only to the unemployed and older people, but to the whole of the population at off-peak time, emphasising participation and regular, cheap tuition sessions. The Brixton recreation centre, which was funded by the GLC, indicates how investment of resources can take such policies forward, including a free crèche and meeting rooms which are open until 10 p.m.[19] Local voluntary groups like the pensioners' art group can display their material in the foyer and use the facilities for conferences. Outreach workers are employed to meet groups who are not making use of the centre, such as Asian women and the elderly, and they are trying to tailor facilities to suit their needs.

A major contribution to life in many communities has been made when local education authorities, along with voluntary organisations, have pursued the ideas behind 'community education' and applied them in the adult and continuing education service. Barriers are broken down between education and life, barriers erected by a system that defines education in terms of teaching formal classes and courses within institutions. Community education recognises all the processes by which people learn, in the family and in the community, and in groups who come together to provide activities for themselves and others. By validating this learning as a legitimate part of education and, therefore, allocating resources accordingly, adult education becomes a liberating process when control remains in the hands of people, not professionals. Many local authorities are beginning to find ways of doing this through specially appointed staff and resource centres, in addition to formal institutional provision. Not only does this offer many more people than before access to education but it also ensures that the effort, ideas and imagination of working-class women and men are recognised properly alongside the more publicly acclaimed activity of politicians and professionals.

Leisure and educational facilities are combined by opening up schools and colleges to the public, or by more ambitious responses to the growing demand for sport, leisure and cultural activities. County councils like Nottingham, Oxford and Cumbria have followed early pioneering by Leicester and Cambridge by building joint school and recreation centres. Some places, like Cranford Community School (Hounslow), the Sutton Centre (Nottinghamshire) and the Abraham Moss Centre (Manchester) include much more: public libraries, health clinics, further education, adult education, youth service and sports facilities. Moves towards tertiary colleges (comprehensive post-16 educational provision) encourage such development. Such schemes are expensive to build and operate but more cost-effective and better used than individual units.

By contrast, private leisure developments now being proposed concentrate on leisure pursuits which will bring a profit with little attention to minority interests and poorer pay and conditions for the staff. Yet, due to a lack of local authority funds, many authorities are engaged in an unseemly scramble for such private centres for the rate income that they can generate. In 1981–2 total leisure spending was estimated at £33 billion, of which only £851 million took place in the public sector. Moreover, while there is no shortage of private funds for projects owned by a few multinational conglomerates, when a local authority attempts to spend on similar leisure provision, it is frequently condemned as wasteful.

For some people, leisure is an escape from work, a time for recovery, an additional dimension to a satisfactory life. For others it replaces the work they do not have, taking on a different set of purposes and meanings. In either case, there is a danger that the quality of life will be defined increasingly for most people by our leisure time, not by our capacity to shape the whole of our lives, at work as well as at play, and our environment. That is why local politics has refused to accept as its sole aim an improvement in the 'great municipal machine', important as efficient services may be. The goal has been to extend rather than retreat from democracy.

Decentralisation of decision making in politics counteracts the drift towards a crude individual relationship between provider and consumer which the private enterprise system promotes. Interweaving needs and opportunities emphasises the interdependence of everyone, rather than the dependence of some and the good fortune of others. It also reduces the dangers which lie in well-meaning paternalism and challenges the drift into a power relationship between the 'expert' and the recipient. Whether in building on the natural network of relations within the community for education, recreation, housing and health, or providing direct support to families coping with dependent relatives, the local authority is moving towards a kind of structure only hinted at by those committed to a 'localist' solution many years ago.

The new Right identify the state as the enemy of liberty preferring Adam Smith's notion that there is an 'invisible hand' in the market which produces what is best for us all. Local politics has recognised dangers in state power but also knows that in the complicated and continuing effort to build a more democratic society, the state can have its liberating and enabling dimension – it is not a fixed monolithic entity. The best of primary education, the best council housing, the best features of the health service, have freed people and expanded their control over their lives. New relations between the town hall and local society have been intended to extend that liberating process as far as possible and enable people to press for the best, and for the democratic social and economic order which can provide it. By these means fewer people become dependent on either the state or on private charity but can act for themselves.

Key political questions about who gets what, when and how are not made easier by changes in the structure of the local state. The more people learn the facts, the more political debate opens up. Those best able to articulate their case and mobilise support can obviously impose pressures which may distort priorities. On the other hand, legitimate demands are uncovered and people who have previously felt excluded from the democratic process are politicised. Decisions about the distribution of resources can only be made by popularly elected political parties, but local politics has been demonstrating how those decisions can be taken as part of a wider democratic process.

In the long term, survival in a highly industrialised urban environment can only come from emphasising the need we all have for each other. Gross inequalities in society must be removed to achieve this, and this requires a political programme which makes effective public services available to all. Where collective values are dominant, people can act as social beings, using and taking care of community facilities – as long as they have some kind of control over them.

Finally, if people are to be persuaded that providing better public services rather than shifting to private enterprise is not only a good thing, but a commonsense way forward, they have to believe that the resources are being spent wisely and that they can be afforded. There is no reason to tolerate featherbedding or waste within local government which must be concerned with the creation as well as the spending of wealth. Part of the process of redefining relations between the local state and society has been, as we shall see in the next chapter, to examine the role of local politics in regenerating the economy and in creating as well as using wealth.

6

Local Politics and the Economy

Economics is not a science that can be abstracted from politics, social relations and social values. Whatever else results from the 1980s, it has reminded us of that fundamental fact. Debate about the economy has been debate about what kind of society we want.

In one respect, the 1983 election in Britain was more significant than that of 1979. Margaret Thatcher's Tories went into the 1979 campaign blaming Labour for unemployment; 'Labour Isn't Working' posters covered the country. In 1979, therefore, government responsibility for employment and unemployment was clearly acknowledged. 1983, however, saw the first election campaign for 40 years in which a major political party seeking government office renounced responsibility for full employment. The Conservatives were going to leave that problem to market forces. Its own job was to weaken trade unions and bring wages down in order to encourage investment. Theoretical argument about the validity of monetarist economic theories should not be allowed to disguise the politics at the centre of the Conservative economic strategy.

As central government moved in one direction, local politics moved in the other. The growing influence of monetarist ideas on Westminster and pressure from international finance over the past decade have led to claims that economic and social policies should be separated. Economic policy, it is said, is about how the nation can create wealth, while social policy is about distributing it according to the social values of the controlling political group. Local politics has set its face against such a separation, pointing firmly to the social values built into the economic system itself which determines who gets what according to the process by which wealth is created and distributed. The one advantage of Conservative Party policy since 1979 is that it has made this increasingly obvious.

At first, it was necessary to read the more serious publications to discover the true debate behind the political rhetoric but increasingly the government declared its hand openly. For example, legislation which had been introduced over the previous century to regulate conditions of work and provide for fair wages and protection for vulnerable groups, was reversed. Now, after the 1986 Wages Act, even young workers under the age of 21 had protective legislation removed. The view was clear: if people wanted jobs, they must be prepared to take low wages. The ghosts in the House of Commons must have stirred uneasily as they recalled the words of Winston Churchill, speaking during the passage of the Bill introducing wages councils in 1909:

It is a serious national evil that any class of His Majesty's subjects should receive less than a living wage in return for their utmost exertions. It was formerly supposed that the workings of the law of supply and demand would naturally regulate or eliminate that evil. But where you have no organisation, no parity of pay bargaining, the good employer is undercut by the bad and the bad employer is undercut by the worst.[1]

In responding to the consequences of industrial decline in their communities, local politicians are in direct line of descent from those working in local government in the late nineteenth and early twentieth centuries who tackled the consequences of the first industrial revolution. They linked social improvements with the economic significance of water supply, gas, electricity and transport, and saw that effective education and decent living conditions were fundamental to industrial progress. By the 1920s, their actions had begun to point the way towards government intervention in the economy.

Then, as now, local politics came into conflict with national government, but there are some important differences. Britain's place in the world economy was still powerful in the earlier days and the underlying feeling was that the nation could sort out its own future. Now, Britain's economic position is much weaker relative to the United States, Europe, Japan and many other countries. Along with economic power, political control over Britain's future is being lost to overseas centres of power and regulation such as the international boardrooms of industry and finance and the EEC. The City of London, as a major financial centre, may be located in Britain but the interests it serves are not those of the British people. Encouraged by all this, the political Right has gained a new confidence, no longer seeing it as necessary to acquiesce when collective organisations of social reformers or of working people press for social justice. It is in that light that the new powerful voice for separating politics and economics must be seen. After 100 years of waning influence, we see the rightwing argument powerfully revived – that political democracy must keep out of economics; that politics is about public order, foreign affairs and facilitating the market, not part of the means by which people's needs and the resources they have created can be brought together.

In these circumstances creative local politics has taken on a new significance. It represents a defence of democracy, an attempt to draw back some control into the hands of the people, and the promotion of social and political values which place justice, equality and dignity at the centre of politics. It is in this sense that the link between economic and social policies at local level should be seen, not in a more mechanical way whereby it is merely acknowledged that schools, home helps, free bus passes and houses can only be provided adequately by a healthy economy.

There is one further difference between earlier efforts in local politics and the present. While the exponents of the free market are moving backwards in their social philosophy, they deploy all the forward power of evolutionary new technology to reshape the social order in their interests. The challenge to politics – local, national and international – is immense. Defence is not enough. There has to be a counteroffensive based firmly on the liberating aspects of new technology.

From the early 1970s, as full employment moved from the top of government priorities, local councils began to take up the challenge. There was support for small firms; closer links between the public and private sectors; promotion of local areas to attract new business. They were adapting the traditional economic role of British local government which offered inducements in the form of grants, free loans, and publicly subsidised infrastructure, and no request for reciprocal involvement with the community, in order to attract industrial and commercial concerns which were looking for suitable sites for investment and trading.

Efforts to attract employment from the private sector into the regions of Britain most affected by structural economic change and the decline of traditional heavy industry and shipbuilding have failed to make a strong impact. Such policies, based on government as well as local authority aid, have involved little planning and virtually no concern for the type of jobs created or the consequences of relocation. Instead of attracting new job creation projects and innovatory footloose capital from around the world as they were intended, enterprises were largely induced by incentives to move from one part of Britain to another. Some, like the motor industry on Merseyside, have taken the inducements to move and subsequently moved on again. Frozen fish processing plants have moved from a moderately assisted area on the east coast of Britain to an area in the North-East with the most government assistance available in the UK. Technologically advanced investment in the new plant has then often led to fewer people being employed in the new site than in the old one. Competitive efforts to increase the attractiveness of host communities, without a proper long-term social and economic strategy, have failed, primarily increasing the profits of those willing to use the system for their advantage at the expense of the national and local interests of the people.

Recognising these facts, local government began to look differently at its economic role. In the 1980s, on a much more substantial scale than in the past and increasingly in a more concerted fashion, a familiar historical pattern has been repeated. Local government and local politics have used all the powers available under the law, pushing them and adjusting them to make possible what was never directly intended by the legislators. New possibilities have been discovered and thought out which do not directly depend on statutory powers but result from the way in which local politics are conducted.

A common debate soon began to emerge as different types of local authority and shades of political opinion started to respond to the particular situations and pressures of their areas. A wide range of initiatives has been shared, even though the scale and nature of the problems in different areas were diverse. Local authorities vary considerably in the functions they perform. The former GLC and the metropolitan counties carried out strategic planning and servicing functions. The metropolitan districts, which cover the main urban areas, provide many direct services, though their size also requires a strategic and research function. The non-metropolitan county and district councils tend to cover the more rural and smaller urban areas and share responsibility for economic development and planning. Population and scale of economic activity also vary enormously; for example, the GLC, before its abolition, covered a population larger than many small nations.

The specific nature of activities also depends on the degree of control different authorities have over their outcome. Over their own operations and workforce, they have considerable control, whether in providing services or in carrying out research and presenting information. Metropolitan districts have direct responsibility for many services and can use their purchasing power to affect jobs in the private as well as the public arena. Many of the largest councils have access to investment resources, including pension funds. Influence over the private sector, however, except where such companies are dependent on the local authorities for their business, is limited, relying on persuasion and the availability of facilities and grants. Therefore any assessment of direct results has to take into account what could be achieved (a) when an authority has a reasonable measure of control over economic activity, (b) when it has little control over the activities undertaken but more control over the infrastructure which makes them possible, and (c) when there is virtually no control – only influence. Taking into account local variations in all these factors, the particular character of the local political economy and the balance of opinion and forces within the local political structure, it is remarkable that a common economic interventionist strategy has begun to emerge within the framework of local government.

The best local initiatives should not be judged by their immediate success in job creation, but by their implications for economic ideas and policy. Two protagonists, for local politics and for the Conservative's free-market approach, spelled this out clearly. Michael Ward, former Chair of the GLC Industry Employment Committee, wrote in 1983:

The government is committed to the free play of market forces as the dominant principle of social organisation. Each successful Greater London Enterprise Board project is a demonstration that there can be an alternative. Where the propaganda of words has failed we must turn to the propaganda of practice.[2]

Geoffrey Howe, Chancellor of the Exchequer, in 1983:

The general policy changes we have been proposing [are] to liberate enterprise throughout the country . . . The (Enterprise Zone) idea would be to set up local market areas or laboratories . . . If we find communities queuing up for Enterprise Zone status, we shall have gone a long way towards *winning the debate*. [Our emphasis]

The institutions through which local government has operated are very diverse. Some councils set up industry or employment committees and departments. The best known are the former GLC, West Midlands, Sheffield, Leeds and Manchester, but districts such as Newcastle, Barnsley and many others should not be ignored. Others have given their planning departments a strategic economic role or established economic development units in a central policy coordinating role. There is no statutory duty to do this. Councils have used their imagination by recognising the possibilities of Section 137 of the Local Government Act 1972 which allows them to spend the product of a 2p rate to benefit the community in ways not otherwise defined in the Act.

Employment and industry departments vary in their emphases: supporting businesses in difficulty; helping small businesses and backing cooperatives; concentrating on local authority employment and economic activity; planning; conducting strategic research and analysis. They reflect the responsibilities of different types of authority, their local economic structure and their political traditions.

Another strategy has been to create and fund enterprise boards, at arm's length from the council and not under its direct control. These are concerned with new ways of investing in the economy.

A proper assessment of the result of institutions and policies will not be possible for some time. Information and analysis is still underdeveloped. A Centre for Local Economic Strategies, based in Manchester, was founded for this purpose in 1985 and has begun to make possible a more comprehensive review. Furthermore, there will be no way of building the appropriate relationship between local activity and national policy until a government places a different politics at the centre of its strategy than has been the case in the 1980s. However, whatever pattern does emerge, the achievement of local politics has already been to offer a quite definite challenge to the values and principles which underlie 'free-market' policies. We shall examine local policies from this point of view in six sections: taking economics to the people; public-sector entrepreneurship; local infrastructures of training, research and development; local investment and financial institutions; improving the quality of working life; and democratic planning.

1. Taking economics to the people

Local politics has opened up the debate about what is happening to the British economy. Research has provided alternative explanations from those of government ministers, and because of the way it has been carried out, along with local people, it can help to link economic analysis with their own practical reality. The banner on GLC's County Hall, spelling out month by month the number of the capital's unemployed to MPs on the Westminster terraces across the Thames, and to Londoners as they crossed Westminster Bridge, was a powerful symbol. When in 1985 the council published its *London Industrial Strategy* report, it spoke for more than London alone.[3]

The major achievement of the GLC was to use its strategic position in local government to intervene in the public debate on economic policy. Other authorities have carried out basic research into the local economy and worked with shop stewards and the community in campaigns to defend jobs, but the GLC demonstrated more than any other council the potential for extending theoretical analysis into local practice. The *London Industrial Strategy* report provides an incisive answer to the new Right's limited and distorted analysis of the economic dilemmas facing Britain's communities. The GLC's analysis came from examining what was happening to people in London and also took full account of the international economy. It showed how Keynesian economic policies, pursued since the war to maintain full employment, were flawed. While economic activity has been maintained through government stimulation of public and private spending (the demand side of the economy), there has been no strategy for production (the supply side). Thus Keynesianism has not been able to solve the problems of overseas competition, the international corporate control of business and finance, the effective use of new technology, and the relations between public spending, private profit and wages. The need to construct a planned approach to technological change has been underplayed, partly because of the disappointing experience of previous efforts in the planning process, and partly because the approach of planning from the community rather than imposing centrally agreed proposals has never previously been on the agenda. The monetarists responded to these flaws.

For the monetarists, 'the main means of solving unemployment is for Londoners to price themselves back into work'. But while monetarists argue that government should stand back from the economy, their policies have in fact required crucial intervention: high interest rates, public-sector cuts and privatisation, anti-trade union legislation, the removal of exchange controls and the downgrading of the quality of training. Central to their policies is the intention of cutting labour costs and bringing workers more effectively under management control. As already indicated, such policies cannot create full employment. Low wages reduce demand. Fragmented industry cannot restructure itself to produce and market successfully, nationally and internationally, and there has been no attempt to address the problem of massive surplus labour in the world economy in the foreseeable future.

There is no mystery about the fundamental nature of the problems facing many of Britain's communities. The international economy is being restructured 'for capital', not 'for labour', by which is meant both producers and consumers. The *London Industrial Strategy* lays out the evidence for 24 'sectors' of London's economy. Its summary draws together the key themes of what is needed in an interventionist approach 'for labour', concentrating on production from these sectors – themes which have emerged more unsystematically in the practice of local politics elsewhere. There needs to be:

- an emphasis on long-term strategic production planning of industries;
- a concern that restructuring in all sectors of the economy should be carried out in the interests of those who work in the industry and use its products;
- a commitment to the development and application of human-centred technology;
- a strategic concern with improving the conditions and hours of work in the domestic economy, and with improved means of integrating domestic work with other parts of the economy in order to improve the living and working conditions of women;
- a priority to extending social control over the public economy through increasing political, trade union and user control;
- a commitment to popular involvement in all aspects of strategic policy making (what in London became known as 'popular planning') and in the operation of enterprises (enterprise planning).[4]

The GLC was criticised for taking too romantic a view of how the economy could be restructured for labour rather than capital, and also for holding out too much hope for local authority intervention. It was said that the strategy document did not recognise how decisions must relate to some kind of market, dealing with real problems of resource distribution, which bring conflict, both between producers and consumers, and between different consumer interests. Critics have responded as much to the tone of the *London Industrial Strategy* as to its content. For there is in fact a central recognition in the document that action is required on a national and international scale, and that economic development brings continuing restructuring as new technology affects production processes and service delivery. But the message is hopeful. It seeks to offer a future in which people democratically build an economy that takes into account the whole of their lives and does not treat them as abstract labour power. We find, for example, the *Strategy*'s refusal to accept that the home has no economic significance, even though it enables people to act as workers and consumers: 'For an economics geared to need, the household is the starting point, for it is in the home that need is experienced and expressed and where caring is concentrated.'[5]

While no authority has matched the GLC's *London Industrial Strategy* in the scope of its research and analysis, many have made a contribution. There is the work of the Coalfield Communities Campaign on the crisis in the coal industry, coordinated by Barnsley Metropolitan District Council; research on the clothing industry involving Nottingham and the Lancashire authorities; *Steel in Crisis*, an examination of the problems facing the Sheffield steel industry;[6] and Lancashire Enterprise's work on the fishing industry. They are all examples of local politics seeing the need to examine problems facing the key industrial sectors of their local economies in close conjunction with the workers in those communities. The work has been undertaken for two purposes – to influence intervention in the economy and to extend understanding in the community and the trade union movement of what needs to be done. The debate is conducted through trade union groups, centres for adult education, unemployed workers' centres and similar organisations, and also through information and study packs. Local politics helps to involve as many sections of society as possible in this debate, including the unemployed.

Basic research enables local government to recognise the central significance of the private sector in its policies, rather than merely to overemphasise public service expansion, which is more under its control. But the truth about public spending and the economy can also be demonstrated by local research and debate. According to both local and national public opinion polls, a majority of people are in favour of more public spending and are prepared to pay more rates and taxes for it. Monetarist propaganda has endeavoured to persuade people that 'good housekeeping' means cutting back on the provision of services and the employment of people to meet need, such as home helps, whilst accepting that available resources can be spent on paying to keep people unemployed. The debate at local level has begun to spell out an alternative which offers the opportunity of spending available resources to regenerate economic activity by identifying need and then meeting it.

Local government is an essential part of the economic life of any community. It raises rates and it spends large amounts of community funds. Its employment of over 10 per cent of people in work generates important economic activity – in spending their wages they support and stimulate a wide range of jobs not directly related to the services of the authority. Along with the purchasing power of the local authority, this activity can significantly affect jobs in industry and commerce, with a chain reaction which has often been grossly underestimated. Local authority capital investment is crucial to the building industry and its suppliers. Contrary to those believing in private economic market forces, who think that raising and spending community funds is detrimental, local councils and their supporters know that sustaining employment and community services is a crucial backcloth to the life of the locality.

What distinguishes local authority assertions from central government propaganda is the factual research that backs them up. The government and the business world have insisted that the level of rates required by the 'high-spending' authorities is detrimental to local employment. Yet a report from the Department of Land Economy at Cambridge University, commissioned by the government itself, has concluded that 'with the exception of office employment in and around London, it is not possible to detect an influence of rates on the location of employment'.[7]

Councils have also carried out their own investigations. In 1985, Sheffield Employment Department commissioned a unique piece of research – a 'jobs audit'. A consortium of research bodies was asked to 'investigate critically and openly, complex and controversial questions, including those raised by opponents of

City Council policy and expenditure'.[8] Through detailed analysis of council spending, the report demonstrated how rate expenditure in Sheffield helped rather than hindered local industry by maintaining job levels, with attendant spending power and council contracts to the private sector.

Local jobs supported by Sheffield Council 1984/5

	Jobs	Jobs supported by spending of workers	Total jobs
Direct council employment	32,564	7,163	39,727
Construction contracts	953	321	1,274
Other contracts	879	180	1,059
Improvement grants	250	99	349
Total			42,409

In the building sector these figures are almost certainly an *under*estimate because of the greater use of the self-employed in the private sector of the construction industry.

As the table shows, Sheffield City Council spending supported – directly and indirectly – 42,409 local jobs or 19 per cent of the estimated 225,000 jobs in Sheffield in 1984–5.[9] The report also explains how almost £100 million spent by the council on contracts for the provision of goods and services by private enterprise far outweighs any burden imposed by city rates. The report concludes that criticism of Sheffield rates is politically motivated. In the business community, it is 'typical of a major recession when prospects of business obtaining financial relief through political action are better than the prospect of financial improvement through economic activity'.[10] As we see in the following table, public spending supports economic activity and creates more jobs than may be lost through raising the cash through rates to sustain such expenditure.

Jobs in local private firms – relative impact of council contracts and business rates 1984/5[13]

	£m	Jobs effect	Jobs per £m
Sheffield Council contracts	33	+1,280	+39
Business rates paid to council	54	−703	−13

Detailed analysis of this kind not only points the way for rational policies in the long term but also highlights the present enormous imperfections of monetarist good-housekeeping policies, as the Association of Metropolitan Authorities has pointedly argued:

Our programme of action shows how a modest increase in public spending could stimulate economic growth, cut dole queues and meet real needs while not adding so much as 1 per cent to inflation.

Our £4 billion package – modest in terms of overall public expenditure consists of:
– £1·5 billion a year increase in central government grants to local authorities;
– £1·5 billion a year increase in local authority capital expenditure;
– £1 billion a year increase in local authority revenue expenditure.[12]

In 1986 it was estimated that the current rates of investment in trunk road maintenance were 45 per cent below what is required to halt further decline; 16 per cent of the country's sewers were over 100 years old, one-third of the water entering the supply system did not reach the consumer due to leaks; 20 per cent of Britain's primary schools were built in the last century with 25 per cent still having outside toilets. Government allocations for spending on housing were far below the submissions made by councils based on their knowledge of local demand (resulting in a 74 per cent reduction in investment in council provision between 1980 and 1984). In 1984–5 local authorities in England and Wales spent over £6 billion in total on capital works and the table indicates how this has fallen behind other areas of public spending.

Local politics is seeking to ensure that communities are fully aware just how far local government services are an economic motor and not a drain; acting as employer, investor, purchaser and producer. And when the blinkers are removed, the Conservative government themselves are forced to recognise the truth. Speaking at the Annual Conference of the Chartered Institute of Public Finance and Accountancy in June 1985, Kenneth Baker acknowledged that Sheffield offered a better deal on the rates, with its low rateable value and high rate poundage, than Westminster with its high rateable value and low rate poundage, but he did not take his argument to its full conclusion: that efficient, high-spending authorities were offering both better value and a greater contribution to the local economy for the

1974 = 100

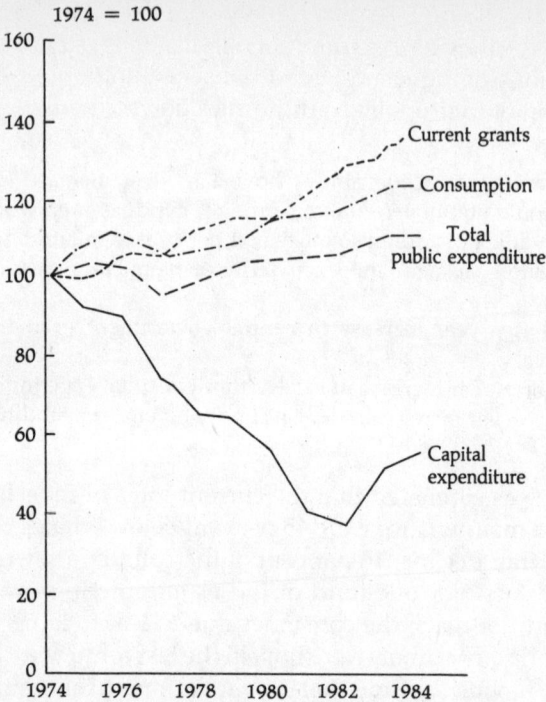

Public expenditure trends, 1974–84
Source: Data derived from Economic Trends, Central Statistical Office.

money spent than lower-spending non-interventionist adherents of government policy.

Although local politics has been attempting to provide alternative examples for future national policy and influencing the political agenda, it has never suggested that a local approach could on its own provide the answer. There has been an emphasis on analysis and research which places the local economy in the context of international patterns of trade, ownership and control, the development of new technology and the availability and best use of resources.

Trade unions and community organisations have begun to develop a two-way process of communication. The debate on industrial decline and the re-emergence of large-scale unemployment has increased interest in the economic and social consequences for many people unconcerned with such issues for many years. The potential for raising consciousness and providing adult and continuing education opportunities has therefore re-emerged in a way not seen since wartime mobilisation made such an exercise both necessary and possible. The numbers involved should not be exaggerated, but the opportunity to know and understand is just as important. For example, in its report, 'Sheffield, The Second Slump (1982)', Sheffield Trades Council showed how employment and unemployment in Sheffield was increasingly determined by the decrease of multinational 'conglomerate' companies like Lonrho and RTZ. Special steel firms like Aurora were closed from a combination of rationalisation and asset stripping.

Carrying out research and providing information is not enough in itself to enable a debate to take place effectively. It is for this reason that local employment departments or units have backed trade union support groups, unemployed workers' centres, community groups and similar organisations as vehicles for seeking two-way communication between the local state and the community on economic issues. A particularly impressive example is the Merseyside Trade Union Resource Centre, funded mainly through Merseyside County Council and opened officially on 1 June 1985, whose objectives were 'to harness the enormous human potential in the area which has been ignored by successive Governments, to integrate the activities of trade unionists and unemployed within a single collective endeavour'.

Large centres like these, where local authorities are sometimes backing up initiatives taken by the Trades Union Congress and local trade councils, are linked in some authorities to smaller local centres which provide neighbourhood facilities. It is a network that tries to prevent the unemployed from carrying the burden of industrial change as individuals, and gives both the unemployed and trade unionists in work an opportunity to contribute to local social and economic policy.

A different form of debate comes from councils joining workers in threatened industrial plants, as when the shop stewards committee at GEC Traction was faced with the proposed closure of their works at Attercliffe, Sheffield. Through the council's Employment Department, they made contact with workers in GEC's other plants, and developed a feasibility plan around a programme of investment in railway electrification and new rolling stock, that would have secured the future of their plant, and of course improved the country's rail network. Such plans were already available at British Rail headquarters, but frozen for lack of government capital borrowing approval.

The work gathered national interest, and a conference on railway electrification held in Sheffield on 10 October 1983 brought together all three main national rail unions, local branches and shop stewards committees of these and other unions in engineering, trades councils and local authorities, to consider the proposals and their implications both for the railways and their supply industries. Ironically at the point when the strength of the argument gained national credibility, the fight of the 750 workers at GEC Traction was coming to an end. The plant finally closed at the beginning of 1984, but the stupidity of the decision was dear.

2. The democratic entrepreneur

Castigating local government for its inefficiency has been part of the same stock-in-trade as the misleading arguments about public spending which have been put about by free-market apologists. Margaret Thatcher set up the Audit Commission as an independent watchdog to ensure that the nation gets value for money in public service. She could not have expected its Controller, John Banham, later Director General of the CBI, to say at the Institute of Housing Conference in Harrogate that:

The best local government is superb and private enterprise could never improve on it . . . with Sheffield as a shining example.

A well-managed direct labour organisation is going to be fully competitive with the best of the private sector. Sheffield collects refuse rather more economically than Southend which is privatised – a fact which went down like a lead balloon in Marsham Street, the DoE headquarters. There is no excuse for lousy management and privatisation is the last resort of a management that has given up.

Local economic activity in the 1980s has supported this judgement by taking the challenge on to the most hallowed ground of the private sector – that of commercial innovation and enterprise.

In the rise of modern industry, pride of place has been given to the entrepreneur – the individual who recognises the need for a product and is capable of bringing together production, marketing, pricing, delivery and the necessary resources in a creative and effective manner. At school we are taught to recognise these qualities in the likes of the Wedgwoods and Arkwrights of the early days and it is said that British industry depends on recapturing that spirit today.

In its study, *The Birth of Enterprise*, the right-wing Institute of Economic Affairs seeks to define the role of entrepreneurship whose

essence is to perceive worthwhile opportunities and act upon them. Both parts of this twin identity are necessary – alertness and action. . .

It is central to the role of the entrepreneur that he is prepared to decide what to do and how to do it, and will back his judgement. . .

Finally the entrepreneur essentially takes personal financial risk since this provides the 'world of uncertainty' which presents the necessary opportunities and spur.[13]

In the world of the microchip and the multinational combine, this simplistic view of the operation of the market economy has only limited value because it focuses on the individual risk taker. It fails to encompass not only the changed scale and nature of economic power and activity, but also how needs are met and resources used for the benefit of all.

Local government today, as in the past, can offer its own entrepreneurship and enterprise in facing the enormous economic and social change which technology and industrial restructuring bring. As with the response to the Industrial Revolution and its aftermath in Britain, so in the late twentieth century local government has something to offer. The examples in the past of local government's role in providing electricity, gas, transport, telecommunications and construction, can all be reflected in the modern initiatives for meeting social need.

The free market is inefficient in matching supply and demand. Unless the form of demand can easily be turned to profit by a producer, it will be left unsatisfied. Democratic political institutions present an alternative way of providing for need, irrespective of the short-term gain to the producer.

Within the local authority the potential exists for workers themselves to generate enterprise. They can see what is happening to their jobs and recognise the obvious things which need to be provided, whether goods or services. They can see where goods purchased are inadequate for the task in hand, or where they are simply not available at all. Skills, initiative, land, property and equipment all exist within the locality and yet often stand idle or are misused because an immediate profit cannot be made.

'Trade waste' is the business of collecting and disposing of any refuse from commercial or industrial premises, including major public facilities like hospitals. Councils have long been encouraged *not* to put this out to private contractors; Alec Douglas Home, later Conservative Prime Minister, was responsible in the 1950s for a report which showed the consequence of the operation of price cartels if it was left to private enterprise. Until 1979, Sheffield City Council regarded the service as part of public health and provided it at no charge, but government policy changes required a direct charge to be levied by the council for the removal of trade waste. Hargreaves, Wimpey, Leigh and others started to expand into this area now that profits could be made. They could invest heavily in equipment and cut prices until a contract was secured and then steadily increase prices again as competition disappeared.

Sheffield's Cleansing Department began to lose contracts to the private sector, some of them big ones like the university. (Sixty-nine contracts were lost between May 1983 and April 1984.) The workforce, whose livelihoods were at stake, were worried. Management in the Cleansing Department wanted to compete but felt unable to match multinational companies in terms of investment. They talked around reducing pay and conditions and possibly the size of the workforce in order to reduce costs. The workforce argued for investment in sophisticated plant, symbolised for them by the private sector's 'big-bite' vehicles which were capable of easily shifting more than any council vehicle could. In the end, neither of these two approaches prevailed, yet contracts were won back and the city's capacity to deal with this public service was greatly improved.

Two trade unionists in the Cleansing Department, members of the local authority shop stewards' association, knew about the work of the Joint Works Group (see p. 98) and the City Employment Department's Public Sector Team. They made the necessary connections, and the entrepreneur in this case, therefore, was not an individual but a group of councillors, officers from a number of council departments, and trade union members. While recognising the immediate problem, a long-term view was taken. How could contracts be won on a stable basis and service firmly established? The answer was versatility, the ability to gain access to the widest variety of premises, and to cope as required with many different materials which large unwieldy vehicles had failed to do. By pooling experience a four-point strategy emerged based on capital investment in new equipment – bins, skips, miniskips, vehicles and adaptors; a low pricing policy; a cooperative approach to work reorganisation; and lively promotion and publicity.

Within six months, £35,000 worth of work was won back, including that for the university and the health authority. Worksite meetings between councillors and the workforce threw up many suggestions about how improvements could be made and how work practices could be adapted to do a better job. Municipal enterprise has an old-fashioned ring to it but it showed itself here to be perfectly capable of competing effectively with the private sector.

In another area of work, Haringey school meals campaign, developed by NUPE and supported by the council, involved parents and school meals workers in designing an expanded service both to counter the threats of privatisation and of rate-capping: 'We see school meals as an essential part of the education service and not merely an ancillary appendage to it.'[14] The project's recommendations took a thorough look at the service. They proposed a food policy which valued women's work and incorporated food traditions of different cultures, the extension of the school meals catering service into breakfasts and community catering, the promotion of a labour-intensive rather than high-technology-based school meals service, the introduction of some 'local' decision-making by promoting nutritional/school meals committees in each school, and the provision of a comprehensive training plan for the school meals service to meet its new objectives and responsibilities.[15]

The same principle often applies in responding locally to businesses outside the local authority. Both cooperatives and small businesses are a way of preventing skills being wasted when mergers and rationalisation cast them aside. When investment, technical knowledge and marketing skills are brought together to help workers continue to produce what they know is still needed, or to turn their skills to new products, enterprise within the community continues to flourish.

One cooperative, sponsored by the Sheffield Cooperative Development Group, was set up to service traffic lights after their previous management had failed through inefficiency; it went on to outbid the two major national companies who control the market. When a machine-tool factory closed down in Sheffield, the workers began to discuss with the local authority the possible production of 'heat pumps' for council housing. (Heat pumps extract residual heat from the atmosphere and recycle it for heating both water and air.) The council's Employment Forum knew the value of this idea, produced by Lucas Aerospace workers almost a decade before. However, continued discussion with tenants on the Joint Works Group led to a recognition that the same engineering principles could be used to design a dehumidifier to tackle dampness in houses, and this would meet a more immediate need. (Dehumidifiers extract the moisture from the atmosphere to help overcome condensation where the structure, design or ventilation of dwellings creates a problem.) What became the Mons Cooperative is now a viable project and this product has been taken up by authorities outside Sheffield.

Recreational and cultural activities play an increasingly important part in the economy but both producers and consumers are often exploited for the profit of a few in the entertainment industry. With 3,000 musicians in Sheffield, many of them young, and with half the 43,569 unemployed in 1983 being under 25 years old, there was a big demand for musical facilities – these were limited compared with other big cities, despite Sheffield having contributed to the national and international music scene with groups such as Human League, ABC, Joe Cocker and others. Instead of leaving it to the commercial market alone, local musicians and promoters, local radio, the polytechnic and university, trade unions and architects were brought together to plan a music factory with rehearsal rooms and a wide range of facilities.

The Conservatives have attempted to suggest that public-service employment does not provide 'real jobs' whilst the service sector in the private-enterprise arena does. Because of local government's vulnerability to suggestions of waste and inflexibility, it has been important to take up this challenge and to show that it is in the provision of jobs to meet the need for clearly identifiable improvements in living standards and the environment that this misleading analysis can be refuted.

3. Training, developing local skills and knowledge

A further area of intervention in which local politics has demonstrated a creativity absent at national level is the exploration of forms of training appropriate to the changing economic and social climate. But while there have been some useful experiments, these should not hide the enormous lack in Britain of local planning for training in line with known predictions of the demand for different skills. This kind of planning for relevant training can only be done through the development of employment plans for the local economy. Such local initiatives could then be integrated into national plans for job creation and the expansion of specific sectors of the economy.

The percentage of British workers with a recognised qualification is half that of our major industrial competitors – indeed, we train as few as one-tenth of the number of engineers trained each year in Japan. In 1985 alone, 27 skill centres were closed and between 1979 and 1986, 16 out of 23 industrial training boards were disbanded. The output of engineering, technology and science graduates actually fell from 27,905 in 1983 to 25,389 in 1986. At all levels of skills and crafts technical change demands training and retraining which requires an enthusiastic partnership between the private and the public sector – one which can be developed more effectively locally. The Manpower Services Commission has functioned not so much as a major training agency but rather as a means of reducing the number of people registered as unemployed. The scale of the problem is so great that local authorities who have tried to develop training programmes have been unable to make a significant impact in terms of numbers. People have therefore had to focus on some specific aspects of training, along the lines of the GLC Training Board which gave its backing to certain projects chosen because they offered potential for the future.

The decline in manufacturing and construction training cannot be reversed by local authorities alone. Colleges and training facilities under their control have traditionally only responded to demands from local industry for apprenticeship and other forms of training. This clearly has to change. Some of the issues which need to be tackled in the future include:

How can training be linked effectively to the quality of production?

How can it offer maximum satisfaction and opportunity for development to the worker?

How can training opportunities be opened up so that they cease to reinforce inequalities in society through their association of skills and status with class, gender and colour?

The most significant field in which local authorities have some control, both over production and over the provision of training, is the building industry. Their actual and potential contribution here is of major national significance. It has become increasingly clear that substantial injections of capital into housing and public projects might present the industry with serious shortages of skill. The responsibility for this can be traced to past government policies towards the construction industry as a whole, which has been squeezed by the continual restrictions on public-sector borrowing for capital projects, and from their antagonism to local authority direct labour organisations (DLOs) in particular. DLOs have always taken responsibility for training more seriously than the private sector. Indeed, private-sector employers have benefited at the expense of DLOs by reducing their own costs through limiting their training facilities and then poaching trained workers with the offer of higher wages. Even in direct labour organisations it has been estimated that the number of apprentices being trained was halved in the five years up to 1986; in the private sector the situation was much worse. Published figures give some indication of the scale of the problem, although they are obscured by the effects of the Youth Training Scheme (YTS) which is included in the figures for all trainees in the private sector, even though YTS trainees may not continue with further training to become fully skilled. By contrast, when local authorities use YTS it is only for the initial year of a full training programme.

Initiatives at local level have stimulated contact and joint working between different educational institutions and research bodies. There are new approaches to traditional apprenticeship training, including workshops for women in trades historically monopolised by male workers. Working men and women, consumers of public services, are offered new kinds of apprenticeships in small, experimental schemes – computer workshops for the unemployed explore the significance of new technology for the community; workshops for women open up opportunities in electronics and computing.

Training and education must go beyond the purely vocational if talents are to be released. 'Taylorism' remains dominant in public service and industry – 'There is no question that the cost of production is lowered by separating the work of planning and the brainwork as much as possible from the manual labor.'[18] Basic training has often exaggerated this tendency by its over-specific content. After initial training, the higher your status the more likely you are to receive time off for more training, conferences,

Building	1975	1976	1977	1978	1979	1980	1981	1982	1983	1984
Craftspeople	69,565	69,250	67,995	66,646	64,090	62,675	56,056	54,893	55,397	53,264
Apprentices	8,624	7,707	6,480	6,574	7,019	7,113	6,897	6,625	5,356	4,125
1st-Year Apprentices	NA	NA	2,000E	2,027E	2,227E	1,854	1,307	1,191	1,177	925E
Craftsperson/Apprentice ratio	8·40	8·99	10·49	10·14	9·13	8·81	8·13	8·29	10·34	12·04

E = Estimate

Craftspeople and apprentice numbers in local government 1975–84

Source: Local Government Training Board.

October each year	Carpenters and joiners	Bricklayers	Plasterers	Painters	Electricians	All trainees
						Thousand
1974	22·6	11·3	2·0	7·2	17·7	81·2
1975	21·6	10·7	2·1	6·6	16·6	77·8
1976	19·8	9·7	2·0	6·4	15·8	74·3
1977	14·9	7·0	1·6	5·5	14·6	62·8
1978	14·9	7·5	1·5	6·1	14·3	65·1
1979	15·0	7·5	1·5	6·2	14·3	65·3
1980	16·6	8·7	1·6	6·6	14·0	69·0
1981	15·0	7·9	1·4	5·8	12·7	60·7
1982	14·0	6·8	1·3	5·1	11·5	56·0
1983	13·8	6·7	1·3	5·0	10·6	54·8

Training by private contractors

Source: Construction Industry Training Board.

discussion of ideas with colleagues elsewhere and intellectual development. Recognising the injustice of this, some local councils have started to negotiate various forms of paid educational leave, offering the same rights to all workers, as we shall describe when we consider ways of improving the quality of local authority work.

Educational institutions also contribute to 'science parks', a phrase which covers many variations in practice. America's experience stretches over several decades; in Britain, with one or two exceptions, science parks are a creation of the last ten years. In order to succeed, science parks must be firmly rooted in the local economy, making best use of existing skills and resources. Unless sited in an area of rapid economic growth, it is no use developing a parkland site with attractive buildings and expecting employment to grow from nowhere. A science park can be an important element in helping to modernise and diversify the local economy but only if it makes use of what is already there.

In Sheffield, it was felt important to develop the supporting resources first. In 1983 a Product and Technology Development Centre was established jointly by the city council and the polytechnic and the Centre for Advanced Manufacturing Technology was funded by the city polytechnic and a skills centre. This offers training on technologically advanced equipment along with support for its introduction in local industry. A Micro-Systems Centre also began work. In 1984 a Business and Management Development Programme was started, again a joint activity between the council and the polytechnic. Meanwhile discussions were under way with the university and Sheffield's five research associations so that their skills and resources could also be tapped.

The physical proposals – land and buildings – were developed as soon as the resource network began to come together. A number of secondments have been arranged from the polytechnic to the city council to ensure that key faculties – Technology, Business and Design – could play their full role. Presentations of the proposals to public- and private-sector agencies at regular intervals brought in their support and enabled them to contribute to the overall development.

The Sheffield Science Park provides a physical base for further development of the Business and Technology Support Network – for example in the Product Development Workshops which are run by SCEPTRE. The park will also provide accommodation ranging from rent-a-desk up to attractive facilities for technology and science-based companies. Beyond this, work is in hand to link the Science Park with facilities in the Lower Don Valley New Employment Park in the east end of Sheffield where the rational-isation of the steel industry has taken its greatest toll on jobs and the environment. As the environment in the valley improves, it should be possible to provide larger and permanent facilities for expanding firms, whether from the Science Park, the New Employment Park, enterprise workshops, or private-sector developments, to facilitate the establishment of new firms in the city.

The links mentioned earlier between different educational institutions and research bodies form a fertile ground for product development. In 1985 Sheffield's Product Development Officer produced the following list of successful council-funded developments:

(a) The Tryad, designed ergonomically for disabled users (this is a shower unit which incorporates a WC and a washbasin);
(b) The washbasin for wheelchair users;
(c) Shower chair, sink units and kitchen furniture for the disabled;
(d) A 'hearing aid' for the profoundly deaf (SESAD);
(e) Early diagnostic equipment for deafness;
(f) Orthopaedic implants such as hip joints;
(g) Radiotherapy equipment such as the collimeter and syringe shields (Medical Equipment Manufacturers, Sheffield);
(h) Hair-care products for the black community;
(i) The advanced dehumidifier to alleviate condensation problems;
(j) MEVA reading aid for the partially sighted (SCEPTRE);
(k) 'Audiocalc' spreadsheet software packages for blind users (SCEPTRE);
(l) Computer Numerically Controlled (CNC) lathe for schools (Abbeydale Engineering – small business);
(m) Metal sensor (Parkway Instruments – cooperative).

Much of this work has been centred on SCEPTRE (Sheffield Centre for Product Development and Technological Resources), linking good ideas with the ability to carry them through to production and marketing of the final article.

Many local authorities have acted as brokers and catalysts for new training and product development networks. The councils deploy their purchasing power, their limited investment funds and the infrastructure of educational and scientific institutions to provide a lever to gain the involvement of banking and industrial concerns. Universities and research institutes, private business and cooperative development agencies all contribute. London's technology network, Leeds's training workshops, Sheffield's Centre for Product Development and Technological Resources, and the Enterprise Centre in a smaller district like Barnsley, are examples of variations on the theme.

In describing the relationship between economic policies and plans for meeting social need, we have outlined the importance of local government as a hub from which new initiatives and job creation measures can be built into the national framework. By providing a way of drawing together the needs of the consumers or users of services with those producing or delivering goods and services, local government in its new role can, in a small way, help the process of making sense of otherwise competing or conflicting interests which the unregulated market economy cannot do.

4. Financial institutions – the local democratic alternative

Under British local government law, the investment role of local authorities is geared to ensuring the prudent use of funds to obtain a satisfactory return on short- and long-term lending, and maintaining adequate cash flow. Investment in the local economy has never been one of the political or financial criteria, and even the development of large employee pension fund holdings through superannuation schemes for council workers has followed this strict accountancy practice. Vast pension fund portfolios are operated purely to maximise return and without any social or employment objective. Some pension fund holdings have tried to break away from this but with only limited success. The West Midlands and West Yorkshire Metropolitan County Councils were breaking new ground when the government abolished them.

The enterprise boards act as limited companies to whom money is allocated for investment purposes. The largest is the Greater London Enterprise Board (GLEB), allocated £32 million in 1983–4. Others include the West Midlands Enterprise Board and

Lancashire Enterprise Ltd, West Yorks Enterprise Board and Merseyside.

Although minute in terms of international capital, GLEB's activities caught the favourable attention of the *Economist* in 1984. Describing GLEB as a company set up by the GLC to create jobs and regenerate London's industrial wastelands, 'part venture-capitalist, part socialist-economic planning agency', its report noted that the board had already committed £35 million to 200 projects and that it claimed to have saved 2,000 jobs during its first 18 months. The *Economist* then commented:

For those who regard stimulus from the public sector as a sure kiss of death, this is bad news. But some who started out sceptical, such as the London Chamber of Commerce, have become wary converts . . . That is, despite the socialist package that comes with the cash.

One example is Whitechapel Computer Works, a new firm making 32-bit computers. Once GLEB injected equity and found a manufacturing site, the City came in with second-round financing. Previously it had hung back. The same went for Airlec, a small company now developing a prototype micro-computer-controlled aircraft loader.[16]

GLEB, like similar initiatives elsewhere, found delivering what the *Economist* calls its 'socialist package' the most difficult feature of the exercise. Whilst most authorities have not insisted on rigorous planning agreements as a condition of investment, useful agreements have been reached on contract compliance. Such agreements are made between the enterprise board, the company and the workforce and stipulate specific forms of training and marketing, staffing levels, equal opportunities policies, trade union recognition, mechanisms for workers' participation and for monitoring the application of the agreement. Planning agreements are notoriously problematical to enforce. In any case, few local firms are 'one-plant sovereign units'.[17] The problems are immense when the government is entirely opposed to them and seeking to free industry and commerce from any obligations beyond commercial profit making.

The West Midlands County Council was the first to support local enterprise in a major way. By 1985, it claimed to have created 4–5,000 associated jobs in 30 businesses supported by venture capital. The GLC claimed a cost of £13,000 for each job created by its programme and Sheffield's Employment Department as little as £2,000 – this compared with £68,000 for each job created under the government's enterprise zone scheme. Despite such local initiatives, the number of jobs created are of course only a drop in the ocean compared with the scale of the problem, but numbers alone are not the main grounds on which to judge their success.

Enterprise boards point the way towards overcoming a failing in Britain's financial institutions – which compared with many other nations have lacked enterprise in making risk capital available to small and innovative manufacturers. They have been more interested in financing mergers and asset-stripping. The new boards are able to mobilise private-sector funds, in addition to their own, and are developing public-sector expertise in economic development with remarkable success. The West Midlands give great attention to the need for risk to form part of the financial judgement required in order to plug the equity gap for small and medium-sized companies; GLEB directs its attention to strategic investment which can help to restructure key sectors of the economy.

The establishment of municipal banks in the late nineteenth and early twentieth centuries was short-lived and never played a central part in British financial policy. Recognition of their potential came not from those who might have been allies but from City of London interests who saw them as a threat. Thus government legislation prohibited the establishment and operation of local-authority-run financial institutions.

The revival of interest in the establishment of city or regional banks under democratic ownership now coincides with the wider debate on democratising the way in which decisions are made about investment. The lack of awareness in Britain of the inter-relationship of banking with the commercial and technological success of the country is due in part to the very real separation of financial institutions from manufacturing industry, in a way not evident in other industrialised nations. We have to turn again to experience elsewhere such as the Sparkasse city and regional network of banks in the Federal Republic of Germany, and in cooperative ventures in various parts of Europe and elsewhere, in particular the Caja Laboral Popular in Mondragon in the Basque country.

A distinct possibility now exists for local government in Britain to provide, as a long-term contribution, banks committed to reinvesting within their own communities. Along with a reappraisal of the use of pension-fund investment, both from public-service employees in local and central government and in the industrial and service economy within the private sector, these offer an opportunity for raising an alternative consciousness within the country to that currently being fostered by the Conservatives.

5. The quality of work

At the heart of these programmes are the men and women who produce the goods and services. Local politics cannot easily overturn centuries of economic and political organisation and power relationships in which the division of labour has produced major inequalities between workers and taken away creativity and control over their work. But somewhere a start has to be made.

Many enterprising policies have been destroyed or soured by resistance from the workers themselves, due to lack of adequate explanation and appreciation of what was intended. In addition, there is always the fear of adverse changes in working conditions, or even the fear of change itself. Lack of interest in the job is understandable from those on the lowest pay and working in the most unfavourable conditions. Sometimes trade unionists are guilty of exaggerated defensiveness and short-sightedness when responding to new proposals; sometimes there is political disagreement; but the main problem is poor pay, status and conditions among workers.

In 1985 Sheffield's employment department funded a project to improve and defend local authority services and jobs. Starting in two departments – parks/recreation and the cleaners and caretakers in the education department – shop stewards and workers were given time and resources to produce a report with the help of an independent national organisation, Services to Community Action and Trade Unions (SCAT), with a brief to look critically at ways of improving both services and the quality of work. The first reports made compelling reading. The cleaners' report was called *We're Coming Out From Under The Carpet*. Levels of satisfaction with work were not high. The reasons were many – rushed jobs, corner-cutting bonus schemes, lack of materials, dirty unpleasant jobs, and again, low pay.

'Management should come out and look at the standard of work, instead of looking at good bonuses on work sheets.'

'Top management do not have the interest or sometimes the practical know-how.'[19]

However, for some people, job satisfaction was high, particularly where there was good management and positive relationships with the workforce. The point was frequently made that more training and more opportunity to use talents and skills would be helpful. Darlington Shop Stewards' Committee carried out a similar exercise with SCAT, reporting in 1987, and the practice is spreading in local authority trade unionism.

Even with very restricted budgets, some local authorities are trying to include in their spending plans special sums for increasing the lowest pay andintroducing equal status in holidays and conditions. Sheffield City Council, along with Glasgow and the London Boroughs of Camden and Islington, have pioneered policies on a minimum wage for their workforce and on equalising conditions between white-collar staff and manual and craft employees. Sheffield City Council has gone farthest in this respect by raising the minimum wage to £100.20 for a basic week from 1 April 1987 and has been involved in campaigning for this important issue to become a key part of the Labour Party's anti-poverty strategy at national level.

The logic of increasing the attractiveness of work, removing the need for those in employment to apply for national and local benefits to supplement their income, and providing the status gained from adequate reward for a job done, is self-evident. For the national exchequer, the gains are also obvious. Benefit payments are reduced, and higher incomes yield both tax and national insurance income to the Treasury. Increased income results in increased consumption of goods and services of an essential nature which rarely include luxury items that threaten the balance-of-trade position.

Improving the quality of work also involves treating public-service workers as more than mere 'hired hands'. In Sheffield 'Take Ten', a programme of ten weeks on paid educational leave for a full day per week for non-vocational education enables low-paid and manual workers in the authority to attend a specially-designed course in the adult education service. It had its origins in a seminar provided for the council by the Northern College of Adult Education in South Yorkshire. The seminar debated Braverman's critical summary of scientific management in modern industry, which has been transferred to the public services with serious consequences. 'The manager assumes', Braverman reminds us, 'the burden of gathering together all of the traditional knowledge, which in the past has been processed by the work people, and then of classifying, tabulating and reducing this knowledge to laws, rules and formulae. All possible brain work should be removed from the shop floor and centred in the planning and laying out department.[20] 'Take Ten' is a small contribution to the process of liberating the creativity of local authority workers so that they can make the full contribution to society of which they are capable.

Of all the difficulties in creative local politics, extending and developing industrial democracy and worker involvement is probably the most difficult to surmount; it requires imagination, inventiveness from workers, trade unions and employers, and above all, a determination to press on. We shall need to turn to tried and tested practices elsewhere such as the worker self-management schemes pioneered in Yugoslavia. The pressure on local government to reduce costs results in those most vulnerable finding their earnings threatened as part-time work is cut back, overtime is reduced and short-term, temporary government job schemes replace long-term, permanent employment.

Improving motivation and providing dignity at work will clearly require both enforceable standards and equal opportunities. This is why 'contract compliance' policies are adopted by councils, laying down agreed standards for workers in the public sector and those employed by private contractors working for the local authority. Ironically, while this is politically controversial in Britain, in many American cities it is a commonplace procedure for public contracts. The GLC contract compliance unit has taken up some of the policies well developed in the United States on monitoring equal opportunities and levels of black employment in a selection of their major suppliers.

In Sheffield contract compliance has centred mainly on the building industry. With its own building and civil engineering department of over 3,000 employees, it is the major single unit in the local building industry. It is itself acutely conscious of the appalling safety record in the industry, and of the growing and serious shortage of skilled workers. In 1981 the city council strengthened its standing orders on health and safety, requiring that for

every contract for the execution of work or services which exceeds £10,000 the tendering contractors shall, unless the Head of Administration and Legal Department advises to the contrary, be instructed to provide with their tenders firstly a copy of their safety policy and secondly a detailed safe working system for the execution of the contract works.[21]

WE PREFER COWBOYS ON OUR SCREENS...

NOT ON OUR CONSTRUCTION SITES

City of Sheffield Council

7   Getting economic ideas across: part of Sheffield's information campaign to maintain and improve the quality of the construction industry.

The recruitment of a team of safety inspectors and a regular reporting system to the council's policy committee about contracts in progress have not only brought one or two 'cowboy' contractors into court but have also made a recognisable difference to precautions on health and safety taken on council contracts as against much of the rest of the industry.

In January 1983 a new requirement that firms of Sheffield's approved list of contractors should train one apprentice for every 10 skilled operatives was agreed. In order to monitor this, all 300 contractors on the council's list have to supply the authority with a quarterly labour return broken down by trade, showing how many apprentices they employ in which trades. This procedure enables the council to build up a picture of the pattern of training in the city. It also keeps it in regular touch with its would-be contractors, and enables it to draw on the powerful attraction of public-sector contracts to persuade firms to recruit extra trainees where necessary to come into compliance.

Other employment conditions are covered in a questionnaire for firms intending to work for the council, which seeks to mitigate some of the worst consequences of subcontracting and lump labour in the building industry, and includes a key question on wages and trade union recognition.

Lord Young, the Employment Secretary responsible for job creation, has said that giving service should not be considered servile, and has rightly suggested that the proportion of jobs in the service sector will continue to grow as fewer people work in the manufacturing sector. However, government policies encourage service through the 'subeconomy', i.e. those who rely on casual, insecure, part-time work with no permanent contract, often having to pay their own National Insurance contributions and receiving none of the pension or other benefits that accrue to those in full-time employment. Pay and conditions offered by private enterprise for leisure, tourism, catering and other services only contribute to creating this subeconomy.

The local public sector can point the way to a better future. New technology replaces jobs, both skilled and routine, but if the benefits of the resultant productivity are spread, then increased automation could increase leisure time and free people to develop their talents so as to reintroduce pride in craftsmanship, both for personal consumption, and high value-added sale. Any such happy outcome is dependent on a fair distribution of the wealth available rather than a divided society where those in work and with access to the new technology benefit, and the remainder are excluded from the progress made.

6. Democratic planning

Traditionally local government has been seen as performing tasks delegated to it by national government. But the approach to popular planning suggests a different model, one that starts from the local and ends with the national – by nature of its power over law, tax, money and the foreign exchanges.[22]

The most vivid examples of democratic planning have been set pieces like the People's Plan for the Docklands in contrast to the plans of the Docklands Development Corporation. In response to the decline of the Port of London the government created a London Docklands Development Corporation which proposed to build an airport for the City of London providing minimal employment for local people and offering no opportunity to redevelop the area in their favour. The LDDC is composed of government-appointed businessmen and has powers to overrule the elected local authorities. Local politics responded in November 1983 with a People's Plan for the Royal Docks produced by the Newham Docklands Forum whose membership included Newham Council, the GLC and trade union and community organisation representatives. The foreword to the plan sums up the traditional establishment's contempt for those who are victims of economic change:

The leading barrister from the Docklands Development Corporation at the STOLport inquiry, for instance, tried to dismiss the People's Plan – 'We are prepared to listen to alternatives from a statutory body, from the GLC or Newham Council, but from the people . . . a people's plan . . . ridiculous. I've never heard of such a thing.' In the end he had to listen for two whole days. The Inspector seemed interested in the details of our proposals. We do not know if the Plan has made any difference to the outcome of the Inquiry, but the demonstration that there are alternatives has certainly strengthened our case against the airport.[23]

The alternative plan looked at the full potential of the docklands for transport in the nation's capital, for leisure and recreation and for the development of new industries which would provide a positive future for the people in the area. These proposals were not based on supposition. Shipping lines were interested in returning to the docks and there is potential for a major transport link at the heart of one of Europe's major capitals with a vast population to serve and an effective national communications system. Both the LDDC and the People's Plan involved economic proposals backed by research and analysis and both had a clear political perspective: one seeking the growth of low-paid service industries supplying the City of London, the other offering substantial prospects for the people of the area and including the development of manufacturing as well as the service sector.

The government's commitment to backing the centralist approach of the Urban Development Corporations can be illustrated by the contrasting sums committed from the Department of the Environment to them compared with those given to inner-area projects for other major urban areas. In 1986 the government allocated £116 million to the Merseyside Development Corporation and £279 million to the London Docklands, but only £4·1 million per year to the Sheffield City Inner Area Programme, for example. The political Right has been willing to commit public funds when their use is centrally determined, but not when local democratic choice is being exercised.

What lies behind the concept of democratic planning, however, cannot be understood by considering specific programmes for new developments in defined geographical areas. It should be understood as a powerful theme that has grown through the mingling of social and economic policies which we have described over the last three chapters, or a dimension of the new relations between the 'local state' and local people which we explored in Chapter 5. It involves combining activities in many areas of the local economy: the spreading of economic information and analysis beyond elite policy makers; bringing voluntary groups and local communities into the economic debate; enabling workers to contribute imaginatively to the development of their industry or service; providing opportunities, support, education and training to local small business and cooperative enterprises in a framework of planned investment, and bringing 'the knowledge of what needs doing as expressed directly by those who want it closer together with those who want it done'. When right-wing theorists attack the efficacy of planning they forget the key role it plays in the investment, production and marketing policies of the giant corporations that dominate the economy. Democratic planning cannot match their strategic power unless we create 'new forms of decision-making through which people can express their values' and needs in terms other than personal spending power and occasional voting.[24]

Whilst key aspects of economic policy must be shaped at national level, local politics presents a framework for an alternative to the approach favoured by Conservatives. Those who are committed to the operation of market forces present a future in which power flows from the decisions of multinational companies and banks, determining national policies and local choices. Local politics shows that people's choices can be built into economic activity in a variety of ways through the ballot box and through the direct meeting of need after public debate and choice in determining priorities. Commercial realism, coupled with agreed economic and social objectives, provides a hopeful view of the future for people who relate best to the place they live in and know, and the workplace and community upon which they depend and which is dependent on them.

The Conservative government has turned its back on democratic ways of dealing with the issues of the time. Its intellectual foundation only appears convincing because there is a vigorous political attempt to undermine the basic values of mutuality and cooperation and assert those of individual enterprise and competitiveness. Talk of bringing freedom to the people is empty rhetoric when account is taken of their own actions as government in increasing economic and social constraints on freedom and opportunity.

Local government creativity has been evident in three major areas: in its response to unemployment and industrial demolition; in its contribution to civilised social policies which directly address Britain's post-imperial dilemmas; in its attention to the means by which democratic public administration can be effective; and in presenting a more effective delivery of goods and services than private-enterprise alternatives through a more open relationship between the state and the people.

The policies and political practice stem from an increasing sense that there is an alternative to the prospect of social division and authoritarianism. Different sectors of the economy may require different forms of democratic organisation, but a model which starts with the local and moves to a regional and national perspective, along the lines we have indicated, has been shown to offer, in the words of one group of economists, 'an imaginative strategy for industrial recovery which can unify the people and generate a new sense of common purpose'.[25] This, they argue, is the only way to prevent an additional 1 million unemployed in the decade after 1986.

One woman is reported to have commented on the government's strategy at a local meeting on the docklands, 'If that is the future, I want no part of it. There must be another way.' Conservative attacks on local government have been based on their fear that more people will say this, and not merely on their own monetarist, public-spending fixation.

7

Turning the Screw

Our problem is the tiny minority of high-spending authorities whose behaviour clearly stands out against the general trend. Suppose that the sort of policies pursued by the minority of councils prove contagious and the disease spread to a much larger number . . .[1]

Patrick Jenkin's argument during the debate on the Rates Act in 1984 directly linked the escalating conflict between central and local government over financial control to divergence in social and economic policies. The disease to which he refers was the alternative agenda being proposed for Britain by local politics. The danger was that this 'propaganda of practice' in a minority of councils might become popular as government policies began to take their toll. Local services had to be cut to the bone so that people rejected them. Councils' control of their finances had to be removed if they did not voluntarily destroy their services. To do this there had to be a complete reversal of Conservative attitudes to the place of local government in national affairs as had been laid out in its 1971 White Paper:

A vigorous local democracy means that authorities must be given real functions – with power of decision and the ability to take action without being subjected to excessive regulation by central government through financial or other controls.[2]

It is important to follow the process which has led to this reversal. Government policy on public spending has long been presented through the rhetoric of good housekeeping, such as the nation 'cannot afford' the welfare state. Resistance by local politics to each step which the government has taken in applying financial controls steadily brought to light the political implications behind the Conservative rhetoric: if there was to be a shift in the balance of power towards capital and away from the majority of the people, the meaning of freedom and democracy had to be redefined – the people must learn to measure it in terms of purchasing power rather than the exercise of political rights. The Prime Minister made this clear in an interview with the *New York Times* on 22 January 1984:

Prime Minister Margaret Thatcher said . . . that Britain was sitting on a 'social security time bomb' and that she therefore felt it essential to reconsider the whole web of public benefits built up since the end of World War II.

Excepting only some system of basic pensions and a National Health Service of some kind, though not necessarily like the present one, she argued that it was time to begin a public debate on the structure and financing of the welfare state.

'I'm going on being radical until I feel we have got the right balance between what the state should do and what the people should do,' the Prime Minister said. . . 'We haven't got there yet. The state in this country is still too strong.' . . .

Mrs Thatcher advocated change not only because of the fiscal constraints that, in an era of low growth, are plaguing governments all over the western world. She also argued that the welfare state was undercutting personal freedom.

'You are redistributing responsibility,' she said, 'and you are taking quite a bit of a man's independence by taking away so much of his income.'[3]

This radical restatement of individual and social responsibilities was part of the Conservatives' break with the broad political consensus which had been maintained in Britain since the 1940s. It also included rejecting government responsibility for full employment, which William Beveridge originally proposed as the foundation of a sound system of state services and social security. However, unemployment means government must pay out more in benefit and receives less revenue from wage earners. In their own attempts to cut public spending, the Conservatives were caught in this dilemma. Central government spending on social security rose dramatically, while the services provided by local authorities received the brunt of the cuts. Between 1974–5 and 1979–80 social security spending rose from £14 billion to £19 billion at 1979 prices. Between 1980–81 and 1985–6 it rose by a further 49 per cent. Social security became the highest-spending department; in 1980 it was the seventh largest.[4]

Councils have been caught up in a vicious spiral. Cuts in public expenditure brought unemployment. The consequence of cuts, especially in capital expenditure, was a steady decay in the condition of city streets and public buildings. Higher unemployment increased social security spending. Consequently central government found it impossible to cut its own spending, so a further squeeze was put on local government. But local government tried to meet the increasing needs of local people as conditions deteriorated and was accused of further overspending while further cuts led to more unemployment.

Local politicians were initially slow to resist, partly because in the first stages of central government pressure, under a Labour government, they shared its perspective. From 1979, as the radical free-market policies of the Conservative government became increasingly apparent, councils found themselves on difficult territory for political opposition. The constitutional position of local government discouraged outright opposition from its political base. Government policies for local spending were implemented through the technicalities of local government finance, and resistance took the form of quick-witted manoeuvring within these technical arrangements. But because central government could continually change the rules, the ground continually shifted. Eventually local authorities came together in a national political organisation against Westminster as never before.

Local spending falls under two heads: capital and revenue. We considered in Chapter 6 the consequences of government control over capital spending which covers purchase of land, building, major improvement and repairs. Local authorities raise their money through borrowing but they are constrained in the amount they can borrow through the capital allocation allowed to each council. Government control is easy to achieve and capital spending is used as a simple economic regulator, often expanded 18 months before an election to increase employment and economic activity. Local government failed to resist central control on capital spending, with serious consequences for housing, roads and other parts of the urban infrastructure.

Local revenue spending meets the day-to-day costs of salaries and wages, heating, lighting and purchase of supplies, repairs and maintenance, as well as the considerable debt charges on past capital borrowing. There are three main sources of income: local rates, charges for rents and services, and government grant. The main political issue in local–central relations over the last decade has revolved around attempts by government to control local authority revenue spending. The grant system, known as rate support grant, which operated in the 1970s created problems

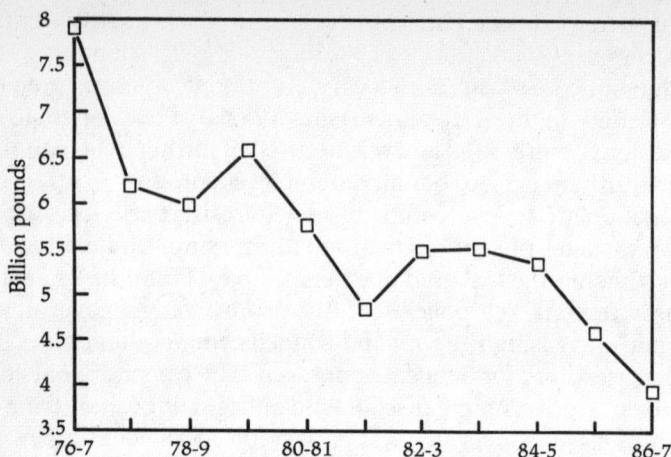

Gross capital expenditure (England)
Real terms with 1984–5 as base year. Source: Association of Metropolitan Authorities, 1985.

for any party in power. In consultation with local authorities, the government decided the total amount of grant available which was then divided among individual authorities according to a formula which contained three elements: the domestic element, the resources element, and the needs element.

These were the technical arrangements for deciding what local authorities received. But technical systems have their political dimension. The resources element[5] in the rate support grant system was where the political problem largely occurred. The size of grant tended to follow the historic trend of local authority decisions on spending – it did not determine them. Decisions by local councils on their own priorities triggered increased grant. The following table shows the consequences:

Local authority expenditure as a share of gross national product

1951	1961	1971	1973	1975
9·8%	11·4%	15·5%	17·1%	18·6%

Local authorities are responsible for many of the key services whose nature led to the public expenditure growth and the growth of employees. Its share of the combined central and local public spending rose from one-quarter in 1951 to roughly one-third in the 1970s.

From the mid-1970s, governments were attempting to exert greater control at the same time as some councils were building a coherent response to the monetarist policies which have been the basis for spending restrictions. Local government was squeezed by successive turns of the screw – starting with gentle persuasion and moving through from pressure, manipulation, punishment and coercion to abolition.

Persuasion – 1974–6

It took two elections in 1974 for Labour to achieve a slender majority of three in the Commons, a precarious basis for dealing with the economic problems it faced. Local government almost immediately asked for more money when the Houghton Report on teachers' pay recommended pay awards which entailed a 30 per cent increase in overall cost. The government accepted that local authorities should not meet this from the rates and agreed to pay it all by putting up the rate support grant from 61 per cent to 66 per cent of relevant spending – that is, spending accepted by government for grant purposes.

Despite this gesture of goodwill, DoE Circular 171/74 (Rate Fund Expenditure and Rate Calls in 1975–6) insisted in December 1974 that it was necessary that the government should offer detailed guidance to local authorities on the way in which limitations in services might be made. Denis Healey, in his 1975 Budget speech as Chancellor of the Exchequer, announced the formation of a new Consultative Council for Local Government Finance, consisting of all local government associations and ministers and officials from national departments concerned with local government spending. Jones and Stewart in their book, *The Case for Local Government*, point out that his purpose was clear:

'I now turn to the cuts in public expenditure which have become inevitable . . . a sizeable proportion of these savings will fall on local authorities, and I realise what this task means. I do not think it would be right to leave them to face it without closer guidance and help from the ministers.'[6]

Tension soon became evident. Local authority representatives on the Consultative Council recognised the importance of guidance from the government but were at the same time concerned 'that such guidance should not prevent local authorities from exercis-

148 *Democracy in Crisis*

ing their own responsibility for deciding on priorities for expenditure in their own areas.'[7]

The following tables show the long-term decline in rate support grant prior to 1979 following the Houghton Report increase, in two quite different authorities, one a shire county (Avon) and the other a large metropolitan district (Sheffield).

Even in this period of persuasion, the politics behind the technicalities were evident to the discerning eye. The Transport Subsidy section of Circular 171/74 insisted that subsidies should be reduced and fares should go up. Transport should be run on a commercially viable basis. A Labour government was both accepting the argument that it needed to control public as opposed to private spending, and also promoting free-market values against a real attempt to use resources for the collective good, as we saw in Chapter 5. Overall, in the first few years of the Labour government, the close working relations between local and central government, particularly in the Consultative Council and its working groups, enabled the policy of persuasion to prevail. It became less viable when the government itself submitted to external pressures.

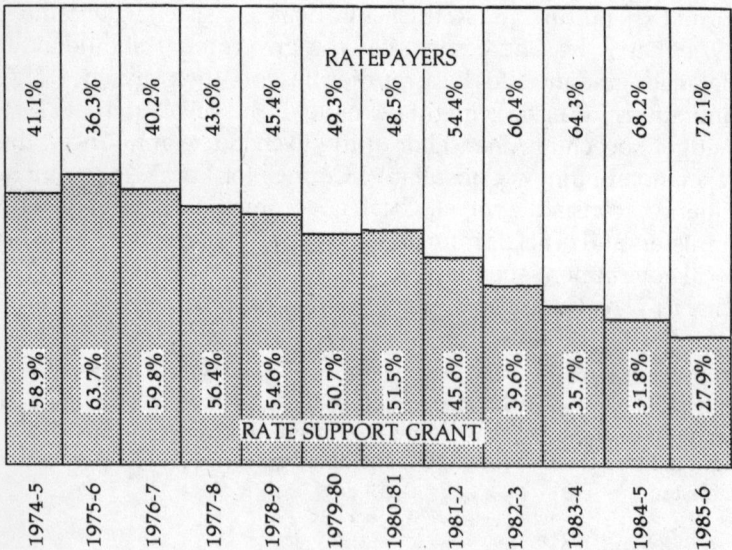

Year	RATEPAYERS	RATE SUPPORT GRANT
1974-5	41.1%	58.9%
1975-6	36.3%	63.7%
1976-7	40.2%	59.8%
1977-8	43.6%	56.4%
1978-9	45.4%	54.6%
1979-80	49.3%	50.7%
1980-1	48.5%	51.5%
1981-2	54.4%	45.6%
1982-3	60.4%	39.6%
1983-4	64.3%	35.7%
1984-5	68.2%	31.8%
1985-6	72.1%	27.9%

Share of Avon's expenditure met by ratepayers and rate support grant, 1974–5 – 1985–6. Source: Avon County Council, in *Local Government Finance* by Ian Douglas and Steve Lord, Local Government Information Unit, 1981.

Year	Rate Support Grant	Ratepayers
1975-6	59.9%	40.1%
1976-7	58.3%	41.7%
1977-8	57.7%	42.3%
1978-9	56.7%	43.3%
1979-80	54.8%	45.2%
1980-81	55.6%	44.4%
1981-2	49.9%	50.1%
1982-3	42.2%	55.8%
1983-4	40.0%	60.0%
1984-5	40.5%	59.5%
1985-6	42.4%	57.6%
1986-7	32.9%	67.1%

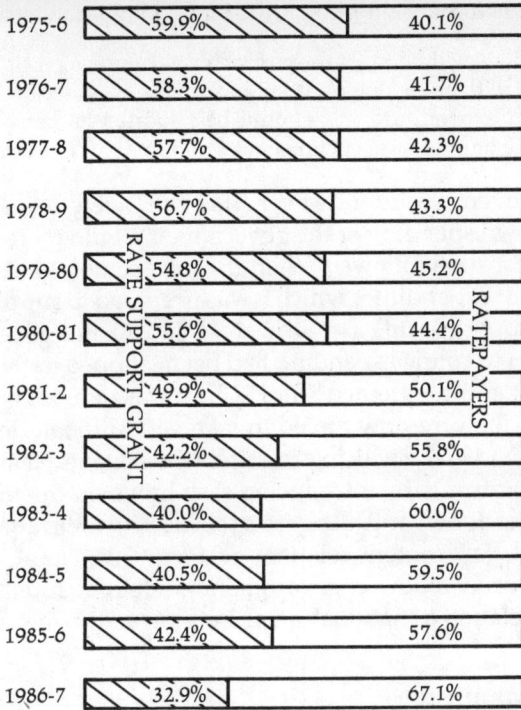

Share of Sheffield City Council's expenditure met by ratepayers and rate support grant
Note: The city council received grant prior to 1981–2 in respect of county council services. The expenditure shares have been based on the combined city council budget and county precept in those years to allow for this fact. Source: Sheffield Council.

Pressure – 1976–9

In the Manchester Free Trade Hall, in October 1976, Tony Crosland told local councils, 'The party's over.' He was responding directly to IMF conditions on loan sanctions. Local councillors, particularly in Labour areas, were not at all sure that the party had ever begun in their communities, but at this stage the full implications of Crosland's declaration was not appreciated in many town halls. Commonly associated with the Labour right wing, Crosland himself is reputed to have put up at least as strong a fight against the bankers as many standard bearers of the Left.

At first the language of persuasion stayed very much the same:

Local authorities will know of the advice given in previous circulars on how to deal with reductions but should themselves decide how the reductions in expenditure . . . should be allocated as between their services in the light of local circumstances and their own priorities.[8]

Councils were aware, however, that they were being told to limit their own spending or the government would try to do it for them. Action soon followed when the government reduced the proportion of expenditure which it was prepared to support from the rate support grant. The upward trend in the government contribution to council spending had been stopped in the 1976–7 rate support grant settlement; for 1977–8 it was reduced by 4·5 per cent. Councils were now forced to take very difficult decisions. Persuasion had given way to pressure, which Denis Healey soon applied more firmly by introducing cash limits on the total RSG available. As Jones and Stewart spell out in their analysis of central/local government relations in the 1970s,[9] local revenue spending closely followed government guidelines and its rate of growth in relation to national spending slowed down markedly.

Manipulation

After the Labour government was defeated in 1979, a qualitative change took place in the nature of central control. Labour had tried to restrain public spending through their allocation of grant to local authorities. With the election of the Conservatives it was not merely a question of how much councils should get from the government, but of how the government could direct their spending decisions, and therefore their policies, on ideological rather than economic grounds. Through a series of measures which continually changed the rules, the government tried to compel high-spending councils to put up their rates and succumb to the expected ratepayers' revolt. This would force them to change direction. At first they did this by manipulating the system rather than openly attacking local democracy.

This change in relations between central and local government was made clear immediately after the 1979 election: though the Conservatives came to office after the financial year had started, they immediately reduced the Labour government's published guidelines for grants to local authorities by 1·4 per cent without any reference to the Consultative Council.

In the autumn of 1979 there were further proposals, later
embodied in the Local Government Planning and Land Act,
which completely changed the whole grant system by replacing
the resources and needs elements of the rate support grant with a
block grant. There were good reasons for such a move which had
already been recommended by the Layfield Commission on Local
Government Finance in 1976. Tom King, Minister of State at the
Department of Employment, said during the passage of the
above bill:

It is not suggested that it [the grant-related expenditure assessment, i.e.
the needs assessment on which the block grant was calculated] prescribes a specific level to which an authority ought to spend . . . I want to
make it clear that that was not its purpose. We are seeking to find the
fairest way to distribute public money to local authorities.[10]

However, the ideological intentions of the government ensured
that this was not how the block grant system would be used in
practice. Consequently, no account was taken of requests from
local authorities, by no means all Labour-controlled, who asked
for delay in implementation to ensure that it worked effectively.
If an authority spent exactly at its grant-related expenditure
assessment level, then it got its full portion of the overall national
block grant, but if it decided, as a locally elected body, to spend
more than GREA, then the extra spending would not attract so
much central grant and it followed that a larger proportion of
what was spent would come from the rates. Unsure that this
would discourage spending sufficiently, the government took
further measures in its first year of operation.

The following graph shows the continuing decline of rate
support grant following 1979:

The Conservatives were embarking on a programme which
brought an accumulated reduction of £17 billion in rate support
grant to councils between 1979–80 and 1986–7, as indicated in the
table on p. 152. How this increased the proportion of local
spending borne by ratepayers in various authorities is illustrated
for Avon County and Sheffield Metropolitan District in the
figures on pp. 148–9.

Each authority was 'given a target' close to recent spending and
expenditure above this level was penalised by 'holdback' of
grant. Councils who refused to modify their plans must from
now on find from the rates more than a pound for each pound of
expenditure. Neither side was sure how to deal with a system

£12848 million	£12332 million	£12200 million	£11531 million	£10799 million	£10394 million	£10006 million	£9079 million	£8988 million
78-9	79-80	80-81	81-2	82-3	83-4	84-5	85-6	86-7

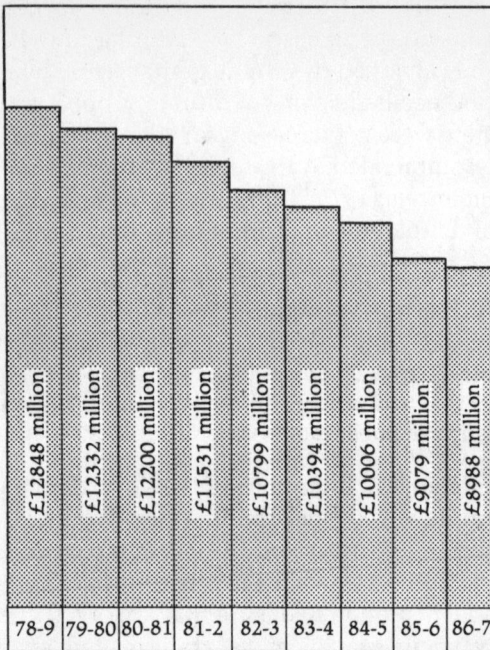

Rate support grant (1986–7 prices). Source: Ian Douglas and Steve Lord, *Local Government Finance, a Practical Guide,* Local Government Information Unit, 1986.

whose hasty and peremptory introduction ensured that it was never considered carefully as a practical contribution to local government finance. This became clear when the government tried to penalise Camden and a number of other individual authorities – the first 'hit list' to come within the government's sights. They were to be fined retrospectively for the expenditure increases in the financial year 1980–81, already under way before the Act became law. Camden responded by challenging the legality of this move and won its case in the High Court.

These early measures were accompanied by various indications of the ideological programme which inspired them. Along with its financial provisions, the Local Government Planning and Land Act forced direct labour organisations to compete with private builders on unfavourable terms. Unable to tender for outside work, they now had to show a return on each area of activity (maintenance, new building, etc.) rather than over the

	England and Wales (per cent)	England only (per cent)
1975–6	66·5	
1976–7	65·5	
1977–8	61·0	
1978–9	61·0	
1979–80	61·0	
1980–81	60·0	60·1
1981–2	60·0	59·1
1982–3		56·1
1983–4		52·8
1984–5		51·9
1985–6		48·7
1986–7		46·4

Rate support grant reduction

	£m.
1978–9	12,226
1979–80	11,733
1980–81	11,623
1981–2	10,196
1982–3	9,565
1983–4	9,205
1984–5	8,585
1985–6	8,489

Accumulated reduction

	£b.
(a) 1978–9 to 1979–80	0·5
(b) 1978–9 to 1980–81	1·1
(c) 1978–9 to 1981–2	2·2
(d) 1978–9 to 1982–3	4·1
(e) 1978–9 to 1983–4	6·4
(f) 1978–9 to 1984–5	8·9
(g) 1978–9 to 1985–6	12·4
(h) 1978–9 to 1986–7	17·0

Grant percentage at main rate support grant order
Source: Hansard 21.5.84, column 332

whole operation, as a private company would. The 1981 Housing Act instructed local authorities to sell council houses at well below market value (which had been created by the investment of tenants, ratepayers and taxpayers in collective housing over the years) to tenants who wished to exercise their 'right to buy'. In effect they were bribing people to support the Conservative free-market manifesto.

Punishment

Most authorities began to submit at this point and curtailed their spending, but those Labour councils where a more active local politics had become evident found support for continued resistance and began to campaign. Sheffield Council, for example, put its rate up by 41 per cent in 1980 and 37 per cent in 1981 and was still supported at the polls. Other authorities received similar evidence that the government was not necessarily 'going with the grain of human nature', as their 1979 election manifesto had claimed. In the May 1981 elections the GLC swung to Labour; Labour now controlled all metropolitan counties and a flush of Tory shire counties as well. The GLC and others went for supplementary rates to carry out their election promises now backed by a popular mandate.

If local democracy was heading in this direction, the government had to stop it. A new attempt to change the rules failed when Michael Heseltine's Local Government Finance Bill (No. 1), which ordered councils to call a referendum in order to make a supplementary rate, was withdrawn in the autumn of 1981, in the face of extreme opposition inside the Conservative Party itself, but he had to try again. Since the courts had failed to uphold his right to penalise individual councils for high spending, the Secretary of State had to content himself with a less discriminatory system applying in principle to all authorities. Authorities which followed central guidelines had grant added back to their previous allocation, those which did not suffered a 'clawback' during the financial year. Councils could respond to the loss of income by levying a supplementary rate, as did Lambeth in March 1981. Frustrated in this way by local authority powers, Heseltine decided to change the law itself. The Local Government Finance Bill (No. 2) first abolished local authorities' power to levy a supplementary rate, and secondly introduced a well-designed weapon to punish individual 'high-spending' councils.

The penalty system was a cruelly simple device. Authorities would be given their grant-related expenditure assessment level and their spending target as before, but now spending over target led to a withdrawal of grant *at a progressively increasing rate*. Grant was not merely withheld after spending reached a certain level, it was progressively reduced for every pound spent, even if, as in the case of Camden, ILEA and eventually the GLC, grant would be eliminated completely.

Local authorities began 1982 with hope that the government's unpopularity could be exploited as the parliamentary term started to run out. Margaret Thatcher's standing in the public opinion polls had plummeted, but support for the Falklands War stopped all that, and the Conservatives were returned to power in July 1983 with a massive parliamentary majority though fewer votes than in 1979.

Facing a further term of radical Conservatism, local councils increased their own capacity to manoeuvre within the grant system and the 'creative accounting' which had already followed Conservative manipulation now became a major form of political opposition. The journal *Accountancy Age* noted in June 1985 that 'council treasurers and finance officers have shown the greatest ingenuity of all local authority officers', and one city treasurer remarked, 'It is now up to the profession to respond to the new environment and maintain what is good about local government.' Just as accountants will seek to avoid their clients incurring the highest rate of tax, so now they were saving ratepayers from the consequences of the highest penalties. If £2.20 was lost for every £1 spent over the limit, then every £1 saved meant £2.20 did not have to be found from the rates.

Special funds were created in one year to be available for revenue purposes in another, when penalty might be lower. Capitalisation exploited the legal imprecision between capital and revenue – for example, some spending on repairs and maintenance can be moved from revenue to capital and therefore does not attract penalty. Rescheduling of debt repayments can also reduce revenue spending on the interest payable for capital borrowing. Creativity extended to ways in which the restrictions of capital allocation could be avoided for example by 'deferred purchase' where spending on a project could be put into another year. (See Appendix 2 and pp. 189–90.)

Local government finance became more exciting than ever before, but this kind of creativity had its dangers. At the national conference of the Chartered Institute of Public Finance and Accountancy, Newcastle-upon-Tyne's Chief Executive objected that financial juggling seemed to have supplanted the provision of basic services in the calls it made on his time and energies. The

Audit Commission noted the serious obstacles to planned programmes which government-induced uncertainties created. In
political terms, also, complicated financial devices served to
obscure the issues which needed debating fully in local communities. The councils were working on the same technical
ground as the government rather than confronting its policies
directly.

One authority followed a completely different line. Liverpool
had occupied a unique place in recent Conservative relations
with local government. After the 1981 riots Michael Heseltine had
been created Minister for Merseyside. He conducted highly
publicised sightseeing tours around the problem areas during
which he committed himself to mobilising private and public
spending for the city. Public concern over Liverpool's circumstances placed the government in a difficult position when
Labour took control of the city in May 1983 after campaigning on
the basis of no cuts, no job losses, no rate rises. Even had they not
adopted this position, the new administration would have had
difficulty in carrying through a programme which satisfied the
electorate. They had followed a period of Liberal/Conservative
rule in which both parties had tried to gain popularity by keeping
the rates down whatever the damage inflicted on services. Thus,
while other authorities had built up resources from the rates in
the first years of Conservative cuts in grant, Liverpool had no fat
to live on.

Merseyside could see what the government's public spending
plans meant for a big city that had been allowed to die for decades
by decisions in the free market. Liverpool's Labour council
refused to balance its budget either by reducing the spending
plans which its winning manifesto had promised, or by setting a
rate at the necessary level to cover fully both spending and the
'penalty' to be paid back to the government under the target
system. Patrick Jenkin, the new Secretary of State, handled the
situation with a mixture of bluster and concession. Although no
major change was made in Liverpool's block grant, adjustments
were made to urban programme money and to housing subsidy;
additional money was offered for environmental works and a
decision was reached that housing repair work would be
'capitalised' so that the cost was spread over a number of years.
£20 million was switched to bridge the gap in this way.

A careful examination of these arrangements shows that the
income could have been generated by the same creative account-

ancy as other councils were adopting, possibly without confrontation. Technically it did not imply a climb down by the government on its 'block grant' policy, but politically it was a major propaganda victory. Liverpool council claimed just that, quoting national press assessment:

Today in Liverpool municipal militancy is vindicated . . . By exempting Liverpool from the consequences of spending above its target the government subverts its whole local government policy for the past five years. (*Times*, 11 July 1984)

Both sides in this battle have, it is true, made concessions. The Labour council will have to put up rates by far more than it wanted. But it is the Tory government which has given away the most. (*Daily Mail*, 11 July 1984)

The Conservative government, which prided itself on taking a hard line with opponents, had been humiliated. They were also failing to curtail the activities of creative local authorities whose policies were gaining wider recognition. The politics behind the technicalities were being exposed.

Political courage on the part of those councils who engaged in creative accounting was increasingly a factor, in addition to Liverpool's more publicised stand. Ingenuity in the Treasurer's Departments required support from politicians and local parties to become policy. Conservative propaganda against the councils created a climate of opinion in some sections of the press that they were engaging in 'fiscal anarchy'. The Audit Commission, as we have seen, blamed the government for introducing anarchy.

Central government was restricting local public services and their contribution to economic and social life in those parts of Britain which were 'underdeveloping', in much the same way as the International Monetary Fund and the world financial community has constantly demanded reductions in essential investment and spending on education, health and housing in 'underdeveloped' countries.

Chaos followed this use of financial power for political ends, in one case at the international level, in the other nationally. The only people who really gained were the banks and the financial interests, free to recoup profit from future interest paid on the money lent to councils, thus adding to the long-term burden on people in areas least able to pay. The difference between the national scene and international politics was that councils could consider the possibility of an alternative government which might adopt more sane and balanced economic and finanial policies whereas there was no equivalent international sovereign body. The councils were holding the fort desperately until such relief could arrive for their communities. Those councils which cut and trimmed, accepting the mantle of 'responsible good housekeepers' which the government placed on them, were politically responsible for helping to create a climate in which national policy was less likely to change as worsening services discredited collective provision.

Coercion

Local politics was by the mid-1980s challenging the government's social and political priorities as we have described, and not merely their public expenditure objectives. The result was that the financial penalty system gave way to legislative coercion removing the powers of fixing a local rate which had existed in every form of local government since 1601.

The Rates Act became law in March 1984. By now the government had become skilled in drafting local government legislation; the new Act was simple, straightforward and far-reaching in its consequences. The government would designate specific authorities considered to be 'irresponsible' – either through recent high spending or high rates. They would be told what their level of spending should be for the financial year 1985–6 and the maximum rate they could fix by law. The detailed calculation of the actual grant to be received by individual authorities would take place along normal lines and then designated authorities would be told the highest rate they would be allowed to set within the law – they would be 'rate-capped'. This rate level would enable them to balance their books only if they spent the designated amount.

Rate-capping was not designed to reduce government expenditure since it would not necessarily reduce the amount of grants flowing from central government. If they followed government instruction, rate-capped councils would naturally not incur the heavy penalties which had reduced their grant previously, and the total sum of government grant *would increase*. The government's aim was now clearly to challenge the political independence of local authorities, based on their right to raise a local tax. They wished to narrow the political choices open to councils as they tried desperately to deal with the increasingly urgent needs of their areas.

Without doubt the most subtle feature of the Rates Act was its offer of 'derogation', the right of local authorities to question government calculations of rate and spending levels and to ask that they might be renegotiated ('redetermined' in the terminology of the Act). This apparent gesture of freedom to councils was in practice exactly the opposite. On applying for derogation a local authority would have to supply the Secretary of State with 'such information in such form as he may require'. Councils would be inviting the Minister into their town halls, giving him full access to current accounts and any records he might consider relevant; they would effectively be handing over any power they might still have to determine social policy.

Eighteen authorities were designated for 1985–6 in the Rates Limitation Report 1984 laid before the House of Commons on 24 July.[11] Rate-capping was a long-term danger, not a headache for one financial year. It was not just a cut, it was a change in the balance of power. After similar legislation had been introduced in Scotland for the financial year 1981–2, Lothian had been capped three years in succession. Cuts of £12 million were imposed leading to the permanent loss of 382 teaching posts and similar effects across services.

With the Rates Act, the 'radical Right' had taken Conservative strategy into the heart of local politics. Democrats in their own party had no hesitation about standing up and being counted. In the Rates Bill Debate on 28 March 1984, Geoffrey Rippon MP, ex-Cabinet minister, said:

It is not right that the Conservatives should say in opposition that we stand for town hall, not Whitehall, that we do not believe that the gentlemen in Whitehall know best, that we want a devolution of power, that we accept the freedom of local government and that we believe that it is one of the twin pillars of our constitution, yet in government produce a Bill such as this.

These are proud words, but like many others in the Conservative Party, Geoffrey Rippon was underestimating the lengths to which his Cabinet colleagues would go.

The criteria for 'designating' authorities were to be changed year by year in order to pick out authorities whom the minister 'particularly wishes to designate, rather than establishing the criteria on an objective basis' (Association of Metropolitan

Authorities Paper, March, 1987). This is how the government interpreted the Rates Act phrase: 'in accordance with principles determined by the Secretary of State'. Criteria were to be determined after authorities had made their budgets and after expenditure returns had been analysed by Whitehall, for entirely party political objectives. Thus, for example, Islington was kept in the list for 1987/88 when its budget was 12.52 per cent above GRE by bringing the criteria down to 12.5 per cent above GRE rather than 20 per cent. Rhodes Boyson put his finger on the 'principle' which was adopted:

'As regards the case for rate capping Ealing in 1988–89, I can only say that my right hon. friend the Secretary of State for the Environment has not yet decided what criteria should apply for selection for rate limitation in 1988–89. Before deciding on the appropriate criteria for excessive spending, he will, of course, need to have regard to all relevant considerations . . . I feel strongly on the matter, both as Minister and as a Member of Parliament, as my constituency is adjacent to that of Ealing North Brent, as well as Ealing, has a hard left authority' (Official Report, Col, 672, 13 March, 1987)

If local authority financial arrangements and the democratic choices of local people could be subordinated to the whims of ministers in this way, local government as it had been understood in Britain could not continue.

Finally, the government proposed to replace the system of rates with a community charge or poll tax and structured the whole system to ensure that cities in the north and inner city authorities paid more than in the shire counties:

What the Poll Tax means in England (average per adult)

Average rate now		*After Poll Tax*
Shires	£189	£166
Metropolitan Areas	£205	£218
Inner London	£337	£558
Outer London	£245	£221
Total	£227	£347

As this table shows, these proposals were made with a political bias and not according to need or the ability to pay.

Abolition

In October 1983, a White Paper entitled 'Streamlining the Cities' had begun the process of abolishing the GLC and the metropolitan counties. The government claimed to be 'eliminating an unnecessary tier and handing power back to the boroughs and districts', but this claim was meaningless. Key functions of the old authorities would be handed to 'joint boards' comprised of appointees from the constituent districts and not directly elected. Joint boards would be rate-capped for the first three years, with their manpower and budgets determined directly by the Secretary of State. In the debate on the Bill which eventually followed the White Paper on 11 April 1984, another Tory spoke up for democracy:

If my Rt Hon. friend sticks to his present course, he will win the vote tonight but he will lose the argument. He will lose the opportunity to reform local government and I think that he will lose a great deal of credit.

A ministerial briefing from the Department of the Environment in February 1984 claimed, 'The government rejects suggestions that abolition is simply a political device to remove Labour councils.' But Norman Tebbit gave the game away a month later on 4 March 1984, at the same time transferring the blame for dividing society from the government to local councils:

The Labour Party is a party of division, in its present form it represents a threat to the democratic values and institutions on which our parliamentary system is based. The GLC is typical of this new, modern divisive version of socialism. It must be defeated. So we shall abolish the GLC.

The legislative passage of the Abolition Bill posed many difficulties for the government, particularly in the House of Lords where some concessions were forced through, most notably the retention of the Inner London Education Authority as an elected body. But a parliamentary majority once more succeeded in overriding rational and constitutional arguments and the Act was implemented on 1 April 1986.

Legislation to remove a tier of local government was not the only form of abolition in which the government was engaged. It had begun a programme of privatising local services, dissolving the activities which gave local government its purpose rather than legislating to remove structures and powers. As we saw in

Chapter 5, the Transport Act destroyed local government policies which had demonstrated an effective alternative to the free market. A 1985 Consultation Paper, 'Competition in the Provision of Local Authority Services', led to government promises to legislate according to its principles in the 1986–7 parliamentary session. (Its intentions were deferred through an overcrowded parliamentary timetable early in 1987 as the Conservatives gave themselves more room to manoeuvre in deciding their general election timetable.) In advance of legislation, Conservative authorities were encouraged to privatise cleansing, school meals and other services in which the effects of removing public accountability were soon apparent in reduction of quality both to the consumers and to producers whose wages and conditions have been ruthlessly depressed. Some examples have verged on the ridiculous, as multinational companies moved in to make as much profit as they could from the government-induced climate. When Wirral District privatised cleansing, Grand Metropolitan's tender proposed a workforce of 60 men who, on careful examination, would collect and empty dustbins each day at an average speed of 8·7 miles an hour, just outside the world-qualifying time for the marathon. This bid was rejected by the Conservative council in favour of Waste Management Ltd who generated 600 complaints a week in the first month of operation.

Conservative-controlled Wandsworth has been the front-runner in implementing government policies on privatisation, having put 13 services out to tender by the end of 1986. They could certainly point to some savings on the rates, but at the direct expense of wages, conditions and stability of service. The turnover of staff in street cleaning was more than 1,000 for 80 jobs over three years. Contracts change from one form to another as standards fail to be maintained.

Not surprisingly most councils have been slow to follow Wandsworth's lead. A survey by Waste Management in late 1986 showed that privatisation of refuse collecting and street cleaning, a profitable area of work, had virtually ground to a halt by late 1986 – with only ten contracts out of 27 tendered going to private contractors since 1983–4. Reporting this survey in the *Guardian* on 13 November 1986, Patrick Wintour and Geoff Andrews go on to quote the Conservative-controlled Association of District Councillors: 'Fragmentation of existing pooled direct labour organisations through contracting out services will inhibit a coordinated approach and limit the flexibility to respond to seasonal changes and emergencies.' Despite its previous experience, Wandsworth Council handed over the cleaning of sheltered accommodation to private contractors, reducing the services because, as one cleaner put it, 'We do much more than clean.'[12] The domestic staff helped in a variety of ways which a private contractor would stop in the interests of 'efficiency'.

We have seen in Chapter 6 that creative local authorities have been increasing the flexibility and responsiveness of services by democratic means, but Nicholas Ridley, the Environment Minister, would rather get rid of democracy except in its most restricted forms. Wintour and Andrews note how he cheerfully admits that 'his ideal council is one where members turn up once a year, have lunch, approve the private contractors and go away for 12 months'. This would be the final abolition of collective public service. Jack Edmonds, leader of Dudley Council, said, 'I make no apologies for attempting to run Dudley Council as a business.' The council spent less per pupil on education than any other borough and had the second lowest personal social services spending, among a catalogue of inadequacies.[13]

By 1985 Conservative policy towards local government could no longer be presented as a reasonable attempt by national government to ensure that 'he who pays the piper calls the tune'. Income from rates and charges had by then far outweighed government grants in local authority budgets. It had failed to deter by financial restrictions councils who decided to maintain and even expand public services. Seeing local politics as a substantial source of opposition in the nation, its only remedy was to remove local powers in one form or another, despite evidence that popular support for such action was extremely low. The independent survey of social attitudes conducted annually since 1983 by Social and Community Planning Research showed a slight percentage shift in favour of less control by central government between 1983 and 1984. More significantly, those in favour of more central control in 1984 were a distinct minority, even in the Conservative Party, while the majority of the electorate, supporters of both the Alliance and Labour combined, thought the power balance should remain the same or shift in favour of local government.

The government was faced by a dilemma of democracy. Margaret Thatcher had said, as we note earlier, that 'you are taking away a bit of a man's independence by taking away so much of his income.' But what if men and women preferred to spend it collectively, not individually? The Conservatives would ignore what people wanted in order to deal with local government in line with their overall political strategy. There should no longer have been any doubt in the public mind of the government's intentions. The political question now raised for the authorities under pressure was how to respond and how to mobilise support.

| | Conservative | | Alliance | | Labour | | Non-aligned |
	partisans %	others %	partisans %	others %	partisans %	others %	%
More control	19	17	24	5	11	11	10
About the same	49	46	34	39	32	43	43
Less control	27	28	39	46	52	38	27
Don't know	3	7	3	7	4	7	16

Attitudes to central control of local government by political identification

Source: *British Social Attitudes, the 1985 Report,* ed. R. Jowell and S. Witherspoon, Social and Community Planning Research, Gower, Vermont, USA, 1985, p. 156.

8

Resistance: The Campaign Against Rate-Capping

'It seems to me,' wrote Professor J. A. G. Griffith, 'that the provisions for rate-capping in the Rates Act of 1984 are little removed from a proposal to replace elected councils by administrative units!'[1] A Conservative Cabinet was using a parliamentary majority, based on a minority popular vote, to push through major structural changes of constitutional significance. This was no mere public expenditure exercise but an attack on creative local government itself. The National Rate-Cap Campaign of 1984–5 grew from this recognition and a realisation that the very principle of universal suffrage was being put in question in local politics. Tory Minister Kenneth Baker wrote in *The Times*, on 14 November 1984:

Opponents of rate limitation argue that local authorities are democratically elected bodies with a mandate from their electorate for what they do and spend . . . But the reality is that the link between the ballot box and the rating system has worn pretty thin. On average over half the nation's rate bill is borne by the non-domestic sector which has no vote, many of whom receive rate rebates or have their rates paid in full, finance less than a quarter of net authority spending . . . such an imbalance must raise questions about the real nature of local accountability.

Speaking in Parliament on the Interim Provisions Bill, on 30 July 1984, Cecil Franks, Tory MP for Barrow-in-Furness, said:

In recent years we have experienced the virtual death of democracy in local government. The reason is simple. The electorate and the ratepayers are no longer one and the same person. The elector, more often than not, does not pay rates, and the ratepayer is totally disenfranchised. Many years ago this House in its wisdom decided to remove the business vote; the removal of that financial discipline led to the gradual decline and death of the cities.

Then, referring to his time as a Manchester city councillor:

Those who were the dross of society, who contributed nothing to, but took everything out of society, had a vote, whereas those who were putting something into society did not.

By the summer of 1984, the other highly publicised local government campaign of the period, against the abolition of the GLC and metropolitan counties, was under way. Campaigning for the metropolitan counties alone would have generated limited public support, despite the contribution some had made to local economic policy, public transport and strategic planning. Their place in the system of local government had been questioned throughout their ten-year lives; they were originally introduced by Conservatives under Edward Heath. They were neither regional government nor local government but somewhere uneasily in between. But national headlines were captured by the GLC. Its case was very strong. Removing a strategic authority from the national capital flew in the face of reason and wider international practice. Margaret Thatcher's known irritation at GLC politics and the flair of Ken Livingstone ensured media attention. There was therefore success in obstructing the progress of abolition legislation through Parliament and in raising public awareness of the issues involved.

Yet in some ways the campaign over the Rates Act was a more significant phenomenon. Conviction that people had to be offered an alternative to 'Thatcherism' led to a higher level of joint action in the major cities than ever before. For some the Rates Act represented the point at which resistance to government financial control of local authorities had to go beyond creative manoeuvring if public services were not to deteriorate disastrously. It was a matter of defending material living standards, particularly those of people for whom the 'social wage' was crucial. For others, the principle of local democracy had to be defended before it was effectively taken out of British politics.

The Anti Rate-Cap Campaign took place on much more complicated territory than abolition, as we have seen in Chapter 7. The public had some difficulty in understanding that the issue had gone beyond a party-political squabble over levels of spending and financial management. Like the miners in the same period, campaigners were defending their communities (though there is no comparison intended with the personal courage of the miners and the loss that their families were experiencing at this time). At its height, the campaign's energy came from the new relations that were created between local communities and the local state. The hit list of Labour-controlled authorities were forced into national action, along with others who were not rate-capped but who recognised the dangers, because the parliamentary Labour Party offered no lead.

Parliamentary leadership always finds proposals to defy legislation difficult to handle since it threatens its future authority. There must be no hint of illegality in local government action according to the opposition environment spokesman.[2] Here it failed to distinguish between, on the one hand, illegal action, and, on the other, dissent in defence both of an important constitutional convention and of people whose interests the Labour Party existed to support. The Conservatives had not bothered about the niceties of the law in pursuit of their own ends. Lord Denning considered the opinion of two professors of law and two senior lecturers on the government's local government financial legislation and concluded: 'To put it bluntly, they have not complied with the law and they admit it.'[3] The story of the campaign has to be seen in this light. Its growth from June 1983 to February 1985 offers evidence that local politics was responding more urgently to the experience and frustration of communities than was the parliamentary opposition. Its outcome in 1985 demonstrated the limitations of what could be achieved within local government traditions and practice.

Building a national campaign

There was little past experience to offer hope for a successful national campaign based on concerted action by numerous local authorities. Proposals to reorganise county borough responsibilities during the 1960s made clear the major common ground for agreement between many authorities, but produced no strong commitment. In 1972, the response to the Housing Finance Act of Heath's government foreshadowed the 1980s more sharply. Nationally determined 'fair rents' were intended to create a surplus in local authority housing revenue accounts, government subsidies would be reduced, and local authorities denied the power to decide levels of rent subsidy from the rates. The Act discriminated sharply in favour of the private housing sector (where subsidy is provided through tax relief), reduced tenants' living standards and challenged the central principles of council housing as a modifying influence on the workings of a free market in housing. Local authorities met together and proposed defying the legislation, but attempts at combined action failed when none of the large authorities could secure a majority amongst their members for defiance. The small urban district of Clay Cross was left to stand alone: its councillors were surcharged and excluded from office. In 1980, Lothian Regional Council, based in Edinburgh, again showed how isolation can lead to defeat even with community support, when it resisted in vain the government's specifically Scottish legislation on local government finance. Aware of this isolation, the government was able to punish Lothian as a lesson to others.

Some permanent organisations exerted pressure on national government. The six 'core' cities (Birmingham, Leeds, Newcastle, Liverpool, Manchester, Sheffield) had met regularly in the 1970s to defend their special position in servicing major conurbations. The Labour Group of the London Boroughs Association (which in 1984 became the Association of London Authorities) had always spoken on behalf of London. In all these cases, contact between local councils was at the formal level, through leading representatives. The official local authority associations[4] acted mainly as the tools of central government by providing advice and expertise rather than criticism or opposition.

Considering the limited amount of joint action in the past, it was surprising that authorities moved so quickly together after the general election in June 1983. Within a month, a large number of Labour authorities met in Sheffield. The meeting drew together virtually all those that were eventually on the list for abolition and for Rates Act designation, as well as those most threatened by the penalty system.

From that meeting there emerged the idea of setting up a National Campaign Unit to facilitate coordination and act as a resource for authorities for the sharing of experience, facilities and campaigning strength. Within a year, over 70 local authorities and all the major public sector trade unions had joined what later became the Local Government Information Unit. During this period, the possibility of local councils taking a stand also began to seem more credible through events in Liverpool. Unique in local government during recent years, the Liverpool campaign had been carried forward by a close alliance between the party and local authority workers.[5] After taking control of the city council in 1983, Labour refused to set a rate in the following financial year with the existing level of government grant. Large demonstrations of workers and supporters made an impact on national consciousness and created a momentum that was eventually reflected in the May 1984 elections, when they achieved a substantial increase in their majority. The government was forced to negotiate and, as we have seen, the Liverpool City Council came away with a major propaganda victory.[6]

In this climate a wide group of authorities met in July 1984 for a two-day conference in Sheffield organised by the Campaign Unit and Sheffield's campaign team under the title of 'Forging the Links'. The authorities present committed themselves to policies of 'non-compliance' along with carefully worded statements indicating the two options that this implied: either refusing to make a rate for the next financial year, or deficit budgeting. (Deficit budgeting means deliberately planning a level of expenditure which cannot be met by known income. The resultant shortfall in the declared budget is illegal.) The phraseology and the policy proposals were echoed in National Executive Committee statements and conference resolutions at the 1984 Labour Party Conference. Early in the same year, the Labour Party for the first time established a local government committee as a main committee of the National Executive. Local government was achieving a political importance not seen for many years.

When the 'hit list' of rate-capped authorities (see list, p. 225) was announced by the Secretary of State, also in July 1984, all the 16 Labour authorities cooperated in campaigning collectively, and when the then Lib-Lab alliance controlling Brent joined them, 17 out of the 18 authorities worked closely together. Portsmouth, under Conservative control, while not actually joining, was unwilling to yield to Conservative spokesmen who tried to separate it from the other designated councils, and refused to seek 'redetermination'. Patrick Jenkin began to soften his line, indicating that redetermination might not mean what it said, deferring the deadline for application and consequently strengthening the resolve of some councils.

By November, opinion within the authorities had solidified behind 'not setting a rate' rather than deficit budgeting. The political climate had not changed dramatically since July. The miners were still on strike, although the chance of a favourable settlement for the National Union of Mineworkers was receding.

Prospects of a winter of power cuts and industrial disruption still seemed real.

It could be said that this was the time to fix a deal with the government – and as quickly as possible, while they were still under pressure. The front bench of the Labour Party advised authorities to work within the legislation, sticking together merely to obtain concessions at the beginning of the process of implementation. Just how strong the feeling was among authorities that nothing would be achieved without firmer opposition was indicated by their rejection of this advice after little debate. Few believed that government would do anything but provide marginal changes for individual councils, while continuing to divide and rule. Secondly, it would not provide an answer for the long term and would fail to deploy fully the hard-won unity and sense of purpose which had been built up. Thirdly, a group of leading local politicians considered the campaign to be not simply about the immediate needs of individual councils, but rather about defending and promoting public spending – holding, if not actually reversing, the tide of monetarism and providing an alternative to the despair and demoralisation which further retrenchment and capitulation would bring. Finally, agreement at this stage would concede the constitutional and democratic principles of the Rates Act. National press, radio and television interest in this rested substantially on the phenomenon of continued unity.

Unfortunately, there were no precise definitions about what eventual 'victory' would entail. For a small group, disruption in the normal processes of local government was the apparent aim, on a large enough scale to prove that Conservative policies were making Britain ungovernable. Most people had the more general intention of increasing pressure on the government as the miners' strike continued, and obtaining such concessions in the application of the Rates Act that its long-term financial and constitutional implications would be reduced.

Ironically, 'not declaring a rate' was favoured in the interests of unity because a decision to deficit budget was believed to place councillors under immediate threat of surcharge. Yet the policy emerged from meetings of the South London boroughs, led by Ted Knight of Lambeth, who favoured confrontation. Because of this confusion, and the blockbusting tactics used to win approval for the proposal, the campaign members adopted the policy cautiously and slowly. It was a caution based on uneasiness, not careful deliberation. Satisfaction at the unity achieved, and the useful propaganda for the local authorities which began to emerge, obliterated a serious desire to examine the precise implications and the very different intentions and objectives of those participating.

The authorities met regularly and reached agreement with the local government trade unions that the climax of the campaign would be 'Democracy Week' in the first week of March 1985. Those authorities most at risk would hold their budget council meetings that week, if possible on the same day, and refuse to set the rate as fixed by the Rates Act. High-profile national campaigning would be coordinated around the stand taken, and each individual authority would run active local campaigns.

It soon became increasingly clear that Patrick Jenkin had learned from his experience with Liverpool the year before. Only when he was removed from office in July 1985 was it fully appreciated how much the government resented his public humiliation. He would not be allowed to concede this time; the government would 'sit and wait' as they were doing with the miners' dispute. A serious reappraisal was swept aside yet again by the political momentum among the campaigning authorities. All that could be done was to ensure a commitment to collective negotiations with the Secretary of State, which were agreed at the Local Government Information Unit Management Committee on 16 January 1985, when furious opposition from the 'all or bust' group was overcome.

February was the watershed of the campaign. A major boost to morale came from the meeting that was, at last, held with Jenkin and his ministerial colleagues. With 26 local authorities and several major trade unions acting as observers, press informants reported that the Department of the Environment had expected a shambles in which the opposition would be picked off individually. In the event, the authorities fielded a tight pack, represented through a single spokesman, David Blunkett, chair of the Local Government Information Unit.

Also in February 1985, the district auditor provided information to the Department of the Environment that Hackney and Haringey would run out of money before the end of the 1984–5 financial year and would not be able to recover their shortfall in the following year if they accepted the government's rate limit. Alterations, embarrassing for the government, were made to the parliamentary orders which fixed rate limits for individual authorities. Leicester's enormous rate decrease of 56 per cent was reduced to 32 per cent. Hackney had their rates increased, as did Haringey a few days later. Delays also took place in parliamentary votes on the level of rate to be fixed for the authorities involved. Despite these encouraging events, the earlier lack of clarity and honesty among campaigning authorities was beginning to have practical consequences.

Satisfaction in maintaining unity, and signs of government difficulties in implementing the Rates Act programme, once again put off discussion about the precise objectives of noncompliance. As March approached, council leaders could no longer disguise the difficulties they would have in obtaining majorities for alleged illegal action, bringing the threat of surcharge and disqualification.

Warnings from legal officers were having their effect on councillors and local political parties. In order to retain maximum support from the waverers, it was proposed at a meeting on 18 February 1985 that instead of not fixing a rate on 7 March, councils would defer the decision. But this only created a further problem. The legal implications of this shift were different for rating and precepting authorities. (Rating authorities are those councils with direct responsibility for levying and collecting rates. Precepting authorities are those councils, like the former metropolitan counties, subsequently abolished, and parishes, that levy a precept on other rating authorities within their boundary.) The metropolitan counties, as precepting authorities, were required by law to make a rate by 10 March. For other authorities there was no legally required date, although it was assumed that they would do so before the end of the financial year, 31 March, in order to avoid the risk of losing income and exposing councillors to surcharge. The problem of how to retain a joint policy taking into account these differences was most acute in London, where the GLC and the ILEA were precepting authorities on the London boroughs.

At meetings in February it looked as though the GLC would fall back to the deficit budget strategy, and ILEA would find itself as the only authority taking illegal action on 7 March by not making a rate on that date, despite the original aim that authorities should stand together throughout.

For that reason, council leaders of both the ILEA and GLC, and their immediate senior colleagues, were asked in Manchester on 19 February 1985 to join Merseyside and South Yorkshire in making a precept and deferring the inevitable crisis which would hit them alone. Not only was their legal position different from the direct-rating authorities, but since they were threatened by abolition they had only one year in which to survive the financial effects of rate-capping. Illegality might deflect attention from their growing campaign against abolition. But in the following fortnight the leadership of the GLC and ILEA explained that the political pressure in London was such that the no-rate strategy had to be attempted, whatever the outcome.

The weekend of 2 and 3 March 1985, just before 'Democracy Week', was the start of a disastrous slide for the fortunes of the campaign, as the disagreement in London broke out publicly and the miners' strike drew to its close. The London Regional Labour Party's annual meeting taking place that weekend offered the opportunity for speeches by both the Leader, Ken Livingstone, and the Deputy Leader, John McDonnell, of the GLC. The two disagreed, John McDonnell arguing for the 'no rate whatever the consequences' line.

The grounds on which they disagreed pointed to confusions in the campaign which should have been sorted out before this late stage. Ken Livingstone suggested that the London borough leaders had been dishonest in giving the impression that they were about to break the law by failing to make a rate and then challenging the GLC to do the same. McDonnell argued that despite the differences between authorities, the GLC should still refuse to fix a rate at the rate-capped level because to do so would mean cutting services. This led to the second area of disagreement, concerning the true financial position of the GLC, about which Livingstone claimed he had been misled. Evidence was available to suggest that the GLC's financial situation would enable them to meet their commitments in their final rate-capped year and not have to make drastic cuts in services.

A third area of disagreement concerned priorities in political strategy. Ken Livingstone placed the anti-rate-capping campaign in the context of abolition. There were still important objectives to achieve in modifying the abolition legislation, including the retention of the ILEA and of some framework of democratic government for London to replace the GLC itself. He argued that losing power through disqualification would reduce the chance of success.

Despite these differences, 'Democracy Day' on Wednesday 6 March could be considered as a major success. Local campaigns came together in a popular and lively London demonstration which even in the official police reports (usually an underestimate) numbered 70,000, the biggest demonstration of support for local government in recent history. Yet the size of the display and its vivacity in the sun could not compensate for the impact of the GLC split evident in the public hostility between the Livingstone and McDonnell camps.

The contrast between this and the stark reality presented by the miners' dignified march back to work on Tuesday 5 March was obvious. Their orderly retreat signalled the success of the government's policy of standing its ground and waiting for time to spell out its dominance. There was no reason to believe that local political campaigning would not receive the same treatment, yet the lessons were still not learnt. With more than a touch of irony it was this very week that Ken Livingstone and his deputy John McDonnell found themselves jointly unveiling a plaque on the Isle of Dogs to the memory of George Lansbury. Neither could bring himself to speak to the other as they honoured the vital tradition of local politics which Lansbury and Poplar in the 1920s symbolised, as we described in Chapter 3.

The effects of the split in London and the miners' return to work were not immediately apparent. Fifteen authorities, four of them not on the Rates Act hit list, but suffering heavily from the penalty system, eventually failed to make a rate on 7 March. A new level of cooperation between councils had been achieved. Nevertheless, the device of deferral, putting off the rating decision into the future, veiled the uncertainties and disagreements in all the town halls and in the relations between councillors, Labour Parties and the campaigning groups across the country. Despite Ken Livingstone voting with London Labour Party policy alongside his deputy for deferral (a serious step for a precepting authority, as we have noted), the Labour Group on the GLC on Sunday 10 March, voted 24 to 18 to set a rate after four days of wrangling. It seemed that the ILEA would hold its no-rate stance, against the advice of the campaign, but this also did not turn out to be the case.[7]

Public disagreement led to a very considerable propaganda blow for the campaign. Whatever the truth of personal accusations about misleading financial reports in the GLC Labour Group, local parties everywhere were experiencing the same problem of distinguishing between the immediate financial situation and its significance for future local spending. Inevitably, the closer they came to the end of the financial year, the more information was available from treasurers on how budgets could be balanced under rate-capping, using reserves and creative accounting, without making cuts in the first 12 months. Waverers and opponents of the campaign, beginning to panic that they might be drawn into illegality by their more determined colleagues, could use the information to discredit arguments for outright opposition to the legislation. Why confuse the electorate, it could be asked, when calling for their support in the campaign if there was no immediate danger that they would suffer?

Against this, the active contributors to the campaign were insisting, as they had from the beginning, that their concern was not one of balancing the rate-capped budget for 1985–6 by whatever means possible, but that rate-capping enabled the government to obtain long-term control over local-authority spending at a time when communities needed more resources as unemployment grew and the urban infrastructure showed increasing signs of gross neglect. Dealing with 1985–6 on the government's terms, whether imposed through rate-capping or penalties, had implications for council strategies in the following years. Reserves would be used up and once they had succeeded the government could tighten the screw further as they had already done in Scotland following similar controls.

The success of the national campaign depended on holding each of the participating councils to this longer-term view. Nowhere had this argument been sufficiently thought through and debated to determine the eventual outcome. Local campaigns which were the lifeblood of the national campaign also contained the same contradictions and instability. This can be illustrated by briefly considering how Sheffield's campaign had built up to the events of 'Democracy Week', and how it responded to the local decision on 7 March 1985 to defer setting a rate.

The campaign in Sheffield

The city had set up a campaign unit to draw together the elements in local politics – the council, the workforce and the community. In January 1985, a joint union campaign group was established bringing together shop stewards and full-time officers of all unions negotiating for local authority workers. Three main areas of activity were promoted: an advertising campaign, an information and education programme for employees through the unions, and a community inquiry into real need in the city.

A MORI poll had highlighted the very low level of commitment and information about council services amongst the workforce. Worksite meetings were arranged, not mass meetings but small enough to allow questions and dialogue. In order to prevent the council dominating the campaign, it was agreed with the trade unions that shop stewards should be seconded for some of their time, to organise, chair and lead the meetings.

By February almost every worksite in the authority had held a meeting, involving 28,000 of the 33,000 workforce. It was a two-way process: the council learned much about the difficulty of defending local government services given the long-held feelings of frustration among many users and workers. Problems with bonus issues and low pay were often raised. A major town hall dispute with NALGO over the introduction of new technology rumbled on through the period as a constant obstacle to unity.

Listening, not just telling people what to do, was a feature of the community inquiry also. An open-ended questionnaire was designed for community groups to identify areas in the city and specific needs where resources were required, and also to give their views on the quality of the services which were provided.

Campaigning activity peaked with a demonstration on 7 March 1985, drawing a wide range of community groups and workers, many of whom were not the usual faces who turn out on such occasions. As they marched from the different assembly points around the city to surround the town hall at the time of the council 'deferral meeting', banners from pensioners' groups, organisations for children's play and local community centres mingled with those of trade unions and political parties.

7 March also indicated the limitations of the campaign. Many councillors pointed to the relatively modest attendance from council workers on the demonstration. Some of the campaigners felt that the council decision to defer making a rate was an anticlimax – very different from outright defiance. As elsewhere, the unity of the Labour Group had depended on legal advice that councillors were not putting themselves at immediate risk. In all the local campaigns the objective was not to make a rate until the government had given way on their major demands. Uncertain councillors had to be persuaded to stand firm and to be convinced

that there was sufficient public support to justify the personal and political risks of their actions.

The campaign drew together a wide range of those who had been active in local political creativity: councillors, council officers and workers, the local Labour Party, trade unions and community organisations. Fervent campaigners had to take into account the more cautious views and conventions of local politics which were by no means dominated by those believing that local government should be in the vanguard of a battle with the government over constitutional and political power. A number of different nuances emerged which defy conventional distinctions of right and left. Although there was an overlap between these positions as the campaign ebbed and flowed, they can be identified as 'enthusiasts', 'negotiators', 'managers' and 'dignitaries'. Campaign 'enthusiasts' wanted a precisely defined and unequivocal no-rate stand. They believed that if council workers and users were to take action which would impress the government that they intended to defend their services, the government would be convinced of the councillors' willingness 'to go all the way'. If other councils achieved the same stand, the government would be faced by an unprecedented wall of local initiative, matching the new levels of collaboration between council leaders at national level.

For 'negotiators', however, the campaign needed only to build up sufficient pressure for the government to give some ground in order for something to have been gained. If possible, personal risk to councillors should be avoided. Unity up to the brink was the objective. This position retained its credibility into the Spring. For the 'managers', the campaign was a diversion and delusion. Local politics was about being elected to do the best for local people, within national legislation, and that was all the electorate expected of them. A final position was represented by the 'dignitaries'. A very small minority in the active politics of these particular councils in the 1980s, their votes in council had no less weight for that. For them, public office brought status and public esteem, which they did not want to put in jeopardy. Disqualification from office was as important as financial risk. Nevertheless, in many councils they supported their colleagues for a considerable time against their better judgement. Personal as well as political pressures shifted the boundaries between groups continually.

'Enthusiasts' – often caricatured as 'the all-or-bust brigade' –

were stronger in local Labour parties, shop stewards' organisations and some community groups and were the political driving force of the campaign. They did not incur the same personal risk as councillors, although efforts were made to share that risk by forming a reserve list of prospective councillors to take on the load if councillors were removed from office. Their efforts focused on persuading and supporting councillors to hold firm at four successive council meetings between the initial deferral meeting of 7 March and the final decision on 7 May. It was considered a success to take waverers through the psychological barrier of 1 April into the next financial year. Between the council meetings, 'negotiators', managers and 'dignitaries' dominated internal discussions among councillors, and campaigners were faced by the dilemma of how to maintain a level of organisation in the community or among the council workforce when there was no means of exerting pressure on the government directly.

Sheffield's campaign locally made the best of the 7 March resolution to defer setting a rate rather than to refuse making a rate under the new legislation. A public petition was launched and meetings continued with the workforce. But to questions like 'What happens next?' and 'What can people do?' the council's deferral of a decision provided no easy answer. The 'enthusiasts' were on ground they would have liked to have avoided.

Meanwhile, on the national scene, two High Court decisions on the position of Hackney, the only council which had passed a definite 'no-rate' resolution, gave renewed hope for the 'negotiators' by allowing more time for a settlement to be reached. On 3 April, by which time Hackney had fallen in with the deferral position, the court ordered them to make a rate. On Tuesday 15 April, in his detailed judgement, Justice Woolf allowed Hackney six weeks to set a rate. The danger of contempt of court, which was the worry of many councillors and which had also deterred the miners, temporarily receded.

If this was a victory it was not without problems. An early 'final' date would have brought matters to a head for councillors, instead of prolonging the now-dwindling hope that the government would negotiate without unequivocal confrontation. The government had no intention of negotiating as they had done when Liverpool made no rate in the previous year. After 1 April they would neither pay normal block grant instalments nor continue to pay their contribution to housing benefit which had helped to sustain Liverpool the year before. The loss of income this entailed for authorities meant that elected members were more at risk of surcharge the longer they delayed setting a rate – circumstances which had not been foreseen from the Liverpool experience.

The debate within Sheffield's local politics reached critical proportions on 30 April. After a heated three-and-a-half-hour debate, the proposition put by the Labour Group and party leadership to switch to a potential *deficit* budget tactic was defeated by the delegate meeting of the district party. An amendment was agreed to 'go illegal' and refuse to set a rate 'until the government provided sufficient resources for the fulfilment of the capital and revenue programmes for 1985–6 and subsequent financial years'.

The local campaign had eight days to gather together the forces to carry this in the council. Traditional political honour and discipline in Sheffield's labour movement would ensure that the majority of the councillors would back the party's agreed decision, whatever their personal misgivings. To support councillors, the campaign had created a pledge fund which had almost reached its target of £40,000. Thousands of manual and craft workers had pledged the income from two hours' unpaid work. The wages saved would be set against any alleged council losses. A 'Pay Your Rates' campaign was mounted to ensure that the council continued to receive income. The party started to plan a programme of door-to-door canvassing. Private-sector unions who so far had been absorbed by the miners' strike now began fund-raising. Against this, the teachers and the biggest manual and craft union (General, Municipal, Boilermakers and Allied Trades Union) opposed the new step, the latter actively lobbying the council meeting to set a rate. One of the six Sheffield constituency Labour parties (Attercliffe) broke ranks with the district party on the issue.

In line with the party decision, the Labour Group leadership attempted to carry the resolution on the 7 May council meeting. But after eight hours of debate an amendment was moved on behalf of a minority of the Labour Group to implement the maximum rate, and this succeeded with the support of 17 Conservatives and 9 Liberals. A rate had been set.

On 5 June the city council met and approved the rate but reinstated the original expansionary budget by the use of creative accounting to avoid a deficit, with particular emphasis on the needs of the elderly and low-paid workers. Sheffield was back to fighting the battle on technical grounds.

A disorderly retreat

Throughout this period the national campaign had been trying to maintain a common front as local campaigns underwent their own versions of the Sheffield experience, and they decided to play another of the few cards left to them: they requested a meeting with the Secretary of State, using the umbrella of all the Local Authority Associations as part of the official machinery of consultation. Jenkin refused, but the propaganda gains which might have come from his obvious belligerence were minimised by publicity on the GLC/ILEA debacle and the obvious failure to hold the authorities to the agreed line.

Of the 15 authorities who originally deferred making a rate, a dozen came through the psychological barrier of 1 April without a rate. But the climate had changed. Councils had started to drift, to fall away one by one, as shown in the following table.

Date on which rate-capped councils set a rate, 1985

7 March	Basildon
7 March	ILEA
10 March	GLC
15 March	Brent
28 March	Thamesdown
28 March	Leicester
4 April	Lewisham
11 April	Haringey
7 May	Sheffield
23 May	Hackney
30 May	Southwark
31 May	Islington
6 June	Camden
8 June	Greenwich
14 June	Liverpool
3 July	Lambeth

Despite this apparent retreat, public opinion was moving in favour of the local authorities. As the *Sunday Times* wrote on 7 April 1985:

Rate-capping was expected to be a vote-winner, ending what ministers saw as the extravagance of Labour-controlled councils such as the GLC.

But 55 per cent of electors disapprove of rate-capping, with only 38 per cent supporting and 7 per cent having no view.

The Consultative Council on Local Government Finance met on 17 April and the opportunity was taken by the Association of Metropolitan Authorities and the London Authorities to place rate-capping on the agenda. They proposed, firstly, to set up a working party jointly between local authority leaders and ministers to look at the future and how the chaotic situation could be sorted out; and secondly, an immediate meeting to facilitate steps towards overcoming the 'no-rate situation'.

At a stormy meeting, the Secretary of State attempted to rule the items off the agenda. He finally agreed to respond in writing but still refused to negotiate. The 'no-rate' tactic was now being pursued in the very cold light of a wet spring. The stress on Labour councillors was beginning to tell heavily. Signs of frustration began to appear. For example, Southwark's council meeting on Wednesday 24 April had to be deferred for 48 hours due to major disruption by members of the public of that meeting along with the following two meetings on 1 and 8 May.

The Local Government committee of the Labour Party NEC intervened on 13 May to clarify what was acceptable or expected from Labour Councils. A resolution was agreed and communicated to the councils involved which said '. . . to this end, no council should be expected to continue with a particular tactic unless it (a) sincerely believes that it is the only option for maintaining jobs and services and (b) has identifiable and specific commitments from Party members, TUs and community groups, to ensure that financial and personal risks are shared with those calling for or supporting such decisions.'

By the time the authorities met on Thursday 16 May, five of the seven authorities left were only deferring by tactical manoeuvring within their groups of councillors, and by very narrow majorities. Their efforts were not placing any pressure on the Secretary of State, but every pressure on the Labour groups and parties in their areas. The district auditors had now intervened in a very decisive way, making it clear that after 31 May councillors would not be able to avoid risk. Meetings rearranged for Hackney and Southwark in the week commencing 20 May, and for other councils during the first week of June, saw the bedraggled end of the 'no-rate' tactic.

On Friday 31 May, after consultation with the local ward

parties, the Islington Labour Group decided to set a rate, significantly choosing to accept that, even with their overwhelming majority, there was now little point in risking disqualification and surcharge in a lost cause. Given the nature of London Labour politics at the time, this was a significant leadership decision by Margaret Hodge who also chaired the Association of London Authorities.

After Liverpool had also finally fixed a rate on 14 June, only the London Borough of Lambeth remained without a rate, until on 3 July the resignation of a Labour member led to a majority of 32 to 31 in favour of setting a rate. With such a small majority in the council, the leader Ted Knight's tactical achievement in prolonging the resistance for so long had been remarkable, whatever may be thought of the wisdom of continuing in isolation to this point.

Both Lambeth and Liverpool councils remained at risk from the separate actions of their district auditors. In the case of Lambeth, the district audit service had identified losses, incurred from the rate-making delay, amounting to £126,000, and a court battle ensued which resulted in disqualification of 31 councillors and surcharge on 2 April 1986. Liverpool first received a threat from their district auditor on the basis of their deficit budget, and later fell victim to the same action on the delay in making a rate as Lambeth, going through the appeal process to the House of Lords and suffering disqualification on 12 March 1987. Fortunately for them it was not within the brief of the Audit Commission to penalise government ministers for the loss to ratepayers and the mismanagement of local government finance which their decisions had produced over the years.

The Liverpool 'go it alone' stand

Because Liverpool was not a rate-capped council the issues were different but the result very similar. On 14 June 1985 they set a rate which did not appear to provide sufficient resources to cover expenditure. The council had chosen a deficit budget strategy and in keeping with their style of independent operation over the previous 12 months, and their success in 1984, had chosen to 'go it alone'. They had withdrawn financial support from the Local Government Information Unit in May 1985 before they set a rate, making it difficult for them to be regarded as part of the collective local authority action being taken, with its objective of mutual support and solidarity across the country. Liverpool's situation and policies were equated with the anti-rate-cap campaign by some Liverpool councillors, commentators and critics. A distinction must be made because, in important respects, the political position and style of Liverpool's leadership was different, and by disregarding this they have been used by government propagandists and the popular press to caricature the quality of creative local politics and to turn away potential support for councils.

Liverpool's considerable success was to build 2,800 houses in a period when virtually no council houses were built nationally. However, employment in the Direct Labour organisation was halved and jobs were mainly created in the private sector with all the consequences for the workers and the industry which this entailed, as we describe in Chapter 6. Official statistics actually showed a decline in full-time employees of the city council in 1985–6 despite claims that jobs were maintained and expanded. The local party and council leadership accepted the old fashioned 'municipal machine' as the vehicle for change and did not develop new ways of opening up the town hall to a more active democracy, nor did they engage in new forms of economic policy and influence. Attitudes to many community groups, housing associations and cooperatives were dismissive; everybody was told to 'work through the party', and there was a major clash with the black community when it tried to express its wishes in an independent manner (Liverpool Black Caucus, *Racial Politics of Militant in Liverpool*, Runnymede Trust, 1986). Liverpool politics in the period owed as much to the 'boss politics' which have been recurrent features of its history affecting all parties and political organisations as they did to the role of the Militant tendency, well-documented elsewhere (Michael Crick, *The March of Militant*, Faber and Faber). There was a complete failure to respond to the energy and ideas of the network of community activities and groups which had enlivened Liverpool in the late 1960s and the 1970s, and offered opportunities to work with the people actively to defend Liverpool.

In this regard their decisions at this stage should be compared with the approach of the Islington Labour group on 31 May. There were also important questions as to how far they had seriously addressed the position laid out in the Labour Party NEC resolution of 13 May as the basis for continued council resistance. A great deal hinged on how one interpreted the phrase 'sincerely believed that it [the tactic] is the only option for maintaining jobs and services'.

For the purposes of political propaganda this strategy had the merit of clarity and immediacy compared with deferral of setting a rate. The council appeared to be refusing to accept that the people of Liverpool should shoulder the burden of Liverpool's economic decline, for which they could not be held responsible. If the government would not release adequate grant Liverpool would not make up the deficit from the rates. Nevertheless, behind the apparently robust stand, the same contradictions appeared as in the local campaigns against the Rates Act. Unity broke down because the council could not manage the consequences of their decision without reducing services and directly threatening council jobs, the very basis on which they had campaigned and received support from the workforce and the electorate.

All spending was rigidly controlled. Every small item of spending had to be signed for by the Chair of Finance, job vacancies were, and remained, frozen until 1986, with individual posts being released by the Chair of Finance and approved by the Chair of Personnel, who was also the Deputy Leader. As the district auditor toughened his pronouncements, and deadlines started to emerge by which money would 'run out', the council continued to manage precariously. Within ten days of each other, in September, there was a statement on behalf of the council by the Deputy Leader that the council would not make any of its workforce redundant and the issue of redundancy notices to all 31,000 employees. The hitherto unprecedented unity of workforce, council and Labour Party, began to disintegrate.

Following the Labour Party Conference in October 1985, in which Liverpool was the dramatic focus of the local government debate, an inquiry into the city's finances offered the chance to get at the financial reality and find ground on which clear judgements might be made. The trade unions, the Liverpool leadership and the party nationally, agreed to cooperate. The Association of Metropolitan Authorities cooperated in obtaining the services of four leading local government finance chiefs, from Camden, Sheffield, the GLC and the Association of Metropolitan Authorities itself, led by Maurice Stonefrost. The situation in Liverpool was indeed serious. Grants had stopped to voluntary groups, the physically handicapped and mentally ill and handicapped appeared daily on television as victims of the deficit budget.

The Joint Shop Stewards Committee, a major strength of

Liverpool's campaign, had collapsed, and the Convenors Groups with it. Unions publicly denounced each other, and the Militant element of the group and party in Liverpool denounced the trade unions at local and national level for not backing them fully. On Sunday 17 November, the national trade union leaders were told that no settlement based on Stonefrost was possible and that the 'fight' would go on. On Friday 22 November, the District Labour Party met in Liverpool and announced that without national support they had been forced to give up the confrontation and turn, like everyone else, to the accountants for a solution to the expenditure gap. On Wednesday 27 November the three major local authority trade unions (TGWU, NUPE, G&MBATU) demanded an enquiry into the Liverpool District Party which became the well-documented Labour Party investigation into the Militant Tendency.

North of the border, legislation details differed but Scottish authorities had joined the campaign. The Secretary of State not only had the power to fix the rate but also to determine how far rates might subsidise the housing account, and was forcing up rents. Edinburgh and Stirling were in the forefront of refusing to comply with government demands by the set date of 5 March 1985, which under Scottish legislation could be unlawful. However, the different legal process of public inquiry and retrospective action followed by the Secretary of State for Scotland delayed conflict and made united action difficult to maintain.

By the second week in July Stirling had agreed to comply in the face of a court case resulting in a rise of almost £3 a week in council rents. Edinburgh continued the battle, taking the matter through the courts on 15 July, where they were given three weeks in which to comply with a decision to raise rents and cut the rate subsidy. On both rents and rates the government's figures were exactly the same as those presented at the annual finance debate, earlier in the year, by the Conservative minority on the Edinburgh City Council. The first order to reduce the rate contribution to the rent account was complied with at a special council meeting on Sunday 21 July. On 5 September the council agreed the 5·2p cut in the rate demanded by the Scottish Secretary, using creative accountancy to maintain services.

Was the campaign a failure?

In the summer of 1984 the campaign against rate-capping had set out to unify as many councils as possible behind an ambitious programme: to return grant allocations to the 1979 levels, to prevent the implementation of the Rates Act, and to abolish targets and penalties.[8] It was considered that if between six and ten authorities refused to carry out their duty of setting a rate, the government would have to acknowledge the strength of opposition and potential constitutional crisis which would arise and which would not be worth risking for the sake of reaching a modest compromise. What did they actually achieve?

On Thursday 25 July 1985, the next 'hit list' of authorities was designated under the Rates Act for the 1986–7 financial year. In a sleight of hand, Patrick Jenkin based his calculation for the 18 rate-capped authorities on the expenditure figures laid down by him the previous year, not on the submitted expenditure figures from the authorities themselves. Consequently, four authorities were removed from the list. Conservative-controlled Portsmouth and the hung London Borough of Brent were taken off, but so were Leicester and Sheffield, whose actual budgets were higher than the figures being used by the government to estimate net expenditure. Liverpool and Newcastle were added to the list, although, in marked contrast to those removed, their own submitted figures for 1985–6 were used rather than government estimates so that it could be argued that spending was higher than in Sheffield or Leicester. Political considerations rather than logic prevailed. There were now 12 rate-capped authorities plus the joint boards and the ILEA – automatically rate-capped under the abolition proposals – all of them Labour-controlled.

The rules for applying for 'redetermination' were altered in a parliamentary answer on the same day, 25 July. The penal clauses of the previous operation were eased. Authorities would no longer have the threat of further expenditure reductions, nor would there be interference in individual spending proposals, if they decided to seek redetermination.

The Secretary of State also announced a change in the target and penalty system. The two-tier system of grant assessment figures and arbitrary spending targets was changed. Grant-related expenditure became the starting point for withdrawal of grant. Tom King, then Minister of State, had said during the passage of the Land and Planning Act, on April Fools' Day 1980,

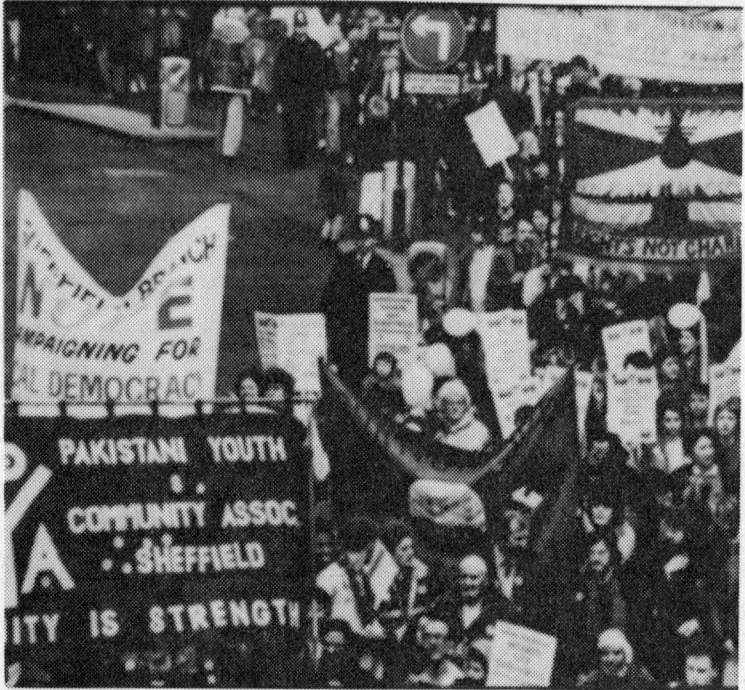

8   Rallying against the Rates Act: a demonstration outside the Town Hall, Sheffield, 7 March 1985, included many who had not been interested in politics before.

'It is not suggested that it [needs assessment] prescribes a specific level to which an authority ought to spend . . . I want to make it quite clear that that is not its purpose. We are seeking to find the fairest way to distribute public money to local authorities.' But as Patrick Jenkin said, when he answered questions in 1985, 'That was then, and now is now.'[9]

While the outlook was bleak for the rate-capped councils, Conservative local government policy was in some disarray. Support for councils and public spending was evident in opinion polls and the government's overall popularity was slipping. The House of Lords had in May inflicted irritating defeats on the government during the passage of the abolition proposals, such as the retention of ILEA as an elected body. In November the government announced that they were delaying legislation on enforced privatisation of local services. The local election results on 2 May 1985 in the shire counties had been disastrous for the

Conservatives.[10] Rate revaluation in Scotland had created such mayhem that the government had allocated large sums to industrial and domestic ratepayers in order to reduce the impact. So although the original, specific objectives of the campaign had only been partly achieved, the climate of opinion was affected.

The campaign also had consequences in strengthening the resolve of local councils to maintain services. If they had given up meekly during the financial year 1984–5, they would have adjusted to the government's views on local public spending. Political pressure exerted by the campaign forced politicians and officers to break new ground and extend the boundaries of financial ingenuity. The larger authorities began to operate more independently in the financial markets, negotiating special loans, known as 'deferred purchase', to cover day-to-day spending, transferring items from the rate-borne revenue heading to the 'capital development' programmes, thus meeting the expenditure from this loan rather than the normal revenue income which had now been reduced, e.g. Sheffield borrowed £110 million in order to sustain its programme for the years 1986–8.

This would have been undreamt of in 1984. Political compliance with government intentions would have removed the pressure on officers and councillors to find such alternatives to cutbacks. (These loans are not to be confused with arrangements for raising a premium through 'lease and lease-back schemes' adopted by some councils in 1987.) It was a resilient and imaginative response by councils who entered the 1985–6 financial year with a commitment to saving services despite a 'government rate' which would not cover their expenditure. The alternative would have been immediate and virtually impractical expenditure reductions. Labour councils seemed less intimidated than a Labour government had been by the IMF's pressure in 1976. The 'crisis' at that time had involved borrowing £3·2 billion or the equivalent of only 30 big financial deals by councils.

Deferred purchase and similar arrangements were protecting thousands of people from unemployment, and hundreds of thousands from the demoralisation which would have followed even more drastic decline in schools, services and the condition of streets and public buildings. These deals counted against income and thus helped to balance budgets by reducing 'overspend' and thereby retaining government grants. The same result could only otherwise have been achieved by reducing services and jobs. (See Appendix 2.) Such measures saved public money although they were not the preferred method for sensible financial planning in the councils which adopted them. As Neil Kinnock pointed out later at the 1987 Labour Party Local Government Conference, 'It is quicker and easier to destroy than it is to rebuild services and the economy'. He might have added it is also more expensive.

In Sheffield, which found itself budgeting for £71 million above the expenditure level fixed by central government for 1987/8, in its second rate-capped year, 7,000 jobs were saved by measures, including deferred purchase, which enabled the Council to find £60 million of the shortfall. The remainder came from income generation and efficiency savings which had been worked on over previous years. 5,000 of the jobs saved were funded within the council and 2,000 sustained through spending in the local economy as indicated in Chapter 6. Redundancy and benefit payments amounting to some £42 million from national funds and £5 million from local government funds were saved, and at the same time the spending power and tax and national insurance contributions of the people working were maintained. It would have been unthinkable to have cut anything like that amount of money from essential services, and the Chamber of Commerce, as well as opposition parties, lobbied the government in the autumn of 1986 to say just that.

The contribution of the anti-rate-capping campaign to all this was to help discredit the government and undermine its attack on local democracy and democratically developed public services. Miscalculations over what was achievable against the government should not divert attention from the imagination and practical skill shown at many levels in the campaign. National unity gave local government more coverage in national news than ever before and achieved more than individual acquiescence could have hoped to obtain. Local campaigns made possible political education and a raising of consciousness about local public services.

The form of opposition which had been mounted could do no more than reflect the constitutional powers of local government and the level of political organisation in local areas. Day-to-day management of local government is difficult within the uncertainties of campaigning, and many elected councillors chose to manage. No direct pressure was exerted on ministers by councillors putting themselves at financial risk through surcharge, unless the disruption in local administration across the country had reached considerable proportions. Once this was clearly not going to happen, the government could sit back and wait for the reality to sink in. It was the councillors who were put under pressure. Individual political careers and aspirations, both locally and nationally, inevitably affected decisions taken about the risk involved and about the reputation which involvement in the campaign would bring on the Left or the Right of the Labour Party.

Local government did not seek confrontation with Parliament, nor wish to raise some of the pointless distinctions between local and central democracy in a unitary state to which it led. The new level of activity and democracy in local politics could not succeed against an authoritarian use of Parliament, but it could ensure that its alternative agenda remained prominent. As we have seen, the campaign failed to achieve its stated objectives through its chosen method, and the realities of power were demonstrated, but this does not imply that the campaign was without effect. The government acknowledged its own frustration by sacrificing Patrick Jenkin's career[11] – local government had not been brought sharply to heel and application of the Rates Act continued to be muddled and inconsistent. The battle may have been lost, but the argument was not – even amongst Tory ministers. John Carvel, political correspondent of the *Guardian*, wrote on 7 May 1986:

The Environment Secretary, Mr Kenneth Baker, has told his colleagues that he can no longer accept the basic intellectual justification for the government's attempts since 1979 to control local authority current spending.

He and his top officials at the Department of the Environment are now convinced that central government cannot and should not try to determine total current spending by councils, now running at about £30 billion a year. They believe that ministers should be content to cash-limit central grants.

How far the argument was won among the people at large is more difficult to judge. The local councils' case had been built around three issues: the political rights of local government, levels of public spending, and the significance of local government spending for people's lives. Some opinion polls show a favourable shift in attitudes towards local government in recent years. According to Gallup polls, the difference between people in favour of rate increases to improve services rather than rate reductions was 35

	Layfield Committee, May/June 1975 %	Gallup for BBC TV's 'Newsnight', April 1980 %	Gallup for BBC, *New Society*, Feb. 1982 %	Gallup, May 1985 %
Decrease in rates, even if it means some reductions in local services	19	26	22	15
No change	53	29	32	29
Extension/maintenance of services, even if it means some increase in rates	28	36	38	50
Don't know	Excluded	10	8	6
Balance in favour of rate increases to maintain/extend services	+9	+10	+16	+35

Opinion polls on rate increases or local service cuts
Source: Local Government Information Unit, 1986.

per cent in May 1985 compared with a difference of 16 per cent in February 1982. The following table suggests that some support was won by the Conservatives in 1980 for their policy of rate reductions and then lost over the years in which local government campaigning increased in intensity.

A MORI poll commissioned by the Audit Commission and published in 1986 found strong support for local government. 53 per cent were satisfied with the way local authorities ran services compared with 44 per cent in 1981. 47 per cent said that council services would get worse if the government centralised decision making, while only 16 per cent said they would improve. MORI's summary notes that 'overall, these figures are in line with other survey findings which consistently show greater satisfaction with local rather than central government'.[12] This is true even of inner London, where there is most scepticism about all government services, but the difference between satisfaction (33 per cent) and dissatisfaction (55 per cent) for central government is much greater than for local government (38 to 41 per cent).

When asked why rates had increased, far more thought it was due to less money coming from central government to local councils than to councils spending on unnecessary activities. Significantly, MORI identified activists within the community, the 'movers and shakers' of society, and discovered that two out of three attributed the current year's rate rise to reduction in government grant. This group was also noticeably more in favour of local government increasing its spending to improve services, even if rates went up. Finally, the MORI poll threw interesting light on the Conservative claim that rates are unreasonably high, bearing in mind the services provided by local authorities. Opinion was evenly divided on whether rates were at a reasonable (47 per cent) or unreasonable (42 per cent) level – it was more favourable during a MORI poll in the final stages of the anti-Rates Act campaign (49 per cent reasonable to 35 per cent unreasonable) – but the margin was two to one against the present level of income tax and VAT for services provided by central government. MORI concluded, 'it is apparent that local government is considered to be fulfilling its responsibilities of value for money from service delivery more satisfactorily than central government.'[13]

Local polls conducted during the campaign tell the same story, but while they were useful for the campaign itself, they were not conducted over a period which can give some measure of change in attitudes. A research study based on a range of different polls by MORI concluded that 'The surveys which tracked these campaigns consistently showed that the local council, *not* central government should be responsible for local spending, that centralised decision-making leads to a deterioration in local services, and that the government takes (i.e. should take) the greater part of the blame for rate increases.'[14] NOP's survey for the Trades Union Congress in October 1986 revealed deep concern about the impact of private contractors in local and NHS services; plans to impose privatisation on local authorities being opposed by as much as five to one.

While it is difficult to ascribe any of the changes to the local government campaigns alone, we can recognise that opinion might have been affected if ministers had been allowed to exploit their dominance of the media and their official publicity without a substantial challenge.

Another important means of judging the success of campaigning was the reaction it provoked from government, which showed its concern over the effectiveness of the arguments presented in local politics by setting up a Committee of Inquiry into Local Authority Business under David Widdicombe (the Widdicombe Inquiry). Its interim report on council advertising and publicity, published on 8 August 1985, disappointed the government by declaring that 'Councils must be free to publish material on the services they provide and on proposals which affect them; that includes abolition and rate-capping.'[15] It insisted, however, that there should be a legal ban on council publicity of a party political nature, and recommended a tightening up of accountancy on publicity. The committee was strongly in favour of 'awareness-raising' campaigns which increase knowledge of services for those who require them and which recognise that 'the health of local government depends much on the strength of its democratic base.'[16] It responded positively to local councils' efforts to increase local democratic activity, hoping that it would have a beneficial effect on turn-out at election.

The committee argued that local government is more than the sum of the services it provides but has a significant political role: 'We do not believe it is wrong in principle for local authorities to issue material dealing with matters of political controversy, nor to express a view on such matters. Local authorities have a long-recognised and important contribution to make to political debate on matters concerning them.'[17] Sir Lawrence Boyle, a member of the committee, saw that it was local government's success in doing this that had led to the inquiry taking place, and said so when summarising his minority report.

Local authority powers of information have been in force in virtually identical terms since 1948. What is it that has caused this to emerge as a 'problem' since 1980 – the date identified by those giving evidence? . . . My main conclusion is that it is the attempt to alter the constitutional position of local government in our society both by legislation and convention. We should bring that issue out rather than hide behind the issue of 'advertising on the rates'.[18]

He was equally clear about the 'party political' issue. If the government, he asked, is of one particular persuasion over abolishing the GLC and metropolitan councils (and he might also have added the right to set a rate) and local councils are of another, are they not equally party political?

Sir Lawrence's judgement about the motivation behind the inquiry was soon vindicated when the government drafted a local government bill, whose recommendations went far beyond Widdicombe in curtailing the political rights of local councils. It sought to prohibit a local authority from publishing 'any material which, in whole or in part, appears to be designed to affect, or can reasonably be regarded as likely to affect, public support for (a) a political party or (b) any body, cause or campaign identified with or likely to be regarded as identified with a political party'. It also attacked voluntary organisations and other groups in the community. A local authority would be prevented from giving assistance to people or organisations who published such material. As the National Council for Voluntary Organisations pointed out, this could include tenants' groups campaigning on housing issues, an advice agency criticising social security reforms, a community relations council campaigning against immigration regulations, even a conservation group campaigning against a new motorway and arguing in favour of public transport.[19] These steps indicate that active local democracy was more than the government could stomach. Its devotion to the free market was stronger than its commitment to democratic debate; the argument being presented by local politics must not be allowed a full airing.

On 29 May 1986, after only nine months in his post as Environ-

ment Minister, Kenneth Baker was moved to the Department
of Education and Science. His successor, Nicholas Ridley, the
architect of the Ridley Plan in the late 1970s with its strategy
for undermining trade unions in the nationalised industries,
could be expected to remove any impression of uncertainty on
the part of the government. On 22 July 1986, the government
took two steps which at first sight appeared inconsistent, but
actually showed that the target it was aiming at remained the
same, namely those authorities which might offer an alternative programme to its own. In the medium term it wished to
neutralise local government opposition as far as possible now
that the next general election was on the horizon. It was
announced that the government would recognise for its planning purposes and allocation of grant what local government
was actually spending, rather than what had been demanded
of them in spending reductions. This gave some prospect of
relief to local government as a whole on rate increases in the
following year, and to some degree justified the campaign by
acknowledging the unreality of the demands made by government and vindicating the decisions of key local authorities to
maintain their spending and service levels. Had services been
reduced, the £2·9 billion which was added back into the sums
on which grant was now calculated might never have been
restored.

On the other hand, the new Secretary of State took a very
different view of rate-capping from that of his predecessor. He
changed the rules retrospectively, using $12\frac{1}{2}$ per cent over grant
assessment rather than 20 per cent as the guideline for designating councils for rate-capping in the 1987 financial year. (See
Chapter 7, page 160.) Nine Labour authorities were added to the
list already designated, making a total of 20. Sheffield was rate-
capped for the second time, Liverpool was taken off the list. All 20
councils were Labour-controlled with the exception of Tower
Hamlets, which went Liberal in May 1986.[20] Deferred purchase
deals were outlawed from midnight on 22 July, closing a key
loophole in the survival strategy of many authorities, although
anticipation of this move had at least secured existing
arrangements.

The limits of power available to local politics were well and
truly exposed. Winning the argument was not enough in the
short term, and the long term would require even more
determination on the part of creative local authorities as their

prophecy of what could happen at the beginning of the campaign proved increasingly accurate.

The government was determined to take control of local government regardless of legal difficulties and contradictions with past policy statements. On 16 December 1986, Nicholas Ridley conceded in the House of Commons that rate support grant and rate-capping legislation over the previous five years had been incorrectly drafted. Their operation had been unlawful. On 18 December 1986, a bill was published which completely revised the rate-capping criteria, changing the machinery and procedures for determining expenditure levels and rate limits. The bill, to be rushed through Parliament before the 1987–8 financial year, threw local government finance – and particularly those authorities affected by rate-capping – into confusion.

Once again the efforts of the government to use central power to control local government decision making and spending programmes had resulted in chaos. As before, the technicalities ensured that the real impact, particularly on rate-capped authorities, was completely obscured even for specialists in local government matters. The right of appeal to the Secretary of State was to be removed – and with it the ability to make out an individual case – and all authorities were to be dealt with according to a standard formula rather than local circumstances. The bill also removed judicial review of past and present ministerial decisions about allocation of grants and accounting practices (i.e. decisions about which items in local authority accounts are accepted as legitimate in determining net expenditure levels for grant purposes). What had been announced as minor legislation to ratify past decisions became in fact a vehicle for further draconian measures.

In the House of Lords debate Lord Denning trenchantly summed up the consequences of the way in which the Conservative government had used local government finance for political purposes. They had simply acted unconstitutionally, in placing 'the executive above the law':

I have a letter in my hand from two professors of public law and two senior lecturers of University College, London. Their comment on the provisions in the Bill is that:
  'The breadth of protection afforded by this Bill is unprecedented, unnecessary and is contrary to the basic principles of executive accountability under law.'
I have studied what they have said and I endorse their opinions. I should

like to summarise the position. The game is given away in the opening words of the Explanatory and Financial Memorandum:

> 'Relevant expenditure and total expenditure, which are essential elements of the rate support grant and rate limitation systems in England and Wales, have been calculated in a way which conflicts with the legislation concerned.'

To put it bluntly, they have not complied with the law and they admit it. . .

It reminds me of the statement made by Thomas Fuller:

> 'Be you never so high, the law is above you.'[21]

The scale of the legislative assault on local government can partly be measured by the sheer volume. Up to December 1986 there had been 39 bills put before Parliament (including the bill on a Scottish community tax) and four more were in the pipeline before Easter 1987.[22] Not surprisingly some were hasty and misconceived – and this from a government that claimed to be noninterventionist.

Winning the argument had thus not been enough if the party controlling Westminster was prepared to overturn the conventions of democratic politics in Britain and use its constitutional powers to the full and even flout the constitution. Local councils, on the other hand, had balked at the prospect of stepping in unison outside the limits of their constitutional powers. One obvious result of their failure to halt or modify the government's policies was that more cautious and conservative features of local government might now be reasserted. The immediate task was to stop this happening. For the long term they had shown that wide support can be mobilised for a radical alternative to the programme offered by Mrs Thatcher's Conservatives. If this could be the basis of a change of direction nationally then new relations between central and local government might be able to play some part in extending democracy, rather than curtailing it, to grapple with major economic and social problems.

9

No Answer But Your Own

The conflict between central and local government has been fought not over economic or technical issues but over different views of the world. The view that the Conservative Party has put forward since 1979 is that the only way out of Britain's economic problems is to allow market forces full play, for it is only through competition between groups and individuals that we can tap our ability to create wealth. For Margaret Thatcher a market-based approach has a natural logic, being, in her view, in line with 'the grain of human nature'. The Tory view finds it regrettable that in the process of competition the weakest may go to the wall – with the collapse of industry, mass unemployment and widespread poverty. But for them this is inevitable, for in their view it is only through such sacrifices that we will allow the best to rise to the top and thus solve our economic problems. Any approach that balks at such sacrifice and seeks a less devastating means of recovery is for them 'bad housekeeping' – a kind of misguided do-goodery that will lead nowhere. According to this view, democracy rests on the freedom of individuals to act in their own economic interests: the freedom to buy and sell confers the freedom to live the life you choose.

Those who espouse market forces as the only answer to our economic and social problems divest themselves of any responsibility for the outcome. This they do by arguing that it is inevitable that this or that part of the economy or sector of manufacturing is collapsing – given the wage levels, the attitudes of workers and trade unions, the location of specific industries, and the state of the market. Any intervention in the past, they argue, has 'interfered' with the natural activity of the market and distorted the normal influences which would have secured a more prosperous future or allowed the productive base to 'die naturally'. In other words, other governments have been responsible for past failures, but politicians leaving it to the market place are absolved of any responsibility for present unemployment or industrial decline. According to this view, government action would only make things worse – it would distort the natural operation of economic forces which must be allowed to function on their own, unfettered by regulation or social conscience. For example, the whole approach to 'privatisation' not only removes any political responsibility for what happens, but also makes it impossible for there to be a democratic response to the needs of society by removing key areas of decision making from the democratic process.

Since the late 1970s these ideas have been incorporated by the Conservatives into a full programme of political action. Politicians like Rhodes Boyson signalled their intentions very clearly in 1978 when he stated, 'Conservatives must actively work for the welfare state to wither away as personal freedom and independent provision takes its place.' The philosophical grounding for this position has been provided by writers such as Frederik Hayek, who has argued:

This obligation [to be benevolent] can exist only towards particular known people and though in a great society it may be towards people of one's own choice, it cannot be enforced under equal rules for all . . . We can choose to whom we are benevolent and this requires that welfare provision should be privately based outside the state sector.[1]

As an economist and philosopher, Hayek has extolled the virtues of private enterprise as being synonymous with freedoms generally. Together with like-minded rightwing thinkers from around the world who formed the Mont Pelerin Society in 1947 in Switzerland, he has worked systematically since the late 1940s to reverse the tide of welfare and interventionist politics that arose after the Second World War by appealing to the instincts of self-interest that were being played down by others. Thinkers such as Hayek have also gained access to political power in many countries and have used the state machine which they have so readily condemned in the hands of others in what has amounted to a planned strategy to reverse the collective gains of the past century. (Chapters 7 and 8 illustrate the use of central state power against local government in Britain along these lines.) With international finance and transnational corporations only too happy to back the views of Hayek and others, their ideas have gained international influence: the Mont Pelerin Society now claims 500 members in key political or advisory positions in capitalist governments around the world.

This simplistic view of the world has been given massive promotion by the Conservatives and the media, precisely because it denies the possibility of a more egalitarian and democratic alternative. It conveniently ignores evidence in the real world that the free market does not exist. The United States economy owes less to free-market forces than to public expenditure through defence contracts. President Reagan's commitment to the Star Wars project is designed as much to save the US economy at home as it is to secure military ascendancy. Britain has looked to pick up as many crumbs as it can.

According to the democratic-socialist alternative, our economic predicament is indeed serious – there is a world recession and Britain is badly placed historically to face it. However, the solution lies not in a return to late-eighteenth-century liberal notions of economic freedom whereby everyone is 'free' to compete in the marketplace. This view completely fails to take into account the way in which economic power has been developed and is dominated by international finance and the multinationals so that the ability of the individual to influence the world through economic activity is an illusion. As we show in Chapter 2, the collective movements that developed in the nineteenth century were a direct response to the squalor, disease and material degradation that had been wrought precisely by the free operation of the marketplace. Those that witnessed this devastation recognised that it could only be resolved through people working with and for each other in collective action. This led to major reforms – the extension of the franchise, the imposition of regulations over unacceptable conditions of work, and the major public health and housing movements which transformed conditions of life in the industrial cities. Unfortunately, these early reforms were not followed later by an appropriate extension of democracy. For example, although the consolidation of earlier reforms and the new measures which brought the welfare state in 1945 were a major advance, we have indicated that they were not built on fully democratic lines. The long-term consequence of this failure to extend democracy, along with the present economic recession, has been to allow a reassertion in the 1980s of the myth of the marketplace. The Tory Party claims that we are approaching freedom – in their sense of 'free' economic activity – after decades of restrictive state control. In fact, it is the illusion of economic freedom that now threatens to stifle the desire for humane, interdependent cooperation as the only way of developing a decent life for all.

In line with their economic myth, the Tory view sees human nature as essentially individualistic and self-interested. In our view, human nature is more complex and contradictory. It contains both self-interested features and cooperative impulses. Which of these sides flourishes depends on which are supported or crushed by social and political forces. A civilised government must encourage the cooperative instincts in human nature and not just pander to self-interest. We have shown how local politics refutes Hayek's insistence that altruism is a private matter, not part of the political order, and that democracy works when people are given the opportunity to act in the manner he rules out of order, namely to give collectively as well as individually, and to receive in a dignified manner, not as someone who is the subject of private charity handed out to failures. Hayek offers the classic old order – the rich man in his castle, the poor man at his gate – not a democratic and just society.

Basing economic activity on cooperative values rather than unfettered private enterprise is also 'good housekeeping'. It allows us to look at the true cost to the community of different economic policies and actions rather than simply assessing the profit to be made by single individuals and companies in the marketplace – it may be possible, for example, to produce certain goods more cheaply for greater profit, but what are the health costs to the community of bad working conditions? What are the costs to the community of industrial pollution? What is the most sensible use of natural resources – private car ownership or a truly efficient system of public transport? Both can exist together, developed in a balanced fashion. Our discussion of the South Yorkshire transport policy in Chapter 4 shows what dramatic economic as well as social benefits it provided for the community as a whole.

It is clear that these two views of the way forward are rooted in two conflicting sets of interests. The view whereby self-interest is the only fruitful motivation is put forward by those most in a position to gain from it. They may maintain that through their policies the wealth that is currently available to the few will become more accessible to all, but this hardly tallies with the fact that the wealth of the few has been created largely at the expense of the majority – a process that we saw increasingly at work with the ever-growing gap between rich and poor that developed as a consequence of the Tories' social and economic policies.

Equally, it is in the interests of the vast majority of people and of true democracy that ways be found to ensure that the principles of cooperation and mutual aid prevail. It is our only hope of making reasonable standards of living available to the population as a whole and of building a democracy that can challenge those who wield economic power. In our view, anyone who wishes to live in a civilised society must follow this democratic path.

Which view will prevail? Two Conservative terms of office reinforced powerful economic processes which take no more account of deteriorating standards of life for millions in Britain than in Asia, Africa or Latin America. The Conservatives have made sufficient ground in disseminating their views to have induced a sense of hopelessness amongst many people who dislike their policies. There is no powerful and outraged feeling as there was at the end of the Second World War to insist that an alternative can and must be found. This is not surprising since the media overwhelmingly reinforce the basic principles of Conservative propaganda, even if they occasionally criticise their programme on individual issues.

However, there is also evidence that most ordinary people still have an underlying commitment to collective values. As we have seen, opinion polls indicate support for the welfare state and an acceptance that it must be paid for collectively through taxation. The beliefs and values which inspired the growth of the labour movement persist, despite assertions that they have disappeared in modern social conditions. An Essex University study,[2] examining people's aspirations rather than their response to existing political programmes, found that they look for equality and social justice, not the survival of the fittest, that they understand the realities of power which prevent this (without accepting its legitimacy), and support a substantial redistribution of resources.

In 1986 a survey on British social attitudes[3] showed that people were expressing these views more widely than at the time of the 1983 election. Most people wanted more redistribution of resources towards the less well off, more government intervention, an emphasis on reducing unemployment rather than taxes, and greater spending on the welfare state, particularly the health service. The Essex study showed that many people were still sceptical about the possibility of political change but this was because it was so hard in the then climate to imagine an alternative political framework, rather than because they were convinced that the existing order was necessary and right. Because local government has always been more closely connected with people's lives and aspirations, it has been able to develop a different view and when it has done so it has gained great local support and involvement. This is why it was such a threat to the Conservative government and came under such sustained attack.

Lifting barriers to local freedom

Local politics does not have the power to pursue alternative policies independently because local authorities are not sovereign bodies. If there is to be continued movement towards local democracy, there will have to be a shift in the position taken by Westminster vis-à-vis local government. The following pages give a brief account of some of the key steps that need to be taken.

Restrictions on the freedom of local councils to initiate policy in response to the needs of their areas must be lifted. They need to be able to decide levels of local taxation in line with the wishes of their electorate, not the government in power. Local politicians are just as capable of judging what people are willing to pay in rates, and the effect of this taxation on the local economy, as are national politicians. It is for them to decide what resources they should raise beyond the money they receive in government grant.

The present rating system has considerable merits: it is easy to administer and, though anomalies exist, partly due to a failure to update values in England and Wales, it is not as regressive as some other forms of taxation. If heavy manufacturing industry survives in the British economy, its reliance on large premises and equipment which attract heavy rates, as compared with cheaper financial facilities required by financial and hi-tech institutions, will need to be recognised in any revision of the rating system. The importance of retaining the ability to raise an independent source of revenue at local level cannot be overstated. At the very least, it is one way in which multinational companies, in particular, are obliged to make a financial contribution to the community which carries the social costs as well as the benefits of their economic activity. Proposals for a poll tax, whereby only those paying taxes would have a right to a local vote, are an unacceptable return to the principle that the right to vote in a democracy depends on payment of taxes. However, some form of local income tax, along with a revised and modernised rating system, would mean that those not paying rates would make a contribution to spending.

Capital borrowing restrictions should be completely lifted: local authorities should be allowed to operate on the same basic principles as the private sector, except where government use the Public Works Loan Board or other such mechanisms to make capital available at lower interest rates for public housing, education, social services, environmental health and essential services. In this way, government could promote particular policies and economic regeneration without central dictation. Public and private enterprise would then be on an equal footing.

There is no satisfactory economic or social justification for restricting public investment whilst allowing private spending to continue without restraint. The issue is not simply one of private profit, it is whether an investment brings financial return, as it did with British Gas and British Telecom when they were publicly owned, or whether there are social and economic benefits, which can be demonstrated, as in the case of South Yorkshire's transport policy in Chapter 4. Whatever impact there might be on the economy by raising funds for investment in particular projects will be the same for private as well as public investment proposals. The notion that the two separate spheres of the economy, public and private, have to be sharply distinguished has been artificially created by people politically opposed to democratic and collective ways of achieving prosperity. The question is not how to separate public and private use of scarce resources but rather how we reach decisions about them so that we have control over our lives, maintaining liberty, freedom and personal responsibility.

Similarly, legal restraints on trading should be removed and local authorities be allowed to use their in-house services such as accounting, personnel administration and purchasing power to reduce the costs of the goods and services they produce. Restrictions placed on direct works departments by the Local Government Planning and Land Act of 1980 deliberately placed local government at a disadvantage vis-à-vis private industry where large companies can spread their costs and prices across different sectors of activity. Legal limitation on municipal trading and enterprise has no economic or social justification. It discourages innovation and imagination which are then seen as characteristics of the private sector alone. Public and private sectors should be subject to the same law if they operate in the commercial field. Equally, if public authorities decide not to act according to the commercial practices of market competition in providing services and facilities, they should be free to do so, if there is widespread local political support.

Clearly, however, local government is not a separate sphere of the economy. We need a new relationship between local and central government in which both can cooperate in creating and carrying out policies. Some idea of the kind of system needed can be seen in the present requirement on local authorities to draw up housing investment programmes or transport policies. Instead of being the means by which local government can be tied down – through controls on capital allocation or revenue spending – the process should be turned on its head, elected councils becoming the means by which coherent industrial and economic programmes are built into plans for the national distribution of resources. There would then be a requirement on local government to develop – with their local industry, trade unions and community organisations – the economic and industrial plans that need to be fed into national planning.

As we saw in Chapter 6, Britain's post-school education and training necessary for the technological future leave much to be desired. Some local councils have begun to plan for our real educational needs, but much remains to be done. The education people received in the armed forces in the Second World War played a major part in building the determination necessary to find an alternative to prewar conditions. Local government must now be given the resources to provide the 'education for life' that will enable people to extend ideas of democratic involvement beyond mere political rhetoric. Comprehensive, post-school education (tertiary level) could make it possible to share resources and expertise between sectors of further and higher education and provide opportunities throughout life for training and retraining. This kind of provision has placed other countries far ahead of Britain in making the fullest use of the human resources within the nation. Local training plans should be drawn up in each locality and integrated into a wider national programme. Such plans should involve all those concerned with present education and training schemes, local councils acting as the catalyst. Plans should include courses on improving the delivery of public services, on community and consumer awareness, and on extending democracy at all levels. The establishment of a network of management, marketing and business centres must be a high priority, including the development of skills in planning, and managing democratically run public enterprise locally and nationally. They should include courses of training, based on experience of the best practice in improving public services, promoting and responding to community and consumer awareness, and extending democracy at all levels.

Difficult decisions about restructuring industry and commerce have inevitably to be made as demands and product methods change. However, it should not be left to a remote central government to decide who should bear the costs or benefit – local government is in many ways in a better position to weigh up all the factors involved in restructuring local industry and commerce. Using local knowledge as well as traditional financial accountancy measures, it should be possible to undertake a 'social audit' which looks not simply at the financial profitability of a certain business under threat, but also at the benefits for the local economy of keeping the enterprise going over a given period of time, as opposed to the total cost of closing it. Such an audit would reveal the often hidden costs of closing a business, for example, the tax revenue lost from employees, and the benefits to be paid out as a result of their loss of employment. In this way a proper judgement could be made on whether it would cost the community and the industry sector more to close the business than to maintain it. All closures involving more than a given number of employees would have to be notified to the council whose area was affected, as well as to the Department of Employment for redundancy purposes. If the local authority decided to undertake such an audit, it would need to initiate an inquiry. It would give notice to the business concerned and would have to complete the audit within government criteria, by a specified date. Initiation of an inquiry would halt the closure for an agreed period.

Even if a business had to be closed, a social audit would make it possible to minimise financial and social damage to the community – for example, by showing what could be gained from a phased rather than an immediate closure. Where closure cannot be avoided, the concept of redundancy payments, at present given to individuals, could be extended to the local community, taking into account the economic and social consequences of industrial change.

Communities should not be faced with the choice of either attempting to resist change or accepting a decline in their quality of life. Areas which have suffered economic decline might be allocated resources to develop better levels of health care, and also recreational and other community services, instead of allowing resources to follow market demand in more prosperous regions. If the health service were democratised by bringing it into local government, as Aneurin Bevan envisaged, it would be possible for local authorities to tailor local health provision to the needs of their particular community. Economic planning based on an understanding of local needs could also reverse the principle of the Thatcher government's 'Manpower Watch', which was designed to hold down or reduce numbers employed in the public services, creating instead a Manpower Drive' based on agreed areas of priority between local and central government. The functions of the Manpower Services Commission would then be democratised by incorporation into local government planning.

If the economy is to be revived on a democratic basis, spending needs to be properly planned in the long term. Local government spending has too often been used as an immediate stimulant to the economy, for example, just before an election: increased spending, particularly on capital projects such as roads and housing, produces a short burst of employment and economic activity solely to win votes. Crash programmes to revitalise inner-city areas, housing and the infrastructure of basic services are an obvious way to expand economic activity and reduce unacceptable levels of unemployment. But unless well-informed proposals for medium- and long-term investment, combining public and private sectors, are included through local and national plans for key sectors in the economy, short-term economic expansion will bring even greater problems than it has done periodically over recent decades: increased short-term activity leads to a demand for goods and equipment that cannot be met by British manufacturing in its present rundown state, so that they have to be imported from abroad leading to an even worse balance of payments crisis. Import controls alone are no solution: they only produce shortages. What we need is a proper system of long-term planning to make maximum use of local and national resources and labour power so as to begin to reconstruct British industry, enabling it to supply more of the demand that comes from economic growth.

We need greater accountability from the dozens of regional and national quangos which use public funds in a variety of ways without any direct answerability to the general public. Public utilities such as the water supply, which used to be democratically accountable, energy-supplying industries, and a variety of government departments and agencies, should also be directly responsible to the public they serve. The large sums of money which they use have a major impact on local and regional economies. This spending needs to be properly integrated into plans for economic regeneration. It is not possible to spell out here the precise structures that are needed for greater accountability and coordination but they must be the central objectives in reshaping local and regional government for the future.

A liberating democracy

The point of liberating local democracy is not just to bring about decentralisation and devolution. Local politics also has a role to play in vital contemporary issues, for example acting as a countervailing force to international finance and influencing the introduction of new technology. The alliance between the political Right and international finance totally discounts local government and local politics. New technology is introduced with the sole aim of increasing profits, not for the benefit of society in general – though the consumer may obtain cheaper goods, this is too often achieved at the expense of workers' conditions or the decline of whole communities. Large transnational companies are able to coerce local workforces into cooperation through their power to invest or withdraw investment. They divide and rule – nation against nation, community against community, workforce against workforce. New technology is thus perceived as inherently threatening, though resistance against it is often fruitless, leading to unsatisfactory, unplanned compromise or to the defeat of whole communities facing overwhelming odds, as we saw in the mining industry in 1985.

New technology need not of itself constitute a threat – properly planned, it can lead, for example, to better working conditions and, through new information systems, allow local industry and authorities to operate more effectively in a worldwide market. It can also be applied to the improvement of health, educational and social services if the political will is there. But this all depends on the ability to challenge the collective organisation of international financial interests. Local authorities working together can oppose divide-and-rule tactics, offering an opportunity for communities to cooperate in building economic plans and investment programmes and generating popular support for them. No reforming government that wishes to deal with the present crisis will be able to move forward without this kind of internal solidarity. During the Depression, active, oppositional local politics helped to fuel the indignation which eventually swept a reforming Labour Party to power in 1945. Despite the limitations of that Labour government's attempts to control the market and overcome business and professional opposition, there was popular agreement that it was moving in the right direction, and the party increased its electoral support right up to the very vote which brought narrow defeat in 1951. Its greatest failure, however, was to extend the rigidities of wartime planning into peacetime and to structure ownership in terms of bureaucratic national boards whose members included people opposed to the whole notion of social ownership. There was very little way in which the broader community could make a collective contribution to the operation of public ownership, either as workers in public enterprises and public services, or as consumers.

Without people's direct involvement in their own welfare state, there was no means of defending and improving it where it fell short. Instead the boom conditions of the 1950s enabled the Conservatives to turn people's attention to improvements in individual and family living conditions through increased personal consumption. Harold Macmillan was able to tell people that they had never had it so good at the very moment at which the seeds of future problems were being sown through lack of investment in industry and the welfare state. What is required now, therefore, is not a system of rigid state planning but much greater intervention in the market. There should be no imposition of a model which has to be adhered to, but a framework of regulation which ensures that important values override purely market factors, as we indicate in policies towards contract compliance or health and the environment (Chaps. 5 and 6). Local government is already seeking ways of doing this: people active in local democracy during the 1980s were not merely prepared to wait for the Labour Party to be in control at Westminster, but have gone ahead on their own in developing alternative policies.

What has emerged from the practice of local politics is a view of planning which rejects a rigid framework involving a neat hierarchy of stages – local, regional and national – but instead considers a variety of combinations between sectors and localities within the national economy. Some localities may develop products that are the basis of industrial activity elsewhere, and planning takes place jointly. Or local policies may create a demand for products being developed elsewhere, for example dehumidifiers in council houses or forms of public transport, or there might be joint planning of production of materials – engineering, micro-technology, software. Planning here is conceived more in the way an international conglomerate would plan its sectors and areas of activity than as the result of a state bureaucracy. This means local politics has to have an active role so that the maximum creativity can be released within the nation.

A view has therefore emerged that the future of our cities and regions should not be placed too firmly in the hands of parliamentary legislators. A new partnership between central and local government is needed for which local politics must be freed from restrictions and enabled to play a constructive part in national policy making. (This is not to forget the central significance of Parliament which needs a reformed and modernised legislative system.) It would not be the first time or the only country in which local democracy has helped to shape events. We have seen at many points in this book the contribution which it has made in the past. The example of Mondragon in the Spanish Basque country has much to teach us.

In the early 1950s the Basque region of northern Spain was refused self-determination by Franco. Under the leadership of Father José Maria Arizmenti, a local Catholic priest, an alternative to submission emerged in the area surrounding the town of Mondragon, which set out to develop local resources through a system of interdependence within the community. An enclave of democracy was thus created within the dictatorship. By the early 1980s, 18,000 manufacturing jobs had been created in modern, well-designed cooperatives. Over the years schools, which taught the Basque language frowned on by the state, were opened with the resources generated. Housing and welfare facilities, shopping and leisure activities, were also provided by the cooperatives. The Caja Laboral Popular, or 'people's bank', provided the financial base and the business expertise to underpin the operation. The bank existed only because local people put their money in it, and its entire objective was the success of local enterprise. If the cooperative failed, the bank failed; if the bank collapsed, industry and enterprise were at risk. The people's money was invested in the people. Each element was inter-dependent on the actions and social responsibility of others. The Mondragon project could not be transferred directly to Britain, but it does show that people can create social and economic policies for themselves on a local and regional base, even in the most unfavourable circumstances. Setting up city or regional banks could be an important contribution to developing this economic and social culture in Britain. Extending the concept of building societies in order to create industrial funding agencies which would provide resources for wealth creation could be an important new initiative. None of this will be possible without democratic control of financial institutions as a whole.

Contradictions and difficulties

Our intention is not to idealise local government. Much needs changing: a great deal of local government is bedevilled by bureaucracy, paternalism and inertia. Long-guaranteed party majorities – whether of the Right or Left – have often led to the emergence of party cliques or bosses who take little account of the needs of the community. Such cliques and their associated pressure groups – whether in business, the professions or unions – can become the predominant channel for influencing policy or distributing resources. Corruption is usually too strong a word to describe the result, but there have been recent examples from both the Left and Right where there is no other term to use.

Council employees can also be a barrier to effective local government. We have perhaps given some of them less credit than they deserve, but many officers still reflect the old social attitude that working in the town hall is somehow better and more genteel than working in industry. Long-standing habits of keeping the system going rather than improving it, and narrow definitions of professional responsibility, may reduce account-ability and responsiveness. Even among more committed offi-cers, professional detachment may mean too little account is taken of the need to produce results for the people they serve. Many officers and workers at every level do engage in self-protecting restrictive practices or abuse the power they hold when people depend on them for essential services and resources. Such problems can be found in all forms of organisa-tion, including private industry: in our view, they can only be overcome by working democratically and not simply by attempting to satisfy customers by replacing public services with competitive private enterprise.

We have shown how local politics has pointed towards a more liberating and enabling form of state and that limited achievements have been possible even under a hostile Conservative government. It must also be said that, just as real progress cannot be made without an appropriate national political framework, so it is true that the atttitudes and actions of workers and trade unions are decisive factors. There has to be a continuing and evident disproof of the radical liberal 'right wing' caricature of the welfare state – that it 'will tend to set up institutions that help the middle class more than the working class, and give a high standard of service to no one very much. It will set up institutions which will serve the interests of the men and women who work in them better than they serve their customers or clients.'[4] Trade unions and professional associations must assume the political responsibility for devising ways to defend their members' interests while at the same time promoting the most committed and effective service to the customer.[5] There is evidence, as we have indicated, that some local government trade unions are addressing this matter seriously within the framework of national and local politics, and that some local authorities are responding without seeking to exploit their bargaining position as employers. Democracy has to be built, it is not handed out on a plate.

What part should the Labour Party play in local politics? We do not advocate a 'vanguard' party which goes out ahead of the people and seizes power on its behalf. Democracy requires active dialogue. Political parties must be prepared to speak out and take a lead, but no party has a special right to be heard or followed. When in power locally the Labour Party will have to take decisions that are initially unpopular in some quarters, including with its own supporters, if it is to promote the kind of changes we propose. When the Labour Party has failed to engage the support of people for radical change it is because it has forgotten the source of its strength and legitimacy in the community and workplace, and not presented there the values of democratic socialism, as distinct from other options open to people as they go about their lives. Responding to what matters to most people is a prerequisite for promoting the interests of those who face specific disadvantage or require special facilities and support.

The party's procedures must be democratic and it must be capable of engaging the interests of other groups who are keen to play a part in developing democracy. Where there are differences of view, the party's task is to make its position clear and to ensure it has a mandate to continue its policies, not to disregard opposition. The party provides a focus for political aspirations and is one important means of obtaining and directing through the electoral process the resources of the state which belong to the people. There are those who argue that the Labour Party and labour movement are no longer, if they ever were, vehicles for change. This hardly tallies with the way in which they have been able in recent years to provide a powerful impetus for creative local government.

But there is urgent need for a new lead to be taken. In our view, the mounting attacks on local democracy are part of a wider assault on democracy in general and we will need great determination and insight to confront this erosion of hard-won freedoms. If local politics is to begin to address the problems facing Britain, it must be on the basis of a commitment to democratic socialism which recognises the equal importance of 'democracy, liberty and fraternity'. It is not surprising that the last of these tends to figure less in public political debate than the others, because it stands for the collective values which present the most direct challenge to the values of the marketplace. Democracy is the only secure basis for a popular commitment to change. The present imperfections of institutions which claim to be democratic should cause us to move further forward. Active democracy, whether in the community or at work, has to replace reliance on arm's-length representation. Politicians in parliament and town hall are necessary to act as enablers, advocates and sometimes protectors, where people suffer obvious injustice; but they are not the sole guardians of democracy.

We do not feel that the state should be the only means whereby people in need can find help and support. Firstly, there is clearly no way in which the state will ever be able to provide for every social and economic need of groups or individuals. Secondly, dependence on the state alone does nothing to foster a sense of social responsibility among people towards each other. It is difficult, if not impossible, to relate in any personal sense to others through the state by relying on the machinery of taxation and benefits alone. Collective community support, of the kind formerly seen in so many towns and villages, is vital, alongside formal state provision. What we need is to do things together, rather than having them done for us, to remove the conditions of poverty and dependence rather than to trap people in them, and thus to develop a sense of supporting and being supported, with structures which foster affinity to those around us and a sense of identity with the community in which we live. The strength which comes from mutual support and from being personally valued through membership of and affinity with a local community should not be dismissed as irrelevant to modern times if that is how people want to live. Equally, the values associated with community imply more than merely local ties.

A recognition of the rights of the individual and the importance of personal freedom is vital to prevent majority views oppressing dissent and personal self-fulfilment. Without liberty we live in a dangerous and distorted world. There is no perfect state of affairs and liberty is as much an ideal as a possible reality, but it is travelling, not simply arriving, that should distinguish democratic socialists. Unlike the Thatcher-led Conservatives we do not believe that the end justifies the means in politics. They belong to a set of internationally organised activists – 'zealots'[6] in Margaret Thatcher's words – who believe that unemployment, low wages, insecure and temporary jobs, and destroyed communities are a necessary price to pay for their particular notion of a 'healthy economy', and they use state power to force their ideas on the people.

Liberty means the free choice of opportunities which democracy can make possible: the freedom to work and to give, as well as to receive; the freedom to choose a way of life that allows us to develop as fully as we wish and are able to achieve. Liberty is the right to be what you want to be, against the insistence of others, whether the state or the conformity of the prevailing norm. Liberty enables you to be alone while remaining a social being. Liberty provides rights for the individual, ensures tolerance of differences but requires intolerance of oppressive, divisive dogma. Liberty offers the right to be involved in political activity with the freedom to choose not to be, which is the contribution of 'fraternity' to effective democracy.

Democratic socialism does not seek to impose conformity and sameness, but recognises that freedom of choice and the liberty to be oneself come only when basic inequalities and discriminatory attitudes or actions are eliminated.

Both individual and communal rights have to succeed against

the interests of property and finance. Equality, justice and fair treatment, together with freedom from fear, are the rights of every citizen. Neither accident of birth nor the accumulation of personal wealth entitle people to undue privilege and arbitrary control over the lives and wellbeing of others.

In a world where individuals fend for themselves and possess power only when they control wealth and property, social morality, democracy and liberty can only be spoken of in a vacuum. Only with collective action do individuals, vulnerable and isolated on their own, turn their weakness into strength, displaying the characteristics of social human beings in caring for and supporting each other while defending and protecting their material interests. From the tribe, the village, the neighbour-hood, the town, we have moved into an era of sophisticated technology in which the fragmentation and disintegration of society can only be reversed by devising a collective response which shares prosperity and recognises needs which must be met as a community. These values are as relevant for maintaining a civilised society in prosperous suburbs or rural villages as they are in inner-city areas and declining industrial towns. They offer hope to the dispossessed, to minorities and to those facing extreme forms of oppression or discrimination, but also hope to everyone who believes the planet has a future worth living in. The choice is ours: defending democracy entails extending it, not merely holding the line.

You tell us

It looks bad for our cause,
The darkness gets deeper. The powers get less.
Now, after we worked for so many years,
We are in a more difficult position than at the start.

But the enemy stands there, stronger than ever before.
His powers appear to have grown. He has taken on an
aspect of invincibility.

We, however, have made mistakes; there is no denying it.
Our numbers are dwindling.
Our slogans are in disarray. The enemy has twisted
Part of our words beyond recognition.

What is now false of what we said:
Some or all?

Whom do we still count on? Are we just left over, thrown out
of the living stream? Shall we remain behind,
Understanding no one and understood by none?

Have we got to be lucky?
This you ask. Expect
No other answer than your own.

(Bertolt Brecht: 'To a Waverer')[7]

Notes

Introduction

1 But see Simon Mabey, 'Local Government Change', *Economic Affairs*, July–September 1984, a product of one of the radical right-wing think tanks we describe in Chapter 5.
2 F. Wheen, *The Battle for London*, Pluto Press, London, 1985.
3 M. Parkinson, *Liverpool on the Brink*, Policy Journals, 1985.
4 South-East Economic Development Strategies Association (SEEDS). The authorities in this association are: Basildon, Brighton, Cambridge, Crawley, Harlow, Oxford, Stevenage, Thurrock.

Chapter 1   The Challenge to Democracy

1 Conservative Party Manifesto, 1979.
2 *North–South: a Programme for Survival*, Report of the Independent Commission on International Development Issues, Pan Books, London, 1980, pp. 46–7.
3 W. Rodney, *How Europe Underdeveloped Africa*, Bogle L'Ouverture, London, 1976, p. 31.
4 André Gunter Frank, 'Taxation Without Representation and Security', *South*, September 1986, pp. 64–5.
5 A. Ganhar, *Talking about Development*, Third World Foundation, London, 1983, pp. iii–iv.
6 *Employment Gazette*, January 1987; Sheffield Employment Factsheet, January 1987.
7 Michael Meacher MP, press release, 15 July 1987.
8 Philip Abrams and Richard Brown, eds, *UK Society: Work, Urbanism and Inequality*, Weidenfeld & Nicolson, London, 1984, p. 40.
9 *Faith in the City*, Report of the Archbishop of Canterbury's Commission on Urban Priority Areas, the Popular Version, Christian Action, London, 1985, p. 3.
10 National Economic Development Committee, HMSO, London, 1963, para 39.

11 See J. K. Galbraith, *The Affluent Society*, Hamish Hamilton, London, 1958. The book was originally written about the United States, but the relevance of Galbraith's argument to British society was increasingly recognised during the 1960s.

12 Anthony Crosland, *The Future of Socialism*, Jonathan Cape, London, 1956.

13 Conservative Party Manifesto, 1983, p. 7.

14 Iron and Steel Statistics Bureau, Country Books, 1984.

15 See A. Altschuler, M. Anderson, D. Jones and J. Wormack, *The Future of the Automobile*, Allen & Unwin, London, 1984.

16 J. Prior, *A Balance of Power*, Hamish Hamilton, London, 1986.

17 Quoted in Sheffield Employment Factsheet, May 1985.

18 There is also considerable organisation and constructive action, see A. Sivanandan, *A Different Hunger*, Pluto Press, London, 1985.

19 Hansard, 6 December 1984; M. Hough and R. Mayhew, *The British Crime Survey: First Report, 1983*; R. Kinsey, *Taking Account of Crime*, HMSO, London, 1985; Merseyside County Council, *Merseyside Crime and Police Survey*, 1985; Labour Weekly 20 March 1987.

20 Jorgan Riber Christenson, *The National Front: Fascism in Britain*, Vejle, 1982, p. 34.

21 Ian McGregor, *The Enemy Within*, Collins, London, 1986.

22 Lord Avebury et al., letter to the *Guardian*, 22 February 1984.

23 We thank Colin Thunhurst for this precise information.

24 The following report is from the *Independent*, 24 March 1987.

25 Clive Ponting, *The Right to Know*, Sphere Books, London, 1985, p. 4.

Chapter 2   The Roots of Active Local Government

1 S. and B. Webb, *The Development of English Local Government 1689–1835*, Oxford University Press, 1963, pp. 129–30.

2 'Of the 385 councillors and aldermen who held office in the years 1843–93, 151 were manufacturers in the staple trades, 49 were professional men and 26 were brewers, publicans or builders.' S. Pollard, *A History of Labour in Sheffield*, Liverpool University Press, 1959. 'The Local Government of towns is almost entirely in the hands of shopkeepers and professional men.' G. C. Broderick, 'Local Government in England', *Local Government and Taxation in the United Kingdom, A Series of Essays*, ed. J. W. Probyn, The Cobden Club, London, 1882, p. 59.

3 R. Tressell, *The Ragged Trousered Philanthropists*, Lawrence & Wishart, London, 1955, p. 207.

4 J. Chamberlain, *Speeches*, ed. C. W. Boyd, vol. 1, Constable, London, 1914, pp. 163–4.

5 In a letter to Earl Fitzwilliam quoted by H. Keeble Hawson in *Sheffield, The Growth of a City 1893–1926*, J. W. Northend, Sheffield, 1968, p. 1.

6 An interesting parallel with present times arose when the courts objected to the city council using rates income for the promotion of parliamentary bills to democratise the water industry.

7 H. Keeble Hawson, op. cit., p. 17.

8 In 1888 the total local debt was over £181 million and nearly £10 million was paid as interest and sinking fund (*The Local Government Board Report*, 1887–8, section 5550, p. 436). Of course not all this money was spent on gas. It also covered such municipal services as water, trams, ferries, libraries etc.

9 *Board of Trade Journal*, January 1889, pp. 76–8.

10 The following account draws on B. Keith-Lucas, ed., *The History of Local Government in England*, Macmillan, London, 1970; B. Keith-Lucas, *English Local Government in the Nineteenth and Twentieth Century*, Historical Association, London, 1977; and B. Keith-Lucas and P. G. Richards, *A History of Local Government in the Twentieth Century*, Allen & Unwin, London, 1978.

11 R. B. Suthers, *Mind Your Own Business. The Case for Municipal Management*, Clarion Press, London, 1905, p. 12.

12 E. P. Hennock, *Fit and Proper Persons, Ideal and Reality in Nineteenth-Century Urban Government*, Studies in Urban History, vol. 2, Montreal, 1973, p. 175.

13 J. Chamberlain, *Speeches*, ed. C. W. Boyd, vol. 1, Constable, London, 1914, pp. 163–4.

14 The following account follows B. Simon, *Education and the Labour Movement*, chapters 4 and 6, except where there are specific references.

15 S. Pollard, op. cit., p. 114.

16 Miriam Lord, *Margaret McMillan in Bradford*, Margaret McMillan Fellowship and the University of London, 1957, p. 9.

17 W. Ashworth, *The Genesis of Modern British Town Planning*, Routledge & Kegan Paul, London, 1954, p. 191.

18 S. Pollard, op. cit., pp. 103–4.

19 *Sheffield Year Book and Record*, 1906, p. 150; *Sheffield Telegraph*, 27 January 1906.

20 John Burns, *London*, 17 February 1898, p. 19. The first piece of Conservative local government legislation after 1979 was the Local Government Planning and Land Act with

measures to undermine the effective operation of direct labour organisations as a democratic public service.

21 *Sheffield Year Book and Record*, 1905, p. 11.

22 G. A. Almond and S. Verba, *The Civic Culture*, Princeton University Press, 1963.

Chapter 3   1945: Labour Rejects Local Politics

1 P. A. Tyan, 'Poplarism 1894–1930' in P. Thane, ed., *The Origins of British Social Policy*, Croom Helm, London, p. 78. This is a particularly useful account of the events on which we have based our argument, along with Noreen Branson's *Poplarism 1919–1925*, Lawrence & Wishart, London, 1979.

2 Ibid., p. 59.

3 Ibid., p. 76.

4 N. Branson and M. Heinemann, *Britain in the Nineteen-Thirties*, Panther, London, 1971.

5 N. Branson, *Poplarism 1919–1925*, Lawrence & Wishart, London, 1979.

6 Arthur Greenwood, in 'Six Years of Labour Rule in Sheffield 1926–32', p. 1 (unpublished).

7 Ibid., p. 3.

8 Ibid., p. 10.

9 Ibid., p. 11.

10 Ibid., p. 12.

11 Ibid., p. 32.

12 The following draws on a paper by Michael Ward to History Workshop 15, Brighton Polytechnic, 8 December 1981; and B. Barker, *Labour in London*, George Routledge & Sons, London, 1946.

13 Quoted in M. Ward, op. cit.

14 B. Barker, op. cit., p. 103.

15 K. Young and P. L. Garside, *Metropolitan London: Politics and Urban Change, 1837–1981*, Studies in Urban History No. 6, 1982.

16 B. Barker, op. cit.,p. 149.

17 M. Ward, op. cit., p. 3.

18 For example, W. A. Robson, *Local Government in Crisis*, 2nd edn, London: Allen & Unwin, 1968; Tony Byrne, *Local Government in Britain*, 3rd edn, Penguin, London, 1985.

19 M. Foot, *Aneurin Bevan 1945–1960*, Granada, London, 1973, p. 69.

20 Ibid., p. 70.

21 Ibid., p. 71, quoting Bevan.

22 Beatrix Campbell, *Wigan Pier Revisited*, Virago, London, 1984, p. 36.

23 Aneurin Bevan, 'Local Government Management of Hospitals Is Best', *Municipal Journal*, 12 March 1954.
24 Foot, op. cit.

Chapter 4   Public Transport: Community, Freedom and Choice

1 House of Lords decision, Bromley *v.* GLC 1981, in which the Lords decided that the GLC was failing in its 'fiduciary duty' by 'misusing' ratepayers' money.
2 See note 1.
3 Transport Act, 1968.
4 Merseyside MCC *v.* Great Universal Stores, 19 February 1982.
5 *Facts and Figures*, South Yorkshire Passenger Transport Executive, 1984.
6 Ibid.
7 A similar argument for operations in urban conditions has been used in London to counter plans to replace conductors and open-door buses with one-person operated vehicles. In central London this increases boarding time fourfold, and in heavy traffic makes a significant extension to journey time. (*London's Buses – Back on the Road*, GLC, 1985.)
8 Ibid.
9 *Jane's Urban Transport Systems*, Jane's Publishing Co. Ltd, London, 1982.
10 Leyland-Lancashire, *Into the Future*, 1985
11 *London's Buses – Back on the Road*, GLC, 1985.
12 Tinsley Park Multi-Union Committee, 'Tinsley Steel Campaign – 1985', 1985.
13 *Morning Telegraph*, 18 September 1984.
14 Department of Transport press notice No. 476, 30 October 1985.
15 Roger Stott MP (Wigan), Hansard, 10 February 1986, p. 917.
16 Sheffield City Council, 'Trapped at Home', 12 July 1986, p. 4.

Chapter 5   Local Politics and the People

1 *Labour Research*, February 1986.
2 See the discussion of the London Industrial Strategy in Chapter 6.
3 Jimmy Reid, *Reflections of a Clyde-built Man*, Condor, London, 1986, referring to 1971.
4 Lucas Corporate Plan, presented to management on 22 January 1976.

5 See, for example, 'Women Against Pit Closures', Barnsley, 1985.
6 The range of activity encompasses single-parent groups, tenants' and residents' groups, mother and toddler groups, environmental groups, women's refuges, anglers' groups, neighbourhood action groups, alternative Saturday schools in the black community, advice centres, unemployment groups, pensioners' action groups, claimants' unions.
7 Beatrix Campbell, op. cit., p. 59.
8 Paul Corrigan, 'The Sound of Listening', *New Socialist*, January 1985.
9 Cleveland Research and Intelligence Unit, *Local Government Chronicle*, 8 August 1984. See also Derbyshire County Council, 'Attitudes to Derbyshire County Council and Its Services', by MORI (Nov.–Dec. 1984).
10 Walsall Labour Party Report, 1981.
11 Hackney Tenants' Association, 'Going Local', December 1984.
12 *Neighbourhood News*, 1986.
13 Sheffield Health Care Strategy Group, *Could We Care Less? Report of the People's Campaign for Health*, 1986, p. 39.
14 Ibid., p. 23.
15 *Sheffield Star*, 22 May 1986.
16 *Yorkshire Post* investigation, 30 June 1986.
17 Specialist at High Royds Hospital, Leeds, quoted in *Yorkshire Post*, 30 June 1986.
18 Institute of Local Government Studies, 'The Future and Organisation of Local Government: Study Paper No. 4. Leisure', John Benington and Judy White, 1986.
19 Brixton Recreation Centre Report, 1985.

Chapter 6   Local Politics and the Economy

1 Hansard, 28 April 1909.
2 Michael Ward, 'Labour's Capital Gains. The GLC Experience', *Marxism Today*, December 1983.
3 *The London Industrial Strategy*, GLC, 1985.
4 Ibid., pp. 58–9.
5 Ibid., p. 19.
6 Department of Employment and Economic Development, Sheffield City Council, *Steel in Crisis*, 1986.
7 Paul Crawford, Steven Fothergill and Sarah Monk, *The Effect of Rates on the Location of Employment*, Department of Land Economy, Cambridge University, 1985.
8 *Sheffield Jobs Audit*, June 1985, commissioned by Sheffield City Council from Labour Research Department, Services to

Community and Trade Unions (SCAT), Birmingham Trade Union Research Centre.

 9 *Putting the Rates to Work*, Labour Research Department Publications, 1985.
10 Ibid., p. 6.
11 Ibid., p. 7.
12 Association of Metropolitan Authorities, 'Spending Works – Improving the Economy by Investing in Local Services', May 1985.
13 M. Binks and J. Coyne, *The Birth of Enterprise*, Institute of Economic Affairs, London, 1953.
14 Haringey Borough Council, *School Meals Campaign Newsletter*, No. 2, January 1986.
15 NUPE, 'Privatisation of School Meals in Haringey', 1986.
16 *Economist*, 4 August 1984.
17 S. Duncan and M. Goodwin, 'The Local State and Local Economic Policy', *Policy and Politics*, vol. 13, No. 3.
18 F. W. Taylor, *Scientific Management*, p. 121.
19 SCAT, *Coming Out From Under the Carpet*, April 1985.
20 H. Braverman, *Labor and Monopoly Control*, Monthly Review Press, New York, 1974, pp. 112–113.
21 Sheffield City Council, Standing Order 40(b).
22 GLC, *The London Industrial Strategy*, 1985, p. 61.
23 Newham Docklands Forum, *People's Plan for the Royal Docks*, Foreword, 1983.
24 *Value for People* (pamphlet) published by Popular Planning Project, Clapham-Battersea Adult Education Institute, 1986.
25 K. J. Coutts et al., *British Economy: Recent History and Medium-Term Prospects*, Department of Applied Economics, Cambridge, 1986.

Chapter 7   Turning the Screw

 1 Patrick Jenkin, House of Commons debate on the Rates Act, Report stage, 28 March 1984.
 2 'Local Government in England – Government Proposals for Reorganisation', HMSO, London, 1971.
 3 Quoted in 'Economic Myths and the Attack on the Welfare State', Society of Civil and Public Servants and Civil Service Union Briefing, February 1985, p. 5.
 4 Government statistics, White Papers on public expenditure, 1986.
 5 The part of government which adjusted the rateable resources of an area, based on their rateable values, up to a nationally determined average.

6 G. Jones and J. Stewart, *The Case for Local Government*, Allen & Unwin, London, 1983.

7 Rate support grant settlement 1976–7, Department of the Environment circular 129/75, para 28.

8 Local Authority Expenditure 1976/78, Department of the Environment circular 84/76, para 10, August 1976.

9 Jones and Stewart, op. cit.

10 Committee stage, 1 April 1980.

11 Authorities rate-capped for the financial year 1985–86 were the London boroughs of Islington, Camden, Hackney, Brent, Southwark, Lambeth, Lewisham and Greenwich; the ILEA and the GLC; Merseyside and South Yorkshire county council; Sheffield Metropolitan District Council; Basildon, Leicester, Portsmouth and Thamesdown non-metropolitan district councils.

For the financial year 1986–87 Brent, Leicester, Portsmouth and Sheffield were removed from the list, and Newcastle and Liverpool added to it. The GLC, South Yorkshire and Merseyside had been abolished and the ILEA was treated like a joint board which was rate-capped when it picked up those duties of the metropolitan counties and the GLC that were not reallocated to other authorities.

For the financial year 1987–88 Brent, Brighton, Middlesborough, Newham, Gateshead, North Tyneside, Sheffield and Tower Hamlets were added to the list and Liverpool was removed.

12 R. Kline and J. Mallaber, *Whose Value, Whose Money*, Local Government Information Unit and Birmingham Trade Union Resource Centre.

13 A. Johnson et al, Dudley Council Ltd, Lookonit Publishing, Birmingham, 1984.

Chapter 8   Resistance: The Campaign Against Rate-Capping

1 M. Loughlin, M. D. Gelford, K. Young, eds, *Half a Century of Municipal Decline 1935–1985*, Foreword by J. A. G. Griffith, Allen & Unwin, London, 1985, p. xii.

2 *Hansard*, 10 February 1987, p. 581.

3 'In reality virtually everything Labour has achieved has been achieved by using the law, by governing in Parliament . . . And any odd hint that parliamentary government can or should be changed other than through the ballot box is unacceptable. Labour in Parliament cannot hint at, incline towards or acquiesce in illegality as a policy in local government.' Jack Cunningham, Press Gallery lunch, 16 November 1984.

4 Association of Metropolitan Authorities, Association of County Councils, Association of District Councils, Association of London Authorities (some still remaining in the London Boroughs Association) and the Confederation of Scottish Local Authorities. The size and unconstitutional nature of the Conservative challenge to local democracy moved these organisations into a position of criticism and opposition.

5 See M. Parkinson, *Liverpool on the Brink*, Policy Journals, 1985, particularly Chapter 2.

6 We do not consider Liverpool to have been involved in the local government practice described in this book as we indicate later in this chapter.

7 Frances Morrell, as leader, had never been happy about the strategy. She had not pressed her point at national meetings until the stage when she publicly dissociated herself from the policy.

8 National Executive Committee statement to Labour Party Conference, October 1984.

9 Hansard, 25 July 1985.

10 The number of shire counties over which the Conservatives had overall control was cut from 18 before the elections to nine after.

11 Removed from the Environment Ministry on 2 September 1985.

12 *Attitudes to Local Authorities and their Services*, research study conducted for the Audit Commission, May 1986, MORI, p. iii.

13 Ibid., p. 26.

14 MORI, November 1986.

15 Local Authority Publicity, *Interim Report of the Committee of Inquiry into the Conduct of Local Authority Business*, chaired by Mr David Widdicombe, QC, HMSO, London, 1985, para 221.

16 Ibid., para 160.

17 Ibid., para 122.

18 Local Government Information Unit, *Widdicombe Interim Report – Some Observations*, 16 August 1985. Sir Lawrence Boyle was formerly Chief Executive of Strathclyde Regional Council.

19 Local Government Information Unit, Information Briefing No. 9, 27 November 1985.

20 Brighton was denied its first-ever Labour budget, although it was in fact rate-capped on Conservative/Alliance spending plans, since Labour did not take over until after the May elections.

21 Hansard, House of Lords Debate 10 February 1987.

22 These were the Finance Bill, the Teachers' Remuneration Bill, the Local Government Bill (abolishing deferred purchase, introducing privatisation and implementing Widdicombe) and the Rate Support Grant Bill (changing the system of clawback).

Chapter 9   No Answer But Your Own

1 Frederick Hayek, *Law, Legislation and Liberty*, vol. 2, *The Mirage of Social Justice*, Routledge & Kegan Paul, London, 1976, p. 165.

2 Gordon Marshall et al., 'The Decline of Class Politics?' in David Rose, ed., *Social Stratification and Economic Decline*, Hutchinson, London, 1986.

3 *British Social Attitudes: The 1986 Report*, Social and Community Planning Research, 1986.

4 David Graham and Peter Clarke, *The New Enlightenment*, Macmillan, London, 1986, p. 31.

5 See Peter Hain, *Political Strikes*, Viking, London, 1986.

6 We might reasonably ask whether the new Conservatives are a 'band of zealots . . . instinctively hostile to the hopes and dreams of ordinary people' through their 'new extremism'. This was the accusation which, ironically, Margaret Thatcher levelled at the Labour Party in her attempt to point at the 'enemy within' at the Conservative Central Council on 21st March 1967. The *Sunday Times*, 22 March 1987.

7 Bertolt Brecht, *Poems 1913–1956*, ed. John Willett and Ralph Manheim. 'To a Waverer' translated by Eva Bornemann, Methuen, London, 1984.

Appendix 1

Government spending in the regions actually increases the disparity between parts of Britain. Far from equalising conditions and economic circumstances, the direction of government spending makes matters much worse.

A comparison between Yorkshire and Humberside and the South-East illustrates this. Taking key public-spending indicators and expressing them per head of population, it can be shown (Central Statistical Office 1987) that Yorkshire and Humberside would receive £900 million more in public spending if the same amount were spent per head of population in that region as was spent in the previous twelve months per head of population in the south-east of England.

	Per Head of Population	
	South-East	*Yorks. & Humberside*
	£ per annum	£ per annum
Public Administration and		
Defence	383	260
Education and Health	502	442
	885	702

Increased spending necessary if government were to spend at the same level per head of population in Yorkshire and Humberside as in the South-East of England £900m

Government Regional Assistance to Yorkshire and Humberside £50m

£850m

Note: For a city the size of Sheffield this loss of investment amounts to approximately £100m.

Appendix 2

Deferred Purchase Arrangements

Almost any Capital Scheme includes an element of deferred purchase. The householder planning an extension to his or her home will only pay the builder after the job has been completed satisfactorily. It is common, on larger projects, to retain a percentage of the overall cost until a thorough investigation of the standard of the work is completed and to insure against defects that emerge after completion. Sometimes this delay to final payment can be quite extensive.

Local authorities were forced, by the change in the capital control system in the Local Government Planning and Land Act 1980, to extend this concept of deferring payment. The capital allocations, or permission to borrow, which Government gave to local authorities, were cut back steadily each year from 1981/82. Small local authorities with large capital projects were simply unable to carry them out.

One of the earliest and most famous deferred payments agreements was the building of Harrogate's Conference Centre. The Conservative-controlled shire district council would never have been able to find the resources to undertake this project under normal conditions. The deferred purchase agreement or DPA in effect allowed it to anticipate future capital allocations, so that the conference centre was built first and the payments came much later.

In 1987 the Government admitted, in an answer to a parliamentary question, that they had provided Harrogate with additional borrowing allocations to assist them with transferring from deferred purchase to normal arrangements in meeting a £16 million debt as well as revenue contributions to help with the debt charges. An important revelation in view of the condemnation of Labour's plans to incorporate deferred purchase arrangements in normal borrowing regulations.

Authorities also used DPAs to expand their capital programmes in response to the continuing cuts in their capital allocations. By far the majority of DPA schemes taken out by local authorities were used to expand mainline capital programmes, either because of the need to fund large projects or to meet growing housing and other needs. The amount used to help solve problems caused by rate capping is comparatively small.

The advent of very heavy grant penalties and, more importantly, rate capping, led to the use of DPAs to help solve the crisis on revenue which an increasing number of authorities faced.

Authorities traditionally charged their revenue accounts with expenditure which could be described as capital. Such things included repairs to roads, houses and other council property and purchases of certain equipment. However, simply to switch such expenditure onto the capital account ran into the problem that capital resources were already fully stretched because of the reductions in capital allocations and the growing restrictions on the use of capital receipts, from sale of council houses for example.

Instead, authorities began to negotiate large scale DPAs, which were used to fund the main-line capital programme so that capital switched from the revenue account could be funded by use of capital allocations.

Lease and Lease-back

Lease and lease-back deals also have a relatively long history and have been used by a wide variety of local authorities for several different purposes. One common use was the leasing of land to developers who would build small factory units on it and then lease the completed units back to the local authority who would then manage the units.

Once DPAs had been made inoperative some rate-capped and heavily penalised local authorities turned to lease and lease-back deals to help solve their continuing revenue problems. These specialised deals were designed to raise capital by means of, in effect, mortgaging council assets, so that the interest on that money invested could be used to finance on-going costs.

A typical scheme might work as follows. The council would set up a private company to act as the financial intermediator. The council would lease some of its assets, such as its town hall or other assets, the company, which would pay the council a lump capital sum for the asset. The council-controlled company would raise the cash to make the payment by borrowing from banks using the town hall as security. Of course the council still needs a town hall to operate from, which it gets by leasing the town hall back from its own company, by means of paying annual rentals. Normally these rentals will be deferred for a couple of years.

What the councils were doing was raising a loan from banks by using its assets as security. As it is prohibited from raising these loans directly it has to dispense of the assets first – thus the reason for the lease and lease-back scheme.

Interest from balances counted as 'negative' expenditure, and therefore helped increase an authority's grant entitlement. As the grant coming back to the authority could in some cases be greater than the extra interest income this was a considerable bonus.

DPAs and lease and lease-back are therefore very different financial devices. DPAs were a way of bringing forward anticipated capital spending approvals by means of deferring payments on capital projects. Lease and lease-back is a way of mortgaging council's assets in order to get access to loan funds. Despite this difference they were both being used to solve very similar financial problems.

We are grateful to Steve Hughes of the Association of London Authorities for his help with this note.

Index

THE HOGARTH PRESS

This is a paperback list for today's readers – but it holds to a tradition of adventurous and original publishing set by Leonard and Virginia Woolf when they founded The Hogarth Press in 1917 and started their first paperback series in 1924.

Some of the books are light-hearted, some serious, and include Fiction, Lives and Letters, Travel, Critics, Poetry, History and Hogarth Crime and Gaslight Crime.

A list of our books already published, together with some of our forthcoming titles, follows. If you would like more information about Hogarth Press books, write to us for a catalogue:

30 Bedford Square, London WC1B 3RP

Please send a large stamped addressed envelope

HOGARTH CURRENT AFFAIRS

RADICAL FICTION FROM THE HOGARTH PRESS

All in a Lifetime by Walter Allen

The Olive Field by Ralph Bates

Twenty Thousand Streets Under the Sky by Patrick Hamilton

Saturday Night at the Greyhound by John Hampson

The Volunteers by Raymond Williams

Hilary Wainwright
Labour: A Tale of Two Parties

We all know the old Labour Party – the party of Harold
Wilson and Jim Callaghan. But a new, less familiar party
has been emerging – in local government, among women
and ethnic minorities, at the base of the unions. Both the
Conservatives and the Labour establishment condemn
this new movement as 'loony'. But why are they so
alarmed? Hilary Wainwright investigates, examining
past defeats and new initiatives, and arguing that radical
socialist politics can be popular, and can offer a fresh
vision for the future. Packed with interviews, detailed
analysis and controversy, here is a book which no one
who cares about politics in Britain can afford to ignore.

John Carvel

Citizen Ken

'A thoroughly readable and entertaining presentation of the life of an exceptionally fascinating man' – *Financial Times*

'There is little doubt in my mind that this volume is the best account of my years in the GLC that we are going to get' – *Ken Livingstone*

'A very fine piece of contemporary history' – *Sunday Times*

'Well, it's very honest, isn't it, dear?' – *Ethel Livingstone (Ken Livingstone's mother)*

Norma Kitson

Where Sixpence Lives

'A remarkable book' – Lynne Reid Banks, *Sunday Telegraph Magazine*
'Magnificent: more than an autobiography; a personal testimony; and one of the best I have read' – Matthew Parris, *The Sunday Times*

Why should a woman, brought up a wealthy, white South African, abandon her life of privilege to espouse the cause of black liberation? *Where Sixpence Lives* is the moving account of Norma Kitson's life and struggle, tracing her path from the ease and security of Jewish Durban in the 1940s to her activities with the ANC and the horror of interrogation and imprisonment. It is both a forceful political indictment and a testament of the indomitable courage of a loving and independent-minded woman.

Michael Cooley
Architect or Bee?
The Human Price of Technology

Is technology friend or foe? Does it destroy our jobs or liberate us from drudgery? Will it free our creativity or reduce us to robots? This path-breaking book gathers together vivid evidence of human wastage and environmental damage but also traces an alternative route to a positive technological future.

William Shawcross

Sideshow

Kissinger, Nixon and the Destruction of Cambodia

'this is a thrilling book, though a terrible one . . .'
– *John le Carré*

Why should a superpower become involved in the des-
truction of a small, distant, neutral country? The year
President Nixon was elected (with Kissinger as his
National Security Assistant) on a promise to extricate
America from Vietnam, Cambodia was a relatively
peaceful and prosperous country. Seven years later,
Nixon was disgraced, Kissinger celebrated, and
Camodia in ruins – its killing fields the grave of hundreds
of thousands of victims of the Khmer Rouge.

This new edition of a stunning journalistic investigation
of American foreign policy contains additional material,
including, for the first time, the final response authorised
by Kissinger to Shawcross's horrifying accusations, re-
vealing *Sideshow* as an invaluable testament of corruption
and deceit in world politics.